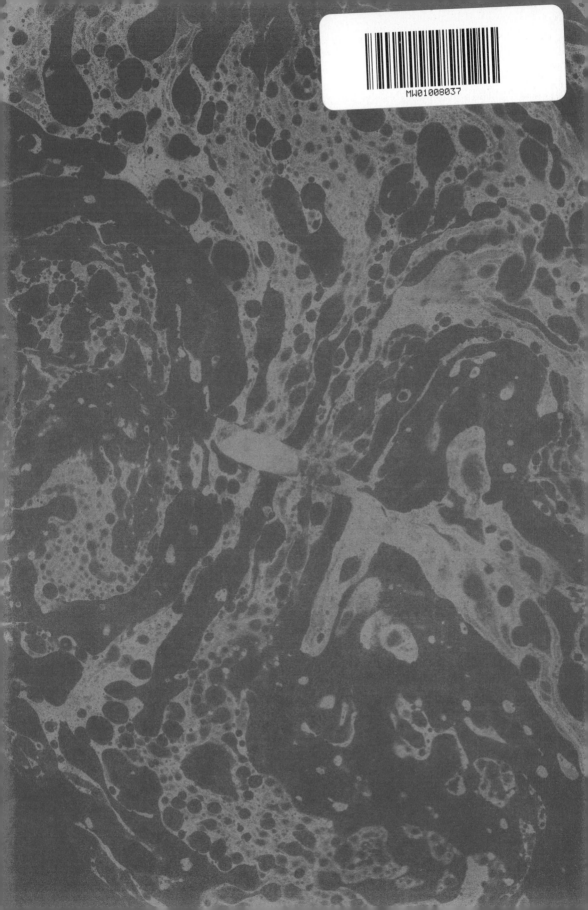
MW01008037

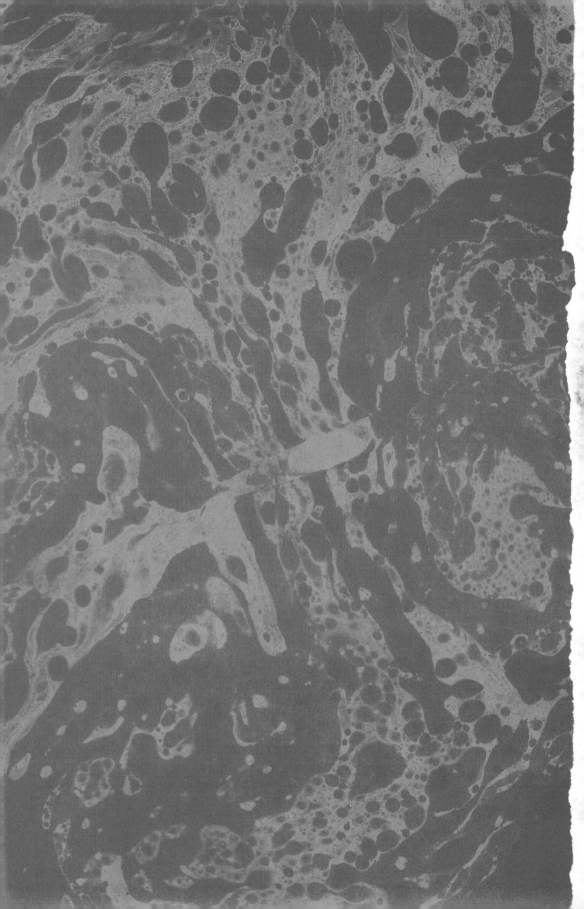

# JIMI HENDRIX
# VOODOO CHILD

**Harvey Kubernik**
and
**Kenneth Kubernik**

STERLING
New York

STERLING
New York

An Imprint of Sterling Publishing Co., Inc.

STERLING and the distinctive Sterling logo are registered trademarks
of Sterling Publishing Co., Inc.

Interior text © 2021 Harvey Kubernik and Ken Kubernik
Cover © 2021 Sterling Publishing Co., Inc.

All rights reserved. No part of this publication may be reproduced, stored
in a retrieval system, or transmitted in any form or by any means
(including electronic, mechanical, photocopying, recording, or otherwise)
without prior written permission from the publisher.

This is an independent publication and is not associated with or authorized,
licensed, sponsored, or endorsed by any person, entity, or product affiliated with
Jimi Hendrix, the Jimi Hendrix Experience, Band of Gypsys, any other artist or
entity featured in this book, or their music. All trademarks are the property of
their respective owners, are used for editorial purposes only, and the publisher
makes no claim of ownership and shall acquire no right, title, or interest in such
trademarks by virtue of this publication.

ISBN 978-1-4549-3738-8

Distributed in Canada by Sterling Publishing Co., Inc.
c/o Canadian Manda Group, 664 Annette Street
Toronto, Ontario M6S 2C8, Canada
Distributed in the United Kingdom by GMC Distribution Services
Castle Place, 166 High Street, Lewes, East Sussex BN7 1XU, England
Distributed in Australia by NewSouth Books
University of New South Wales, Sydney, NSW 2052, Australia

For information about custom editions, special sales, and premium and corporate
purchases, please contact Sterling Special Sales at 800-805-5489
or specialsales@sterlingpublishing.com.

Manufactured in Malaysia

2 4 6 8 10 9 7 5 3 1

sterlingpublishing.com

Cover design by Igor Satanovsky
Interior design by Gavin Motnyk

Picture Credits—see page 294

Page ii: Jimi Hendrix at the Marquee Club, London, 1967; pages vi–vii:
Photographer Henry Diltz captured the scene at a club in San Francisco,
June 18, 1967 (see page 73); pages viii–ix: Hendrix onstage, 1968.

"We play our music, 'Electric Church Music,' because it's like a religion to us."

—Jimi Hendrix to Hugh Curry of the CBC

# Contents

"A GIRLFRIEND RANG UP AND SAID YOU'VE GOT TO HEAR THIS GUY JIMI HENDRIX.... SO I WENT ALONG TO SEE HENDRIX AT BLAISES.... IT WAS LIKE A BOMB BLOWING UP IN THE RIGHT PLACES."

—Jeff Beck

# Introduction

**A** lot can happen in just four years, barely a blink in the transit of our earthly pale blue dot but an eternity when the humdrum of daily life is overturned in dramatic, ungovernable ways, when the prosaic becomes suddenly, daringly, rhapsodic.

Writ large, it is Lincoln's inauguration on a late winter's day in March 1861. By April 1865, he's gone. But not before dragging his beleaguered countrymen toward those elusive better angels, his lyric eloquence a kind of timeless song, tragic and transcendent, a poet in the political world.

On a slightly less momentous stage, a pop group from Liverpool released their first single on October 5, 1962, a pastiche of Everly Brothers close harmony, dotted by a sly harmonica obbligato. "Love Me Do" enchanted listeners with its air of innocence and deft songcraft.

This innocuous little ditty initiated a seismic shift in the cultural landscape that reverberated throughout Britain and beyond, way beyond anyone's most-addled imagination. The Beatles, as unlikely agents of change as the long-limbed lawyer from Illinois, brought their flying circus to an abrupt halt on August 29, 1966, the climax of four kaleidoscopic years.

Following their last concert performance at San Francisco's moldering Candlestick Park, they said goodbye to the road, to their ravenous fans, to the insensate tempo of their professional and personal lives.

They retreated to the comforting cloister of Abbey Road Studios, a salutary acknowledgment that killing the "Fabs" would allow the Beatles to persevere. Their exodus created an unexpected vacuum; for those of us living through those expectant months ("Strawberry Fields Forever," their next release, would not surface until February 13, 1967, an epoch in pop music time), there was

Jimi Hendrix, newly arrived in London, 1966.

a visceral sense of dread, of finality. Unbeknownst to even the most acutely attuned music maven, this was all a prelude to something more transgressive, something . . . bolder.

On September 23, 1966, Jimi Hendrix, twenty-three, an itinerant, jobbing guitarist, boarded a flight from New York to London's Heathrow Airport. His worldly possessions would have made Huck Finn blush: a couple of shirts, some pants, a toothbrush, skin cream for his "spots," plastic hair curlers ("Style makes the man."—Oscar Wilde), and a few bucks he copped from a soft touch on the way out of town.

His life up to that point had been one grinding obstacle after another: high school dropout, Army Air Force dropout, lurching 'cross the country like a Depression-Era train-hopper, finding solace only in the iridescent depths of a guitar chord he alone could hear. Within the confines of that battered, six-stringed muse that he kept as close as his heartbeat, he found beauty, rapture, when the world around him offered indifference and often, contempt. He didn't play it so much as exercise it like another limb, a third arm that packed the punch of Ali, the supple elegance of a Koufax curveball, the snap, crackle, and pop of Indiana's bullwhip.

The blues were his ur-text, his spirit guides the Alberts—King and Collins—and the Kings—B. B. and Freddie, with a dash of Lightnin' Hopkins and a spoonful of *Electric Mud*. He was caretaker to an African American legacy of innovation beginning with Robert Johnson and Charlie Christian. Every note was struck with a reverence for this exalted past, but there was glimmer of something distinctly different, a hint of things to come. He could shear the veneer off a stock blues riff, taking you straight to its Delta origin.

There were occasional gigs (they paid occasionally) where he could exercise his ideas, earn his stripes, backing a succession of razor-sharp hip-shakers and Baptist blues belters who rode the "Chitlin' Circuit" like marauding cavalries, liberating the locals with their seductive beats, their prodigious young guitarist hiding in plain sight. Jimi was always soft-spoken, well-mannered, and open to direction but only to a point; he wasn't going to be gulled into playing a role that diminished his own sense of self-worth, however threadbare he appeared.

He remained steadfast in his belief that greatness awaited him. And deliverance came in the form of a big-hearted "Geordie" from Newcastle, England, whose own musical trajectory from workingmen's clubs to *The Ed Sullivan Show* afforded him entry to the sanctum sanctorum of the burgeoning pop aristocracy.

Chas Chandler had just vacated the bass chair of the chart-topping group the Animals. He was keen to leave the vicissitudes of the road for the soothing climes of the recording studio, where, as a record producer, he could hunt for big game in the form of hit records.

While on safari in New York, he first encountered Hendrix performing as "Jimmy James" in a Greenwich Village club, prowling the stage with a predator's swagger, clawing his guitar like a trapped animal emitting cries of anguish and ardor. Where others plucked and strummed, Jimi took aim and fired with a marksman's eye. Chandler felt it in the marrow of his bones, this mesmeric charge, and he was all in, putting his reputation, his connections, his living space (they shared a flat for a considerable amount of time) in service of making Hendrix "happen."

But first they had to get through passport control. On arrival they were met by the inscrutable gaze of the authorities; Jimi's legal documents were in no better shape than his finances. He was finessed through customs, under the watchful eye of his soon-to-be-manager, Mike Jeffery, a shadowy figure with a bankroll, contacts, and just enough gangster cred to put fear, real and imagined, in his confederates. He'd partnered with Chandler because the Animals belonged to his stable, and they were both invested in seeing where this feral creature Hendrix would take them.

Chas Chandler (far right) was the original bassist for the Animals; the group is seen here posing on the Victoria Memorial, London, c. 1964. Other band members, from left: lead singer Eric Burdon, drummer John Steel, keyboardist Alan Price, and guitarist Hilton Valentine.

LLIARDS
NOOKER
TRE & CLUB
LONDON INSTITUTE
&
MORRIS SCHOOL
OF
HAIRDRESSING
LTD
CAMEO
MOULIN
GAMBLING
SALOON
CINEMA
LYRIC
THEATRE

In retrospect, he took them further than the most distant horizon. He ignited with the speed and spectacle of NASA's moonshot, an improbable confluence of raw talent with the rigor of that alchemical right stuff. "The substantive issue is not that Hendrix was ahead [of his time]," writes Paul Gilroy in his W. E. B. Du Bois lectures collected in *Darker than Blue* (2010), "but rather that he was able to pronounce another time-sculpting temporality itself so that his listeners could, in effect, be transported from one time to another."

On September 18, 1970, almost four years to the day after he began his ascent, the peerless musician perished in an indiscriminate whisper, an act of such quotidian misjudgment that it seemed incomprehensible to his bereft and bewildered fans. Jimi Hendrix was an artist in the floating world, and like some ethereal, untethered spirit, he drifted off into the beckoning silence, the stars his destination.

Few mortals have had their lives so exhaustively documented, so forensically examined, as Jimi Hendrix. Hendrix scholar Ken Voss, who operates the *Voodoo Child* website—a dizzying descent into the rabbit hole of all things Jimi—reports that his book collection totals over 300 titles. Hendrix contained Walt Whitman's multitudes, a fantasia of indiscreet appetites. He rejected the title of bluesman, arguing that it limited his scope. Many of his songs lasted little longer than the two-plus minutes afforded the pop format, but they were rife with structural and technical innovation, executed with a devil-may-care impertinence that demanded the listener's undivided attention. Hendrix's sonic signature was as indelible as Dylan's adenoidal whine or Townshend's churning windmill.

Jimi arrived in "Swinging London" at its delirious zenith, a cool cat stalking a breathless hothouse. He took it all in with the glee of a child unwrapping an endless stream of birthday presents; bouncing along King's Road in Chelsea, he draped himself in brocade and batik, in velvet frocks and paisley prints, aglow in ultramarine and tangerine—a Fauvist vision come to life. Pop Art was all rage; Hendrix's music, like the fish-eyed cover of his debut LP, *Are You Experienced?*, conveyed the antic energy that visual artists like Richard Hamilton and Peter

**Opposite:** The scene in Swinging Soho, London, in the 1960s.

Blake brought to painting, collage, set design. Jimi was ever mindful of the different stages on which he performed, a stroll down Portobello Road as calculated as a show at the Marquee Club. He lived his life like a total artwork.

Jimi was always in the act of becoming—"radical incompleteness" is Paul Gilroy's trenchant take. There was a bit of Robert Heinlein's "stranger" about him, a

> **"HE WAS SO SPECIAL, SO EXTRAORDINARY, HE'S UP THERE FOR ME WITH MILES DAVIS AND CHARLIE PARKER AS SOMEBODY WHO WAS A VIRTUOSO, AN INNOVATOR. HE WAS DIFFERENT, EXTRAORDINARY AND NEW."**
>
> —Pete Townshend

bedazzling outlier who could enchant with a wink, a lascivious tongue wag, a swooping attack on his precious Stratocaster. But virtually no one claimed to know him—not fellow musicians, not his many lovers.

For all intents and purposes he was homeless, hopscotching from friends' flats to stately hotel suites to a comely stranger's bed, a princely vagabond soldiering forth, a shining, evanescent beacon set upon a distant shore.

The trappings of his runaway success—the sex, the sycophants, the reckless self-indulgence—were suffocating. There was never enough time to get one's bearings, only stolen moments to write, rehearse, record. And then it was on to the next gig, and endless, enervating charivari.

By all accounts Jimi was a sensitive boy, thoughtful and kind, navigating a turbulent family life. His father, Al, was caring but he was emotionally distant; his adored mother, Lucille, immortalized in "Little Wing," died when her son was in his teens, occasioning a crippling heartbreak that Jimi carried for the rest of his life.

Seattle, his hometown, was years away from its future stature as the economic hub of the Pacific Northwest, a technopolis on the edge of tomorrow. In the 1940s and 1950s, its black community experienced the familiar lashings of social, racial, and economic injustice. Families provided as best they could, but good jobs and a good education were rarely within reach.

Young Jimi and his father, Al Hendrix, c. 1945.

Jimi found solace in the far-flung world of science fiction; the lure of a Buck Rogers adventure, the exploits of John Carter on Mars, provided a safe harbor for a dreamy adolescent, a portal into an alternative future that found its terrestrial footing in his music years later. Indeed, his entire body of work, so infused with imagery redolent of speculative fiction, can be viewed as fulfilling this early inner urge to escape his all-too-real circumstances. That he also drew pictures of his favorite Pacific Coast Conference college football players, resplendent in their university colors, was evidence that even genius was not immune to the appeal of America's brutal ballet.

All the fractious patterns that cohered into his singular gifts were nurtured here, creating the rattle and hum of an inner-city identity. That his grandmother was part

Cherokee only furthered his outlier standing. For a time, Jimi sported a "process" or "conk"—hair straightened with lye-based chemical—a style popular among many black entertainers of the period.

It was, ironically, his future bandmate, Noel Redding, as white as the chalk of the Dover coast, who first modeled that era-defining poodle perm—"fuzzy wuzzy" in the parlance of the British press at that time—that, coincidentally, mirrored the nascent Black Power movement's push to reclaim their "Afro" heritage. When Jimi was asked about his radically chic new look, he chuckled and said, "It's groovy, man." Political statements weren't in his repertoire.

Then came 1968 and the sobering realization that peace and love were on trial. The blunt force trauma of the King and Kennedy assassinations, the discord over Vietnam, the breakdown of any consensus between the generations, took their immiserating toll.

Jimi was not immune to the ruckus; music, the clearest expression of black culture, placed him in the eye of the hurricane. Whether he asked for it or not, he was cast with other dignified black voices like James Brown and Dr. Martin Luther King Jr., Malcolm X and Harry Belafonte, who were fearless in their advocacy for human rights, for American minority rights. It was time to put away the rococo adornments of psychedelia; something more authentic, more rigorous, was required in the desperate search for a deeper truth.

"Many of Hendrix's immortal articulations of the slave sublime," declares British historian Paul Gilroy in his lecture series, "transposed into genre-defying statements of human suffering, yearning and hope, were, after all, created far from home, his birthplace, his homeland and his kin."

Just days after first arriving in London, Jimi realized his fondest ambition: to jam with Eric Clapton. Chas Chandler had arranged for the two to meet at an early Cream gig at a local polytechnic. Clapton was the darling of the British blues scene—"God" to his many enthusiasts—and fancied himself an honest broker between authentic American blues practice and the earnest interpretive advances of their English admirers.

Jimi and Eric Clapton together at the Bag O'Nails Club in London, in a photo by Herb Schmitz, February 1967.

When Jimi ripped into Howlin' Wolf's "Killing Floor," it was clear that the gulf could never truly be bridged. For all their thunderous sound and fury, Cream were taken to the woodshed by Seattle's own, a skinny kid who could no more talk falsely than he could play a bum note.

Nine months after fleeing the country of his birth, that kid returned to its shimmering West Coast, to the Monterey International Pop Festival. He mounted the stage a cipher and left it as triumphant as Spartacus, exerting a gravitational pull unmatched among his pop music cohort. He had become the high priest of an electric church whose choir rapturously sang of zebras and fairy tales.

This book, like the many others that have preceded it, is, at best, a mere testimonial to Jimi's timeless, universal appeal. Perhaps only Bob Marley merits inclusion in that sanctified space where mind and moment meet with shattering implications, a creative critical mass. Jimi Hendrix circled the sun just twenty-seven times. It makes you wanna holler.

# 1
# The Meaning of the Blues

The quixotic journey of James Marshall Hendrix, starting with the most parsimonious of beginnings and ending with his becoming a figure worthy of his own constellation, plays out like some mythic configuration as imagined by Joseph Campbell. Jimi was a hero with more than a thousand faces; he enraptured a radically transforming world, and its citizens, then and now, have embraced him as so much more than a wild-eyed guitarist.

**Y**ou could travel to a village in Ghana or visit an island in the South China Sea and discover locals wearing T-shirts with Jimi's impassioned profile emblazoned upon them. Have they heard *Electric Ladyland* or performed air guitar to "Foxy Lady"? Not likely. But they're keenly aware that he is important, a shamanic presence who commands respect like an elder, someone who resides on that spatial plain that gods inhabit, between the right here, right now, and somewhere over the incandescent rainbow.

For our purposes, we'll mark the beginning of his sojourn at September 1, 1957. Elvis Presley is performing at Seattle's Sick's Stadium. Jimi is fourteen years old, as impressionable as a Little Leaguer on opening day. He makes detailed notes on every song Presley performs—"Hound Dog" in particular captures his ear, and will get the "Experience" treatment in years to come. But at this moment, music is seeping into Jimi's bloodstream, consuming him body and soul.

"Hound Dog" was initially written at the request of Johnny Otis, the bandleader and A&R man for Big Mama Thornton. Otis wanted Jerry Leiber and Mike Stoller to listen to his acts and see if they could write some songs for them.

**MIKE STOLLER** | songwriter and record producer

"Elvis knew the Big Mama record, because he was a student. And it was a woman's song. Jerry wrote the lyrics for Big Mama and I think we recorded it in 1952, and it was released in early '53. It was a big R&B hit. In 1956 Elvis heard a lounge act doing it in Las Vegas."

**JANIE HENDRIX** | Jimi's sister; CEO and President of Experience Hendrix

"There's a scene in the Royal Albert Hall [1969 film footage] where my dad and Jimi are in Jimi's apartment and just kind of making up songs along with 'Hound Dog.'"

> **"My dad had a wonderful saying that I'll always remember. And that is, 'Jimi never played a note I didn't like.'"**
>
> —Janie Hendrix

## JERRY MILLER | guitarist, singer/songwriter, cofounder of Moby Grape

"In the early- and mid-sixties we used to watch together a lot of the touring bands who would visit the Seattle area. All the guitar players would show up then at the Spanish Castle, the Tiki, or Birdland. Jimi, myself, and Larry Coryell would all go.

"There was a guy we would check out, Jerry Allen, who was funky to a rat. He'd get up there with his Stratocaster guitar and arch his ass out. Man, he was the funkiest. We saw the Wailers, too. One time we saw Gene Vincent, Chuck Berry, Fats Domino, and Little Richard. Chuck Berry was unbelievable."

Chuck Berry at the Miami Pop Festival, December 28, 1968.

**Later, after he was established,** Jimi wrote a song called "Spanish Castle Magic." The Spanish Castle was a venue in Midland, right between Seattle and Tacoma. Originally a popular local dance hall, in 1959, famed Seattle deejay Pat O'Day booked the Wailers to play the first of many rock 'n' roll teen dance concerts there.

## JANIE HENDRIX

"In 'Spanish Castle Magic,' he's talking about a Metro bus here in Seattle that drove him from the Central District to almost Tacoma. It was a Metro bus, but he named it the 'dragonfly.' He talks about the clouds. And the thing about Seattle, we have the fluffiest clouds, these blue skies, these really puffy clouds, and he totally describes this fantasy place, but part of it is his reality and what he lived here in Seattle. But then it's to one's interpretation what it is and a lot of times too what he is saying."

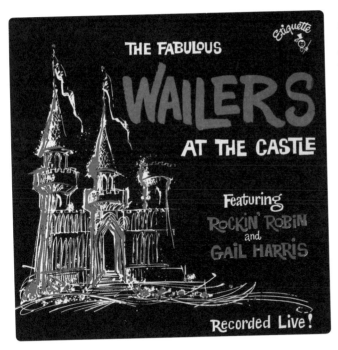

Record cover of *The Fabulous Wailers at the Castle*, recorded live at the Spanish Castle Ballroom in Seattle in 1961.

**DON WILSON** | guitarist and cofounder, the Ventures

"Jimi Hendrix was from Seattle. He saw the Wailers live, and Dick Dale at least a couple of times, and probably heard or saw the Ventures as well."

**During 1962–63, James** Marshall Hendrix enlisted in the army and trained as a paratrooper in the 101st Airborne Division in Fort Campbell, Kentucky. After he was discharged, the rhythm guitarist with a dream went to Nashville, Tennessee, to pursue a music career playing clubs like the Jolly Roger, the Del Morocco, and Club Baron.

**BOBBY WOMACK** | guitarist and singer/songwriter

"The first time I saw and met Jimi Hendrix to really know him was late 1964 when he was with a guy named 'Gorgeous' George Odell, who made clothes and always thought he could be Sam Cooke or Jackie Wilson. It was on a show when I was playing guitar for Sam, on a bill with Sam and Jackie Wilson. But George never had that kind of talent for me, but you couldn't tell him that. And he had Jimi Hendrix playing for him. George is going crazy and Jimi is setting his guitar on fire in a routine. And George said, 'Hey man, you're trying to steal my gig. If you do this again and start the act, I'm gonna fire you.' And Jimi replied, 'Man, I'm just trying to help you.' And George responded, 'I don't need that kind of help.'"

**STEVE CROPPER** | guitarist, songwriter, record producer

"Around 1964, Jimi Hendrix was in Memphis and came by to visit Stax Studios. At the time I was filing records, logging tapes, and producing recording sessions. I was busy, but we talked. I then went out to a local diner, met him, we had hamburgers, and he then told me he did the lead guitar introduction on Don Covay's 'Have Mercy.' I was knocked out by that funky intro riff and had heard it earlier on the radio. He came to the Stax studio and we jammed a bit."

# Lost Angeles

Little Richard toured across the South and Southwest in the first months of 1965. He was promoting a greatest hits package, screaming his tutti frutti head off while his backing band, the Crown Jewels, teetered back and forth behind him, the whims of their mercurial boss dictating the vitality or indifference of each performance. Jimi was one of two guitarists slipping and sliding between the grooves and Richard's Napoleonic demands, such as no puffy or frilly shirts (so as not to upstage Richard)—

Little Richard during an appearance on *The Glen Campbell Goodtime Hour* TV variety show that aired October 26, 1971.

"You get rid of that shirt, boy! . . . I am the one who's going to look pretty of stage!" The road offered some upsides: Jimi jammed with heroes B. B. King and Albert Collins, cousin of Texas blues titan Lightnin' Hopkins.

It was during this tour, in places like the Harlem Duke Social Club in Pritchard, Alabama and at the Club 500 in Houston, that Jimi was formally initiated into the blues brotherhood—copping licks, trading eights, unraveling the endless permutations of the 1-4-5 structure like a strand of DNA.

On February 5, they arrived in Los Angeles to headline the Red Velvet Club on Sunset Boulevard in Hollywood. It was a desultory affair: Richard was in a protracted pout, there were no other gigs lined up, and Jimi was left to his own devices. He auditioned for Ike Turner, who'd never met a young player he couldn't break. Jimi was too free and easy for Ike's perp-walk commands, lasting barely long enough for it to register on his CV. But LA had many other inducements to keep him occupied.

The band Love in Los Angeles, 1967. Top row: Arthur Lee (left), Johnny Echols (right); bottom row, left to right: Ken Forssi, Michael Stuart, and Bryan MacLean.

**JOHNNY ECHOLS** | songwriter and guitarist, record producer, cofounder of Love

"Before Love, Arthur [Lee] and I started playing in bands. Jimi Hendrix, then Jimmy James, had come down to the California Club in Los Angeles because the O'Jays were looking for a new guitar player and to kind of audition for the job. And I don't think he got the job, but that was when I first met him. He was a nice guy. Arthur knew him previously and was closer to him.

"When I came into the club, Jimi had my guitar. That's a no-no. A stranger especially does not pick up a guy's guitar and start fiddling with it. This was a 1961 Esquire guitar. At the time he did not impress me as a guitar player. He was basically like a pedestrian, workmanlike guitar player. He was playing what most guitar players did at the time. He also wore his hair in a process. And a cardigan type of suit sports coat jacket, and real tight pants that we all wore at the time.

"The first thing I remember about him, which is weird, was that he used a lot of Right Guard deodorant. Because at that time Jimi didn't have a lot of money, hell, none of us did, and he just reeked of Right Guard. What he would do, instead of having his clothes at the cleaners, he'd just kind of have them dosed with Right Guard. And everything started to smell like that. So that was my first impression of Jimi.

"Because, you know, the white kids from Hollywood had not gone to the 5-4 Ballroom [in LA] and had not seen Johnny 'Guitar' Watson and those guys play with their teeth or behind their back. All of the things Jimi did. They thought this was new. When we all knew from the 5-4 Ballroom and the California Club that this was a staple of guitar players going way back playing like that. But people just weren't aware.

"Guys like Johnny 'Guitar' Watson were vocalists as well as guitar players. But Jimi Hendrix kind of pushed that out there with the flamboyance and got a lot of pointers from Little Richard and the clothing. . . .

"Billy Revis of Revis Records was working with Arthur and this lady named Rosa Lee Brooks, and he wanted Arthur to write a song for her. So that was 'My Diary,' which was about his girlfriend and their breakup. Jimi played on it. Rosa Lee was the vocalist. It was mastered at Gold Star studio."

"**I met Jimi in 1964** or maybe very early 1965, around the time he was with Little Richard at Ciro's on Sunset Boulevard in Hollywood. He was playing or had been playing before with the Isley Brothers. First of all, during that time, most guitar players and myself we were basically in the background or we tried as it was our job to make the vocalist look good. And that was who we were. We were not really flashy or showy."

—Johnny Echols

The Byrds and Bob Dylan onstage at Ciro's, West Hollywood, March 1965.

### CHRIS HILLMAN | bass player, the Byrds

"We got to know Jimi in 1965. Drummer Mike Clarke and I went to Ciro's on Sunset and he was playing guitar for Little Richard. Jim [aka Roger] McGuinn went as well.

"He was a sideman on the end of the stage playing left-handed.

"The best part of the night was we had these stupid suits that [manager] Jim Dickson bought us, and we left them in the Ciro's dressing room, and Little Richard's band stole them. And we went, 'Thank God,' because they were like these velvet collar Edwardian Beatles suits, but there was Hendrix.

"You could not help but look at him and hear the sounds he was making on the guitar, and playing lead star in an R&B rock 'n' roll band, you're not the showcase. It's the horn section carrying it. Very few guitar solos, mostly rhythm and stuff, but we said, 'Who is that?' because the guy was so good. And then a year and a half later, there he was at the Monterey International Pop Festival."

# 2
# New York, New York, a Helluva Town

When you got nothing, as Bob Dylan once sang . . . you suck it up and take the job. In spring 1965, Jimi had no choice but to re-up with Little Richard, however much sass he had to put up with. This time they were headed east, culminating at New York City's Paramount Theater in Times Square for Soupy Sales Easter Show. It was a riotous week-long engagement, a revue showcase featuring British beat bands like the Hollies; name-gamer Shirley Ellis; comedian Soupy Sales; and a sixteen-piece orchestra conducted by the brass knuckle horn man King Curtis, who would soon pinch Jimi for his band.

**I**t was during this residency that the unassuming bassist for the Animals, a certain Chas Chandler, wandered backstage in the company of some of his British mates. At one point he found himself in an elevator with Richard's unprepossessing young guitarist. A year later it would be Chandler who would strong-arm Jimi into leaving not only New York but America altogether, with nothing more than a wish and a hope.

Jimi's months in and around New York were an admixture of pickup dates, the odd studio session, another round with Richard—who fired him after a show at Harlem's Apollo Theater—and gigs with R&B singer Curtis Knight, the Isley Brothers, and Joey Dee and the Starliters of "Peppermint Twist" notoriety.

# Jimi Goes R&B

The Isley Brothers brought a touch of gospel to their powerhouse blend of R&B and dance-steady beats. They also embraced the legacy of a short-lived member who put them in touch with another kind of soulful discipline, put to scintillating use by brother Ernie for his solo on their hit "Who's That Lady?"

Ernie Isley shared the backstory with writer A. Scott Galloway in a 2008 *Wax Poetics* #30 article:

**ERNIE ISLEY** | singer/songwriter, multi-instrumentalist,
the Isley Brothers

"Somebody told my brother about a guy in Greenwich Village [named Jimi Hendrix] that could play better than whoever was playing with James Brown, Wilson Pickett, or anybody we could name. . . . So they went on a search for this guy. He didn't have a regular place he was staying. They finally found him and asked him if he'd like to play for the Isley Brothers. He said, 'Hell, yeah'—because he was broke.

"They said, 'Play something.' He said, 'I can't, man. I had to hock my guitar.' So they got his guitar from the pawnshop and bought him new strings. . . . They told him to get all his gear together and come stay in our mother's house in our back room. Then they looked at his guitar and said, 'You play that thing you've got very well, but suppose we get you a new one . . .' 'What!' 'Yeah, man. What kind do you want?' 'Can I get a white Strat?' 'Sure.' 'Oh my God!'

"He was quiet, well-behaved, and minded his own business. I used to think, 'Why is he practicing?' He didn't need to. He often played looking out our front window. If an ambulance went by, he'd try to make his guitar sound like that. Then suddenly, he thanked my brothers for everything but said he wanted to do his own thing. They wished him well and told him he could keep the guitar." [Hendrix played guitar on the March '64 recording session of the Isleys' song "Testify (Parts I & II)."]

The Isley Brothers perform at a farewell party for R&B disc jockey Nathaniel "Magnificent" Montague at the Rockland Palace in Harlem on June 19, 1964. Jimi Hendrix is seen at far left.

**Ed Chalpin was a savvy music** business executive and independent record producer in New York. In late 1965, Chalpin was introduced to Hendrix by Curtis Knight. Chalpin signed Jimi to his PPX production company with an exclusive three-year recording agreement. And, like so many before him, Hendrix put a signature to a contract that would have ramifications for years to come.

After Jimi became successful, PPX brought a suit against him in 1968. An in-court settlement was reached between Hendrix, Chalpin, and Warner Bros. in July. The media reported that "The United States and Canadian rights under that agreement have all been sold to Warner Brothers as part of the settlement and Chalpin will participate financially until 1972 in all of Hendrix's past, present and future recording ventures."

### JAMES CUSHING | poet, English professor, deejay

"Before the world knew the name Jimi Hendrix, there were live gigs and a recording studio stint with Curtis Knight.

"There's *Get That Feeling—Jimi Hendrix Plays, Curtis Knight Sings* (1967) and *Live at George's Club 20,* recorded in December 1965 and January '66. Knight is an adequate singer who is long on ambition and short on originality. He imitates Wilson Pickett, Otis Redding, and Levi Stubbs on some numbers.

"There are several of them. Some were issued in Jimi's lifetime, and one reissued on CD by the Hendrix family called 'You Can't Use My Name,' which contains a selection of Hendrix with Curtis Knight.

"Even though Jimi is not himself in control and the music is much more conventional R&B, it certainly gives you a sense of where he was coming from. You hear the root work of Jimi that becomes way more obvious when he made his first recordings as a bandleader. Jimi also did sessions with Lonnie Youngblood and has generally better music than the studio stuff done by Curtis Knight."

### JERRY SCHATZBERG | photographer

"We used to go to my club, Ondine [New York City]; I was a stockholder—[I'd] sit at the bar and hang out. I didn't take photos of the bands that played. We put on West Coast bands like the Doors and Buffalo Springfield. The kids, the club goers, and the groupies really loved them."

"Andrew Loog Oldham and the Rolling Stones would come in. Chas Chandler from the Animals came into Ondine's and heard Jimmy James and the Blue Flames and convinced him to go to London. He then returned to America as Jimi Hendrix in 1967, and he opened my second club, Salvation. It was a special time, and a bit later, 1967, the Summer of Love."

Curtis Knight and the Squires pose for a publicity portrait in 1965. Jimi Hendrix, left; Curtis Knight, center; Marion Booker, top; Ace Hall, right.

**"I knew Jimi Hendrix before he was Jimi Hendrix. He had played with the Isley Brothers and they hired him after hearing about him in Greenwich Village. I knew him when he was Jimmy James and the Blue Flames in New York City. We used to play gigs together at clubs. He was always flamboyant, and he always played with his teeth."**

—Carmine Appice, drummer, Vanilla Fudge

**The Druids of Stonehenge** were the house band at Ondine in New York City during the summer of 1966. At that point they were still called simply the Druids. They became the Druids of Stonehenge in 1967 when they signed to UNI Records.

### CARL HAUSER | guitarist, the Druids

"Ondine was the place to go. The Mamas & Papas hung there when they were in town, Eric Burdon and the Animals came in, and Jimi Hendrix.

"Jimi was playing in the Village as the guitarist with Curtis Knight and the Squires, and we used to jam together—the Druids and Jimi. In fact, he wanted to join the band. But there were five guys in the band and we already had two guitarists— we'd have had to split our money six ways instead of five! This was one of our high points in terms of decision-making!

"I liked Jimi a lot. He was a smart guy; he was not a dumb budding musician. He spent a lot of time with us. In fact, the interesting story from that is that Jimi was over, sleeping on Dave's floor one night [Dave Budge, Druids' singer], and Billy [Bill Tracy, the Druids' other guitarist] came over. Billy Tracy was an English lit major at Columbia and he was showing Jimi some poetry by Rimbaud—which Jimi had never seen before—one of which was 'Le Bateau ivre' (The Drunken Boat). One of the lines from 'Le Bateau ivre' is '*Libre, fumant, monté de brumes violettes / Moi qui trouais la ciel . . .*' or '*who ridden by purple mists, steaming and free / pierced the sky . . .*'

"So, in point of fact, 'Purple Haze' is taken from Rimbaud's 'Bateau ivre,' and I think it was Billy Tracy, who was turning him onto Rimbaud, that gave him that line."

# Girl Talk

There she was, peeking out from under a furry mitten of a hat in the gossipy pages of *16 Magazine*, her come-hither pose the essence of one of London's "it girls." She had all the prerequisites: lissome build, pouty-mouthed, feline temperament, and, most sensationally, a pop star boyfriend.

In her case, it was no less than the Rolling Stones' knife-edge, Keith Richards. She was Linda Keith and, like fellow "Dolly Birds" Pattie Boyd and Chrissie Shrimpton, sashayed in her Courrèges boots in the envious company of Britain's pop aristocracy. The three ate at Alvaro's, shopped at Biba and Mary Quant, and danced the night away at the Scotch of St. James.

In the summer of 1966, Linda accompanied Richards to New York as the Stones prepared for their grandest bacchanal across North America. With Keith on tour, Linda found divertissements around Manhattan. One fateful evening she joined friends at the Cheetah Club, the extravagantly chic new discotheque/concert venue in Midtown, an exhibitionist's field of dreams. Curtis Knight was holding center stage, but Linda was smitten with his guitarist, whose stylish, leonine motions were catnip to a young girl's heart.

She invited Jimmy (not yet "Jimi"—he'd tweak the spelling in the weeks to come) to her table. It was a memorable night.

Linda was indefatigable in her support of Jimi, going so far as to abscond with one of Mr. Richard's prized Stratocasters for Jimi to use while his was again in hock. She opened her glittering Rolodex and invited every mover and shaker she could to come down and see him play, mostly under the name of Jimmy James and the Blue Flames. She hit pay dirt when Chas Chandler was dragooned down—literally—into the subterranean squalor of Cafe Wha? The Greenwich Village coffeehouse was a refuge for aging folkies, protest singers, activist comedians, and any young group of stragglers who'd work for the thrill of it all.

Chandler was no Prince Charming and Jimi wasn't exactly Cinderella, but in some bizarro world fairy tale, the two had an instant alchemical bond that burned hard and fast. As if by magic, Hendrix was whisked off to London, to a looking-glass play-ground of like-minded troubadours tantalized by a sound that lay just beyond their grasp. And let's not be coy about it: leaving was the most liberating action he could take, given the restraints placed upon a man with his aspirations and of his color.

Model Linda Keith posing on a Vespa, August 1963.

**JOHN RIDLEY** | screenwriter, novelist

"When I was writing *Jimi: All Is by My Side,* when it got to the point that I really started to explore this particular 1966 year and these events and [the] rapidity that these events happened, certainly the song that sent me on this journey was a Hendrix recording of 'Send My Love to Linda.'"

The scene at New York City's famed Cafe Wha? on MacDougal Street, April 21, 1966.

## RONNIE SCHNEIDER | Rolling Stones road manager

"In 1966, I'd just finished a tour with the Rolling Stones. I was working for Allen Klein [ABKCO Music & Records founder]; my job was 'You're representing me and the box office.'

"There was a big club scene at the time and I was always out and about. Places like the Cheetah Club and Cafe Wha?

"I was a regular at Ondine in Midtown. We always had a reserved table there for the Stones and manager Andrew Loog Oldham when they were in town. And this is where I caught Jimmy James and the Blue Flames. All the top local talent played there; it was a prestige booking.

"My memory is of him just taking that guitar and doing everything you can think of with it—you felt he could play it with his ass. Usually I don't pay attention to the music. He was different.

"Linda Keith was Keith Richard's girlfriend at that time. She was a long, leggy model but a real homebody. When Keith was in town, they kept a low profile. Keith brought her 'round to my apartment in Newark, New Jersey. That place was stocked with airline stewardesses; every night there was a party going on. We had a pool on the ground floor, and Keith and Linda were totally cool just jumping in and hangin' about—no rock star trips at all. Then we'd go up to the roof, smoke pot, look at the stars, and it was just very mellow.

"Cafe Wha? was a hangout for beatniks. I was a nice Jewish accountant from Miami, you know, but it felt good to me. And Jimi comes to the Village and briefly meets Dylan at the Kettle of Fish as well. So there's a nice connection.

"I'm just floating in this wild world and watching as all these brilliant artists sort themselves out.

"And there was a close connection between Brian Jones and Jimi—mutual respect, mutual weaknesses. And let's throw Dylan into this mix because he was close to Brian—just a single degree of separation."

## BARRY GOLDBERG | keyboardist

"I was at the Cafe Wha? when Chas Chandler discovered Jimi Hendrix. Chas was with Eric Burdon. I was playing with John Hammond Jr. when Hendrix was playing with us for the whole week and did 'Hey Joe.' That changed his whole trip."

## AL KOOPER | keyboardist, Blues Project

"I had seen Jimi play live in Greenwich Village with John Hammond Jr. at Cafe Wha? And you could tell he was pretty special."

**JAMES NEWTON** | composer, flutist, professor of jazz studies

"If Hendrix remained in America, he would have never achieved the kind of acclaim that he did by going to England. The racism would have marginalized him, without question. The artistic freedom he fought for, the air of experimentation that defined that time, the critical help he got from Chas Chandler, all happened by virtue of leaving. This is something the British musicians heard when he first came over, that he was speaking from a position of authority. Clapton, Townshend—they knew what they were striving for was now fully realized in this audacious upstart. His guitar spoke languages from all over the world."

"**I feel without Chas, Jimi** would not have been quite [as] advanced in his career. Who knows how Jimi's career may have developed if Chas had not been involved. I dread to think.

"Very simply, not only in the beginning did he discover Jimi and figure out within a nanosecond 'This is the guy, I want to have him record "Hey Joe."' He goes into the Cafe Wha? [and] Linda Keith drags his ass down there, and Chas had in his head this song and trying to find an artist to record 'Hey Joe.' Wouldn't you know, Jimi plays it. [Laughs.] Apart from the fact that Jimi completely blew his mind as a guitar player and performer, and he had this song and he just knew it immediately that this is the guy. Boom. 'You're coming with me back to England.'"

—Eddie Kramer, recording engineer, producer

# 3
# Ready
# Steady . . . Go!

From the moment he touched down in London on September 23, 1966, Jimi was thrown into a whirlwind of introductions, club-hopping, jamming, networking run amok. By the end of his first week, auditions had produced Noel Redding, a guitarist with some middling successes, who balked at playing Fender bass. But their musical rapport was genuine, and Redding dutifully accepted the position. One week later, John "Mitch" Mitchell, having recently left Georgie Fame's steaming R&B ensemble, mounted the drum seat. He was a jazzer but fit in with Noel and Jimi like a missing piece of the puzzle.

Mitch Mitchell during a sound check before performing at the Saville Theatre in London, 1967.

**B**ut there was another claimant, Aynsley Dunbar, who also demonstrated some serious chops, and it came down to a coin toss. Mr. Dunbar, who would go on to a distinguished career working with Frank Zappa and Journey, among many others, would have been an equally inspired if stylistically more conventional choice.

History records that Mitch was the right man; his raspy snare, swinging like a pinwheeling Gene Krupa, would prove to be a defining characteristic of the Experience.

### MICHAEL DES BARRES | actor, musician

"I attended the Corona Academy drama school in London and appeared in several plays. I had a teenage band, the Orange Illusion. This is before 1967 and doing the movie *To Sir, With Love*.

"Earlier, 1963, '64, '65, and this follows the whole trajectory of Steve Marriott, Ronnie Wood at art school, so many different guys who were in bands that came from drama and art school. There was Mitch Mitchell. I knew Mitch as a young child actor. I met him in a ballet class. We were in tights. And he told me he played in a band.

"Mitch is the greatest rock-and-roll drummer that ever existed. Because, as you know, he just didn't keep that four-four beat. And that was his character. He had this kinetic magic, and it was a completely different range than everybody else.

"At the drama school, Mitch and I were doing a Shakespearean piece, and we all did the same monologue. But Mitch would improvise Shakespeare. Can you imagine that? My relationship with him was very cool because I was trying to be, you know, James Dean on a different level, and Mitch was doing it naturally. . . .

"I kept in touch with Mitch. Late '66, Mitch said to me, 'Look, Michael, I'm gonna go do this thing with this left-handed geezer. He's very sexy and he's gonna be doin' this gig at the Marquee and you have to come down.' Even at age sixteen I rolled my eyes.

"I come into the Marquee venue and it is packed. I saw Hendrix and it changed my life. If you look back, that was Jimi Hendrix. And he had a little bit of Cherokee Indian in him, and English kids are so obsessed with cowboys and Indians. And then we saw Jimi on the TV—we were fascinated by that. And Jimi, who was a black dude but an Indian dude, with a fucking headband in velvet, and the two hundred girls in the front were masturbating looking at him.

"Jimi was about fucking in the galaxy and fucking in the stars. And those young white girls in the front saw this and the sweat hit their brows and their hands were down their cheeks and I'm telling you man, this is the truth."

### KIM FOWLEY | songwriter, record producer

"I had just left Hollywood and met Jimi Hendrix the first time in 1966. I produced the Soft Machine previously in England, who, like Jimi Hendrix, were managed by Michael Jeffrey, who also had the Animals at the time. In 1966, I was his neighbor in England at the Bayswater hotel.

Songwriter, Soft Machine producer, and controversial Hollywood music business figure Kim Fowley, June 1967.

"In our first forty-five-minute meeting in the hotel lobby, Jimi was wearing a green suit. I was literally the first person he met when he got off the plane from New York. We talked music, and he said he wanted to play science-fiction rock 'n' roll. He mentioned a song, 'Martian Love Machine,' that was influenced by Ray Bradbury.

"Jimi liked the fact that I knew about the Spanish Castle venue in the Seattle area. I was the record promo man for 'Tall Cool One' by the Wailers from his neighborhood, since I was tall and cool, and I was a producer of LA–based Richard Berry, who wrote 'Louie, Louie,' who wrote 'Have Love Will Travel,' that were regional hits, and Jimi knew them.

"Jimi and I bonded in trivia over singer Gail Harris, who had 'I Idolize You' on the Carlton label. I knew Gail played the Spanish Castle venue. She had Janis Joplin's voice and was good-looking. Gail was like a sensual stewardess with a Janis voice."

### JOHN MAYALL | singer/songwriter, multi-instrumentalist, founder, the Bluesbreakers

"Jimi came to England and a blues world, which had been all my life, going back to Cyril Davies and Alexis Korner who started the British Blues boom. This attracted a lot of musicians who now had something new to inspire them.

"Blues had an audience in Britain. And Chas Chandler of the Animals [sort of] discovered Jimi not doing very well in America and brought him over to England, and that really positioned Jimi on an international scale.

"Jimi was very thrilled, of course, that people in Europe were blown away by his playing. He was really recognized for what he was. It was something he hadn't experienced in America. English and European audiences really put him on the map. And Chas Chandler was the one who saw that was coming and did a lot to advance his career on an international basis.

"When Chas Chandler brought Jimi over to England, everybody was totally impressed by his personality, his singing, and his playing. I think it was a shot in the arm for all the British guitar players to have someone that they had never heard before. And it all started from there, really. It was important for Jimi to have had Chas Chandler, who himself had reached great international regard with playing with the Animals.

"Jimi and I loved the music of Freddie King. We both included his catalogue in our sets. Freddie King was a revelation to a lot of people who played guitar. When Jimi mentioned Freddie King, we were all very well familiar with him in England. King's *Getting Ready* [1971] is one of my favorite albums."

Hendrix and John Mayall inspiration Freddie King performing in Holland, 1973.

**EDDIE KRAMER** | recording engineer, producer

"Jimi lived with Chas, which I think was a very good move because it created this tremendous bond. They sat up nights and were very compatible. They loved science fiction. They loved comic books. They loved anything to do with space and shit like that. Jimi was totally into it.

"And Chas kept saying, 'Jimi. You gotta write. Jimi, you gotta write.' Fortunately, he does a cover song there, and Chas is now pushing him early on. He then gets this thing, 'I can write.' He's got the confidence.

"Because Chas was that kind of guy and a disciplinarian. If you go back in history and think of the disciplinarians in Jimi's life: his dad, then the army, then the Chitlin' Circuit, and then Chas. 'Come on, man. I gotta sell my bass to pay for this session time, and we have three hours to track.'"

# In the Clubs

Journalist Peter Jones of *Record Mirror* caught one of the Jimi Hendrix Experience's earliest gigs when they debuted at Blaises Club, November 26, 1966, and touted them before anyone in the British music press:

> NOW hear this—and kindly hear it good! Are you one of the fans who think here's nothing much new happening on the pop scene? Right . . . then we want to bring your attention to a new artist, a new star-in-the-making, who we predict is going to whirl round the business like a tornado. Name: Jimi Hendrix. Occupation: Guitarist-singer-composer-showman-dervish-original.

**DAVE MASON** | singer/songwriter, cofounder, Traffic

"I saw Jimi play in one of the semiprivate clubs in London, maybe the Bag O'Nails or Scotch of St. James. Chas Chandler paraded him around before he ever did anything. I saw him there and play with a group on stage. 'Wow! Okay. Need to rethink things.'

"I later ran into him at one of the clubs people used to frequent. And he was just sitting there alone at a table. So I just sat down and started talking with him. We had a mutual fan thing. Jimi was a big fan of Traffic. And I was a fan of his. Out of that there were times when I would try to get him or at least get the other members of Traffic to invite Jimi down to the cottage and invite Jimi to come play. They weren't too enthusiastic about it, frankly. So I kept a very loose sort of relationship with Jimi. We'd get together sometimes at a restaurant or a couple of times we went out to clubs and got up to jam, or tried to."

## BRIAN AUGER | keyboardist

"I knew Chas Chandler from the scene. We used to hang out at the Scotch of St. James. There was always a jam session going on. One I remember distinctly had Stevie Winwood singing, Chas on bass, Mickey Waller on drums, and Eric Clapton on guitar. After a gig, before heading home to Richmond, we'd stop at Zoot Money's place. Jimi lived upstairs for a while, so you'd always see him around and some of the players from Zoot's band like Andy Summers.

"Chas called me one day and said, 'Hey Brian, can you come 'round the office—we want to talk to you.' I'm thinking, 'We' means Mike Jeffery.' . . . I'd already put my new band, the Trinity, together. Chas says, 'We've brought over this incredible guitar player from New York. And we want him to front your band.'

"I said, 'Well, I've already got a guitarist, Vic Briggs, and [singer] Julie Driscoll fronts my band. Are you suggesting I kick them out and install your guy who I've never heard play, nor has anybody else? Look Chas, we're playing the Cromwellian on Friday. Why don't you bring him down, he can sit in with the band and it'd be a kind of showcase'—'cause everyone in the scene always ended up there because it stayed open till the wee hours.

"They showed up with Jimi at the break—literally the moment I first laid eyes on Jimi. He looked, you know, hip, nothing outrageous or outlandish. He seemed really

> "I said, 'So, what do you want to play?' And he proceeded to show me this sequence of guitar chords, told me what key it was in, and I was like, 'Yeah, we can jam over that. What's it called?' "'Hey Joe.'" All right then.
>
> "Now at this moment Jimi wasn't singing; that came later, when Chas really impressed upon him the importance of that. So we counted it in and he started to play, and oh my God . . . I'd never heard anything like that—it was a unique voice."
>
> —Dave Mason

Keyboardist Brian Auger, 1968.

sweet and shy and kinda asked quietly if he could sit in. At that time, our set would have included some originals along with some heavy R&B like Mose Allison and soul jazz like Jimmy Smith.

"The club circuit at that time was run by Johnny and Rik Gunnell. The Flamingo was their mainstay—it was a dancing, raving club. I'd come straight from playing Ronnie Scott's, which was a heavy jazz vibe, very serious, and end up at the Flamingo, where I'd get into a Ramsey Lewis 'In Crowd' groove. Bag O'Nails was another . . . [and] the Marquee, of course. They were all in the West End, just minutes apart. Jimi would routinely show up at these clubs and check us out if we were performing. We jammed at Blaises, another of the hip clubs, on Queen's Gate off Cromwell Road.

"You know, it was a great time for players because the music industry hadn't quite taken hold yet. Everyone was looking for new things. We could take chances: jazz, blues, pop, all dressed up in velvet frocks! Jimi was a perfect example of that; maybe you could call it advanced R&B.

"Also, the economy was starting to show signs of life. England struggled for so long after the war—rationing, shortages, austerity—and suddenly, there's color. Designers and artists started to get some power in the marketplace. The striped trousers and the bowler hat got swept away. Jimi was an obvious fashion icon, but the scene was really changing even before he arrived."

# Opening for Jimi Hendrix

JOHN ETHERIDGE, GUITARIST, SOFT MACHINE

"The first time we heard about Hendrix was around September 1966, when rumors went around that this 'cat' had turned up at a Cream gig in London, sat in and blew everybody away. (A friend of mine was in the audience.) At this time (between September '65 and all through '66), the absolute, unchallenged star of the guitar was Eric Clapton, whose use of the Les Paul, Marshall sound single-handedly revolutionized guitar playing. This had been a quantum leap forward, and his style became the template for what became standard rock guitar.

"The first time I saw Jimi would, I think, have been in Windsor, at the Ricky-Tick Club [on November 26, 1966], which holds about one hundred people. Hendrix came on looking amazing—Afro, colorful military jacket, velvet trousers, etc.—and the first thing he did was play a left-hand trill (right hand in his case, of course) and point his other hand at a girl in the audience and move his tongue lasciviously! As an eighteen-year-old, I remember thinking, 'I could never get away with that!'

"The trio then launched into an extraordinary mélange of everything that up until now had been possible to play on the guitar—wailing blues, rhythmic, funk, extravagant antics, guitar behind the head, on the floor, between the legs, Bob Dylan songs.

"My initial feeling was that this guy had summed up everything that had gone before but put it together completely naturally with the most graceful and balletic movements that flowed completely organically with the sounds . . . after all, we'd seen people play the guitar behind their heads and with the teeth—T-Bone Walker—or smash it around—Pete Townshend—but with those guys, it always seemed premeditated. With Hendrix, this seemed like a natural outpouring of soul, grace, and feeling.

"I also thought the competition with Clapton was not apropos; Eric was a classic player, orderly, soulful, elegant, superbly poised. Jimi was a force of nature—a Romantic Expressionist. And of course he went on to pioneer so much sonic invention.

"Then one day in about January '67, the drummer in our little band came running in breathless and said, 'We're playing the Speakeasy on Sunday.' Now the Speakeasy was the hangout joint for all the dudes—Clapton, Hendrix, Stones, etc. (Very important to remember that this was a small scene at the time, so everybody knew each other.)

"Our drummer, who was an extrovert, talked to Hendrix, extolling the virtues of our band (very bold!), and Jimi agreed to hear us and spoke to the manager. 'OK boys, you can open up for a half hour on Sunday.' Agh!

"Nervously, we arrived to set up at 6:30, and there was Jimi. So he came and had dinner with us. He was very polite and mild-mannered offstage and had a sweet vibe. I, being some sort of idiot, got it into my head that I should pass some opinions.

"So I said that I didn't think much of the guitar sound on *Are You Experienced*? What I meant was that the record didn't capture the beauty and depth of his live sound, which is true! It came out all wrong and he was bit taken aback (not really—why should he care about some spotty teenager!). Of course I was immediately mortified.

"Anyway, we played our music, basically blues, but I particularly was striving for what would be later called a fusion style (horrible phrase!), as I was a huge Django

Jazz pianist Michael Garrick and guitarist John Etheridge play at the Stables in Wavendon, Buckinghamshire, c. 1980.

Reinhardt man and was trying to put this together with a rock sound. Jimi seemed to really appreciate this because when we finished playing, he sought me out and said, 'That was great, man.'

"These words were of course taken straight to my heart! When you are that age, encouragement from someone who was already emerging as an all-time great were nectar!"

# A TV Star Is Born

Britain's *Top of the Pops* and *Ready Steady Go!*, coordinated by Vicki Wickham and Elkan Allan, entertainment head of Associated-Rediffusion, were lenses into secret tunnels that prepared our world to eventually discover and investigate the Jimi Hendrix Experience.

On December 3, 1966, Hendrix made his first television appearance on *RSG!*, premiering "Hey Joe."

### MICHAEL LINDSAY-HOGG | director, *Ready Steady Go!* (1963–66)

"It was a black-and-white program. I think people were stunned by the comparative substance of the rock 'n' roll that was on television.

"It was the kids who had been children in World War II. The world was opening up for them. They could have long hair, the pill for pregnancy, and music if they wanted, too. And so a whole nation was open for young people and freedom. The paper was ready to be lit, and the match came."

### HUGH BANTON | organist, Van der Graaf Generator

"London was overrun with groups whose styles veered wildly from starry-eyed pop wannabes to intrepid space cadets droning on aimlessly in the Dorian mode, waiting for the acid to kick in with its parfait of visual counterpoint.

"This 'Progressive Music' scene was composed primarily of some precociously talented young miscreants, who rejected their class-bound expectations in favor of the phantasmagoria that surrounded them.

"They practiced Bach, quoted Blake, read Burroughs, revered Spike Milligan, and were all enthralled by Jimi. Van der Graaf Generator and Soft Machine were two prime exemplars of this studiously uncommercial, avant-rock sound. The Softs shared many bills with Jimi, while Van der Graaf scored an invaluable spot opening for him at the fabled February 24, 1969, concert at the Royal Albert Hall.

"I vividly remember Jimi's first appearance on BBC's *Top of the Pops*. 'Hey Joe,' of course, December 29, 1966. In fact, everyone I knew were phoning each other the following day. 'Did you see *that guitarist*?' I was seventeen, had only just left school, and was having a . . . ummmm . . . gap year, during which I spent a vast amount of time listening in particular to *Revolver*, *Are You Experienced?*, and *Sgt. Pepper*. Plus Stravinsky. This is all more than a year before I moved to London, which wasn't until January 1968, so just my teenage view from the suburbs

Organist Hugh Banton during a Van der Graaf Generator performance at the Robin 2, Bilston, Wolverhampton, UK, June 26, 2013.

of Edinburgh. An incredible time to be seventeen, but in truth I'd been well into pop music since I was seven or eight, ever since Elvis, Everly Brothers, and Eddie Cochran, etc.

"I reckon the UK was ready for Hendrix; along with the incredible progression in pop music we'd experienced here throughout the sixties, there'd also been a massive surge of interest in American blues the previous year or two, particularly if it involved wild, overdriven guitars, and JH just seemed to nail it somehow. Eric Clapton and Jeff Beck were both huge in '66, but at a stroke Jimi managed to eclipse them both. And he was full of mystery too, especially the drug/psychedelia thing, a whole other world out there to wonder about."

**On January 18, 1967,** the Jimi Hendrix Experience was in Shepherd's Bush at Lime Grove Studios for a taping of the BBC's *Top of the Pops* show, which aired the following day. Photographer Barrie Wentzell was in attendance.

**BARRIE WENTZELL** | photographer

"'Purple Haze' was out, and I asked Jimi if I could take a few snaps at the BBC, and there was very little light. I took some pictures on one stairwell where a couple weeks before I had been photographing Cream and Eric Clapton. That's how I found the spot, and the only place where I could get natural light, but there were always people coming down the stairs interrupting us. I told Jimi that a couple of weeks ago I took some pictures of Eric. 'Oh man. He's my hero.' And Eric was saying exactly the same thing about Jimi.

"From an English point of view, anybody from the States was a legend already, from years earlier. Elvis Presley, Gene Vincent, and the blues artists like Willie Dixon, Muddy Waters, and Howlin' Wolf.

"I think the same with Hendrix. Chris Welch at *Melody Maker* was telling me about Jimi's first gig. Then I heard the first track: 'Wow!' That's different. That's magic. May not be going over in his own country, but he's adored here. Musicians, especially jazz and black American musicians who came to England, were stunned that people paid, listened, applauded, and treated them like royalty."

The Jimi Hendrix Experience recording for German TV
at the Marquee on Wardour Street, London, March 2, 1967.

## KIM SIMMONDS | guitarist,
### cofounder Savoy Brown

Jimi Hendrix arrived in England when a lot of the listening music public had never seen anybody like that before. I was aware that Jimi had taken some things from Buddy Guy, and before that [from] T-Bone Walker, you know, the playing behind the head. It was a time-honored thing that I recognized. When Jimi hit the scene: 'What is this?' And, of course, he was very, very dangerous. A dangerous look about him, you know. All of a sudden on *Top of the Pops*, like you see him doing 'Hey Joe.' This guy was like John Lee Hooker untamed. It was something that most of the public had never seen.

Savoy Brown guitarist Kim Simmonds, 1973.

"In 1967 I was very involved with Savoy Brown. I saw one of his [Jimi's] first appearances on TV and he was just astonishing. I was a big fan straightaway. Right away, 'Purple Haze' stuck with me. Suddenly we have this great guitar with a fabulous blues lick. We had it in our stage repertoire in the late sixties in 'Savoy Brown's Boogie.' It left an indelible impression. Now I look back. . . and I realize that's the nice thing about getting older. All the pieces of the puzzle start to fit together."

**In the January 21, 1967,** *Record Mirror,* reporter Bill Harry hailed the arrival of the Jimi Hendrix Experience at the Bag O'Nails club in London:

> Beyond any shadow of a doubt The Jimi Hendrix Experience is the 'in' thing with London 'in' clubs—he's worth a fortune to any West End Club sensible enough to book him. Last Wednesday he appeared at the Bag O'Nails—'sensational' is not a word adequate enough to describe his success there.
>
> The club was so packed it was almost impossible to breathe. Among the 'faces' who gathered to watch him were: Bill Wyman, Paul McCartney, Mike Wilsher, Donovan, Keith Moon, Tony Hall, Brian Epstein, Viv Prince, Tony Booth, Georgie Fame, Twiggy, Bobby Elliott, Eric Clapton, Pete Townshend, Liza Minnelli, Allan Clarke, Chris Denning, John Entwistle, Ringo Starr, Denny Laine, Twinkle, Phil May, Peter Kenton, The Fourmost. etc., etc., etc.

**DAVID KESSEL** | multi-instrumentalist, cavehollywood.com founder

"In a circumstance of being at the right place at the right time and having inside connections, I was able to see the Jimi Hendrix Experience gig at the Bag O'Nails.

"I was going to school in Switzerland, along with my brother Dan. Our dad, jazz guitarist Barney Kessel, was touring Europe and England and suggested we all meet up in London. By sheer luck our dad had a connection at Polydor Records and was able to persuade (mild terminology) them that it was imperative that they arrange for us to get in to see Jimi at the club.

"Here's this black guy going crazy on the guitar and owning the stage, with these two frail-looking white English guys holding up their end quite excellently. Having grown up around the jazz guitar and jazz in general, it was easier to assimilate what was happening. Jimi had great showmanship, but I could see he was channeling a new guitar vision for rock-and-blues music.

"It also stood out to us that Mitch Mitchell was playing from a jazz drummer's mindset. The bottom line here is this was a jaw-dropping, mind-altering musical UFO landing. The kinds of thing that gives you actual goosebumps and makes you have to rethink a lot of things."

Hendrix captured mid–guitar smash, London, February 1967.

**DAN KESSEL** | record producer, multi-instrumentalist

"While a teenager, I was living in England for a while and was heavily into the whole UK music scene—listening to pirate radio and reading the music trade publications and teen magazines. With the emergence of Cream, and the Yardbirds' Jimmy Page now adding to Jeff Beck's guitar onslaught with their release of 'Happenings Ten Years Time Ago,' and then my seeing Syd Barrett's Pink Floyd at All Saints Hall, it was obvious to me the whole scene was on the brink of exploding. Then, astonishingly, and seemingly out of nowhere, Jimi appeared like a prophet descending from the sacred mountain of another planet. The world was waiting for him even if the world didn't know it yet.

"I know about guitarists. My dad, Barney Kessel, was one of the greatest. Aside from his own jazz career, he played guitar on classic rock 'n' roll records by the Coasters and Elvis Presley and tons of others, from the original 'Bony Moronie' by Larry Williams to *Pet Sounds* with Brian Wilson.

"I avidly listened to 'Hey Joe' and then 'Purple Haze' on pirate radio and bought the first album the day of its release. I soon played it for my dad, who appreciated that Hendrix had taken essentially a blues-based format and created a whole new hyper dimension from that.

"At the official press debut gig for the Jimi Hendrix Experience at the Bag O'Nails in London, I, a lad of fifteen, and my brother, David, twelve at the time, were present to witness something astounding. And after the unbelievable performance we were thrilled to get to go backstage and meet Jimi, Mitch Mitchell, and Noel Redding, and even members of the Beatles, Stones, Yardbirds, Clapton, Townshend, and many other major players in London. Jimi was very gracious. Everybody's minds had pretty much been blown."

**Later that January, Marijke Koger-Dunham**, cofounder of the Fool, a London-based Dutch art design collective, discovered Jimi Hendrix:

**MARIJKE KOGER-DUNHAM** | cofounder, the Fool

"I did not hear anything about Jimi Hendrix until I was commissioned by Brian Epstein to design the program for the Saville Theater's Sunday rock concerts and we were invited to the first performance: Jimi opening for the Who, who were no wimpy performers either, on January 29, '67.

"That was a mind-blowing show, Jimi playing exciting new sounds and looking fabulous in turquoise velvet and polychrome silk.

"I was introduced to Brian by a friend, Simon Hayes, owner of Mayfair Publications, who was on board to do the publicity for the concerts, and after looking at my portfolio, Brian commissioned the program cover design from me.

"The Saville program was designed by me alone and I used the image of Apollo and the Nine Muses for the illustration, thinking it appropriate for a theatrical production. Brian liked it enough to use it in different colors for the remainder of the concerts that year.

"Consequently, the Beatles became aware of Simon Posthuma and me and visited our studio, after which we became involved with many projects for them. Simon and I painted John's piano, did a mural at George's house, and of course the Apple boutique. Not to mention the various garments. . . .

"I did not design any clothing for Jimi and the band, but we met them several times at Eric Clapton's pad. Jimi, like me, was very quiet and shy in person, but he had a cool, kind, laid-back vibe, unlike the firestorm on stage.

Marijke Koger-Dunham, cofounder of the Fool, a Dutch psychedelic design collective best known for the clothes and artwork they did for the Beatles.

"Obviously, it is the iconic combination of unique talent and personality that makes him still outstanding to this day. I myself like the hard-ass opposed with lyricism yin-yang quality of the music."

## HUGH BANTON

"The Saville in '67 was a very traditional-styled regular London theatre, with heavy stage curtains, balcony, and boxes to the sides. On the May 7, 1967, gig I went to, JHE [Jimi Hendrix Experience] played the whole second half of the show, and in the interval none other than Brian Jones (and party) suddenly appeared in the box seats; naturally, he got his own burst of applause. We were sat on the balcony, and in the row behind me I had spotted Mike Hugg, drummer of Manfred Mann. Hendrix caused so much excitement that spring that everyone wanted to see him play.

"I remember hearing these monstrous guitar chords as they plugged in, and had never heard its like before. They started off with 'Foxy Lady,' with the curtains only opening during the sustained opening guitar flourish and descent. Unbeatable—great way to start a show, guaranteed to pin you—open-mouthed—back in your seat! Hendrix used three Marshall stacks with 6×4×12s, and Noel Redding two, with four 2×15 cabinets, unheard of then.

"Can't remember the whole set list, but it certainly featured 'Purple Haze,' the brand new 'Wind Cries Mary,' 'Like a Rolling Stone,' and finishing with 'Wild Thing,' which featured the customary guitar V-amplifier abuse.

"We'd already had the full display of solos played with teeth, behind his back, between his legs. I note that on this gig he's been quoted as saying something about 'fans sound like herds of squealing piglets'; yeah, that actually rings a bell, but it was a joke and was treated so. He was a very funny guy—I remember him discarding his 'military' jacket early on—'dammit, they told me I have to wear this stuff'—and I also recall him tuning the Strat between numbers, asking the audience if he sounded in tune. Then immediately plays E major at shattering volume level— massive applause—'Okay, I guess I must be in tune then!' In 'Purple Haze' he sang, ''Scuse me while I kiss this guy" . . . and he'd constantly throw in bits of 'Stranger in the Night,' Beatles' guitar riffs, all sorts of topical musical quotes. A masterclass."

### ANYA WILSON | music-business veteran

"When I first moved to London with my friend in 1967 at age seventeen, it was a paradise for young people. The fashion and music scenes were exploding with people exchanging their flowers and caftans for the uniquely styled clothing lines from BIBA and Bus Stop, and laced-up boots were worn on all occasions. Later, the platformed creations of SACHA would take over the young ladies of London's footwear fancy and make us all so much taller. I was able to morph from being 5'5" to 5'10" in my maroon boots, which I still have!"

Anya Wilson, 1967.

"As I had been schooled in secretarial skills at home in the north of England, I found numerous jobs as a temp. A few evenings a week I worked as a waitress at a basement restaurant, Le Sous Sol, and fell in with a crowd of music lovers. This is where I learned about Jimi Hendrix, who was the buzz of London.

"My date from the restaurant got tickets for the show at the Saville Theatre. There isn't a word to describe his performance to me. I hold this as one of the truly mesmerizing moments of my life."

# 4
# Are You Experienced? We Are Now

One month to the day after he left America, Jimi and the Experience began recording at De Lane Lea Studios, laying down three takes of "Hey Joe," his first single, which entered the charts at the end of the year and reached #6 in the UK.

The single had first been presented to Decca Records, but they declined. Yet again, Decca had to live down the embarrassment of having passed on a momentous artist, as they had in 1962 with the Beatles.

**A**fter much hustling, Chandler was able to land a deal with Track Records, the brand new imprint of the Who's management team, Kit Lambert and Chris Stamp, who recognized the scope of the talent before them.

Recording proceeded into the New Year, moving first to CBS and then to Olympic Studios, where Jimi encountered engineer Eddie Kramer. Kramer had previously worked at Pye Studios and Regent Sound before joining Olympic, where he recorded the Rolling Stones, the Beatles, and Traffic.

Jimi had a clear sense of what he wanted and how to get there; he'd run through the song's chord changes, the keys and tempo, and, with professional élan, Noel and Mitch were right with him, cutting a master in one or two passes.

Chas was reveling in his role as producer: cracking the whip—time was truly money, encouraging risk—"Backwards guitar solo? Brilliant"—crafting arrangements, and, critically, providing an anchor when Jimi began to list under the weight of his own expectations.

### EDDIE KRAMER | recording engineer, producer

"De Lane Lea studios. Small room and underneath a bank, which was problematic—couldn't play loud at certain times and all this stuff. Even though some of the sounds they got were cool. They did two songs: 'Hey Joe' and 'The Wind Cries Mary,' and maybe one other track. I wasn't there.

"But from there they went to CBS studios, and they were never happy there.

"Very soon thereafter, in 1966, I'm at Olympic, and in January '67 I start recording with Jimi. Olympic was the greatest independent studio in the UK. Cutting edge.

"All the major recording studios in London at that time—Pye, Decca, Phillips, EMI—the record companies owned their own studios, and they forced their artists to record in their studios. So they were all kind of buttoned up, if you know what I mean, whereas the indie studios like Olympic had the edge that I feel. And I was fortunate enough to be there.

"Chas had heard about it. Brings Jimi in, and from the first day we met [it] was completely overwhelming and stunning for me. But Jimi and I just got on very quickly. He realized I could get him a sound, and we kept trying to top each other . . . I'd get him a sound. He'd run out into the studio and try to make his amp sound different and try to top what I just did. And then he'd come back in, [we'd] look at each other, smile and laughing.

A contemporary view of the facade of Olympic Studios in Barnes, London; the building went back to its early roots as a cinema in 2013.

> **"** Olympic was a big studio. It was about 75 feet long by about 45 feet wide and 35 feet high [23 × 13.7 × 10.7 m]. And it was designed so you could record symphony orchestras and big pop sessions. They had big 35 mm projectors above the control room, so we could do music to picture, which was for TV and film stuff. **"**

—Eddie Kramer, recording engineer, producer

**RICHARD BOSWORTH** | engineer, record producer

"In Olympic they had a similar large orchestral recording space as RCA Studios [had] in Hollywood, where Andrew Loog Oldham produced the Rolling Stones during 1964 to 1966. Olympic was well equipped with state-of-the-art custom audio consoles designed by the chief technical engineer, Dick Swettenham."

# Shots Fired

Released in Britain by Track Record on May 12, 1967 (not until August 23 on Warner Bros.' Reprise label in the States), at a cost of £1,500 (approximately $3,700 at that time), *Are You Experienced?* was the opening salvo from an artist as enigmatically disruptive as the decade he would come to define. Two weeks after the Experience's debut album appeared in stores, the Beatles' *Sgt. Pepper* exploded and the sixties were wheels up—it was going to be a bumpy ride.

**JAMES CUSHING** | poet, English professor, deejay

"*Are You Experienced?* exists in separate UK and US editions, with different covers and songs and running order—a situation that indicates a lack of total artistic control. The 'music business' was, at least in mid-1967, making some key decisions about how to sell this risky property (a loud, mixed-race trio in the summer of the Newark and Detroit riots?). But in either edition, Hendrix has already made the musical decisions and his mind, as he insists in 'Foxy Lady'—that result in an original sound.

"Yes, guitarists Willie Johnson and Pat Hare had used extreme distortion in backing up Howlin' Wolf in the fifties, but their blasts and wails were additions to the music, not the center of it. They provide emphatically earthy commentary to Wolf's unearthly vocals. Hendrix was not nearly as powerful a singer as Wolf, but he makes that fact work for him; his voice portrays cool intimacy, inviting the listener into a space where the guitar does the deeper talking.

"The order of songs on side two of the US edition is impossible to improve: the gentle country-western of 'The Wind Cries Mary' leads into the jump-blues of 'Fire', then we catch our breath in time for the sound experiment of 'Third Stone', which anticipates the eros of 'Foxy Lady', after which the processional march–rhythm of the title piece (are those bells on the verses?) takes us out."

### BRIAN AUGER | keyboardist

"When I heard Jimi's first album, I had to play it over again because there was so much in the production I couldn't digest all of it in one go. It's like hearing a great jazz album, but in a much different way.

"The Trinity scored a hit with our cover of an Aretha Franklin tune called 'Save Me'. We were invited to play the Olympia Theater in Paris. Our then manager, the infamous Giorgio Gomelsky, suggested that Jimi and the Experience open for us, which I thought was a great idea. Parisian audiences could be tough; if they didn't like you, you'd better duck, because things would come flying. But if they liked you. . . . Jimi had them eating out [of] his hand. At the end of the show, all the bands come onstage for a bit of a rave and the crowd's going crazy. I stood in the wings and was mesmerized."

# Back in the States

The Experience were quickly acclimating to the rarefied air of incipient pop stardom. April found them twitching impertinently on a glossy packaged tour of Britain, headlined by crooner Engelbert Humperdinck, a nattily attired Cat Stevens, and the current teen sensation, the Walker Brothers. Hendrix dismissed it as a silly little tour, frustrated by the promoters who accused him of being vulgar and obscene. But if the adage that "any publicity is good publicity" is true, the JHE were clearly marking their territory.

"Purple Haze" was the follow-up single to "Hey Joe," furthering their momentum. The song featured that sinister guitar hook, a bold embrace of the "flat 5" voicing—often call the devil's interval—which produces more of a scent than a sound. It's dark, illicit, and reeks of sex. With the release of *Are You Experienced?* in May, Hendrix provided an arousing new liturgy for fans to obsess over, to torment their oblivious parents with, to groove behind a taste of the big muddy in a sparkling new package.

**KIM FOWLEY** | songwriter, record producer

"In spring 1967, I was the one who told Warner/Reprise label head Mo Ostin about Jimi in his Burbank office and that it would be a good idea to sign Hendrix for [the] North American market. Jimi was already with Track Record in England. I thought Jimi could be 'the psychedelic Chuck Berry for the late sixties.'

"I was a briefly a criminology major at San Diego State College, and when Mo asked me how to play the manager, Mike Jeffrey, I gave him negotiation guidelines, record deal suggestions, and Jeffrey's home phone number.

"An hour later, Brian Jones and Jack Nitzsche visited Mo in Burbank and confirmed what I said and lobbied on behalf of Jimi. We all knew that Jimi would be [a] great acquisition for America.

"Bobby Womack, Sam Cooke, and I shared the same music attorney, Walter E. Hurst in Hollywood. Bobby kept his pit bull dog in one of Walter's offices. Bobby cited Jimi and Curtis Mayfield as guitarists to me from tours he did when he played guitar in Sam's group when they did shows with the Impressions, Dee Clark, and Jackie Wilson.

"Jimi was an experienced performer, and everyone else was suburban white kids trying to be English or black.

"I also realized the impact [of] the spring '67 Stax/Volt Records label tour of England and Europe. It galvanized everyone who checked it out. [It was witnessed by Eric Burdon, Stevie Winwood, Brian Jones, Paul McCartney, Peter Gabriel, Pete Townshend, Rod Stewart, John Mayall, Roger Daltrey, Hugh Hopper, Mick Jagger, Keith Richards, Bill Wyman, and Andrew Loog Oldham]. Because black people invented rock 'n' roll. . . .

"I was a dancer on the *Beat Room,* which was on BBC2 in 1964. In 1965, I appeared and sang on *Ready Steady Go!* on

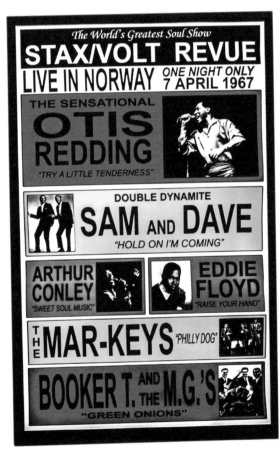

Poster for a 1967 Stax/Volt show.

TV. I was well aware of the late 1966 musical climate Jimi had arrived into. Otis Redding on *Ready Steady Go!* in September '66. I knew Jimi would take over in summer 1967 in England and America because he had Chitlin' Circuit experience, and he knew how to work a crowd."

### RUSS REGAN | record executive

"At the time I was general manager of Loma Records, the Warner Bros. R&B label. Joe Smith brought me to Warner Bros. Kim Fowley had praised Jimi to us. I had an office next to Mo Ostin.

"In 1965, AM radio station KHJ in Hollywood changed their format to Boss Radio. I loved the RKO radio programmer, Bill Drake. Play the hits. Keep the talk down to a minimum. He understood the repetition of Top 30.

"In '67 I noticed the growing development of the LP away from the 45 rpm. FM radio really starts in 1967. My friend, deejay Dave Diamond, was really doing some wild and different programming on the AM dial with KBLA 1965–1967 after he left KHJ in 1966.

"Around April '67, Mo Ostin called me into his office and played me the acetate of 'Hey Joe' by the Jimi Hendrix Experience. 'Listen to this!' And then puts on 'Purple Haze,' and I said, 'It's either gonna be huge or nothing. There's no halfway on this.'"

A c. 1966–67 handout for LA rock station KBLA-AM. Dave Diamond's shift on KBLA in all probability debuted the first Hendrix acetate regionally, courtesy of Russ Regan at the Burbank-located Warner/Reprise record label.

### KIM FOWLEY

"Mo Ostin subsequently visited me in LA at the House for Homeless Groups, which was LWG Studios, where I was living in a back room. He arrived in a Cadillac.

"Later, after Jimi signed to the Reprise/Warner Bros., label, Mike Jeffery came by as well, who was very thankful for my help.

"I connected him with Buddy Walters, who was doing the light show for the West Coast Pop Art Experimental Band. Buddy then set up the light show for Jeffrey's clients Jimi Hendrix and the New Animals with Eric Burdon.

## DENNY BRUCE | record producer, A&R manager

"In early spring '67, [musician and record producer] Jack Nitzsche and I were living at the Sunset Marquis Hotel in West Hollywood. We were between pads. Jack got an advance copy of 'Hey Joe' and it blew his mind.

"Jack knew Mo Ostin at Reprise very well and did 'The Lonely Surfer' for the label and all sorts of arranging and producing in the early sixties. And then Jack got the advance first Hendrix album in mono. It sounded better, with more punch to it, than what Warner/Reprise put out later in stereo."

## JOE SMITH | former president, Warner Bros. Records

"Hendrix became an acquisition for us in North America. I took out the first Hendrix album to our independent distributors during summer '67, and I would make the pitch. And I'm in Chicago with all our distributors from the Midwest and the South. And I said, 'This is the music that will change the world. Now, you've been listening to Frank Sinatra and Sammy Davis Jr. records here. This is what we're going to be dealing with for many years.'

"And our deal used to be with our distributors that they bought seven and they got one free. And then I looked at the order from Minneapolis and they ordered seven records. I called them in. 'This is the future!' And I added three zeroes. 'You just bought seven thousand of this fuckin' album and you'll get a thousand free.' You had to convince these older guys who grew up with Dean Martin and Frank Sinatra records."

## GENE CORNISH | guitarist and harmonica player, founding member of the Rascals

"When the Rascals were recording at the Atlantic Records studio in New York, Aretha Franklin, Wilson Pickett, and Otis Redding would come into the studio. Cream would come in at night.

"Murray the K, the famous deejay, came to my house with the first copy of Hendrix's 'Wind Cries Mary' and 'Hey Joe.' . . .

"The sixties were all about sharing. Jimi opened for us at his first American gig in New York [July 5, 1967] at the [Rheingold] Central Park Music Festival after I heard 'Hey Joe.'"

Gene Cornish of the Rascals, May 25, 1968.

The Jimi Hendrix Experience poses for "jam" photos in a hotel room in New York City before Rheingold Fest in Central Park, July 5, 1967. Jimi's girlfriend, Roselyn Morris, looks on.

# 5
# Pop Goes the Festival

Packaged tours had long been a staple of pop music, a stream of mostly one-hit wonders parading before a distempered outburst of girlish enthusiasm. It was a profitable formula, perfected by Barry Gordy and his Motown stables and by the ever-enterprising Dick Clark, with his various American Bandstand productions. There was also the Hollywood-based Teen-Age Fair, a three-day carnival presented at the Hollywood Palladium on Sunset Boulevard throughout the mid-sixties.

**N**ew York deejay Murray the K—aka the "fifth Beatle"—booked his own multinight music extravaganza in March 1967 at the RKO Theater on 58th Street. He branded it "Music in the Fifth Dimension," and it featured a disparate congeries of old-time rock 'n' roll, white boy blues, hard-core R&B (Wilson Pickett—yeah!), and, from England, the Who and Cream, making their American debut.

But this was all a preamble to the monumental Monterey International Pop Festival, that career-making jubilee held on June 16, 17, and 18 in the sylvan setting of coastal California. It celebrated the growing sophistication of both the artists and the music industry, that this was a unique moment in time to harness all the groovy feelings, the good vibrations that swirling around young people and bring it all under one unifying tent. Music was now more than an entertainment; it was a prism through which society to reinvent itself in a more harmonious, peaceable direction. That was a lot of baggage for a music festival to carry and it succeeded in ways that still resonate today. The event was masterminded by producer Lou Adler and by the Mamas & the Papas' John Phillips, along with entrepreneur Alan Pariser and publicist Derek Taylor.

This was the "Summer of Love," a powerful hook, a "Happening," that catch-all concept for a little societal transgression seasoned with a hint of surrealism, leavened with a dash of Dada, and garnished with a hit of LSD. It had its origins in the febrile imagination of French poet and bohemian gadfly Jean-Jacques Lebel, who unleashed his madcap scheme—the first European version of the "Happening"—in Venice, Italy, in 1960.

Associate producer of the Monterey Pop Festival, Alan Pariser, shown here in March 1967.

Seven years and numerous convocations later, in February 1967, *Life* magazine splashed the following headline on its iconic cover: "HAPPENINGS—The Worldwide Underground of the Arts Creates the Other Culture." Lebel himself articulated the movement's mission statement: the experience was about "a chance to communicate with others on the level of their fantasies and dreams."

On Sunday night, June 18, following the Who's auto-destruction routine and an uncharacteristically sedate set from the Grateful Dead (who perhaps were feeling the pinch of the British assault), Jimi Hendrix fulfilled Lebel's hopes and even more.

### ERIC BURDON | singer/songwriter, the Animals and War

"I departed London Heathrow for New York, spending one night in New York City then onward to Monterey. The next day I traveled with Brian Jones, Jimi Hendrix, Mitch Mitchell, Noel Redding, Chas Chandler, and Jimi's management personnel. Honestly, I do not remember the flight from NYC to Monterey, except Jimi chugging on a bottle of Jack Daniels which he had wrapped in a blue bandanna. This was a great overture to the wonderful madness that we would face the minute we landed in Monterey, California—step one in the cosmic joke."

### ANDREW LOOG OLDHAM | Rolling Stones manager and record producer

"In 1966, I met Jimi at Cafe Wha? but didn't see him play that evening.

"Paul McCartney and I simultaneously recommended Jimi to Lou Adler for [Monterey Pop], and I also suggested the Who and Otis Redding."

### JIM SALZER | concert promoter

"I go back with Jimi to Monterey Festival. I had already booked the Jimi Hendrix Experience as a concert promoter in Ventura because I was into the first album right away. I was always looking for entertainers who were cutting edge and who I wanted to see. So when I got to the festival, I looked up Jimi."

### JENNI DEAN HARTE | Jimi Hendrix friend

"I knew Jimi from Greenwich Village before he went to England. Loved him, loved his music.

"I was with Jimi, driving around Monterey before his performance, trying to find lighter fluid (for you know what!). We had to drive around for a while because most of the stores were closed, but we finally scored. He didn't want to go on after the Who and they didn't want to go on after him. We all knew what kind of impression he was going to make, and it was a fuckin' thrill a minute for everybody."

Backstage at Monterey Pop; Jenni Dean Harte sits to the right of Jimi.

### AL KOOPER | keyboardist, Blues Project

"I was the assistant stage manager. As a songwriter, I was signed to Aaron Schroeder, who was a music publisher. He signed Randy Newman, Gene Pitney, myself, and Jimi Hendrix for publishing before there was a record out on him.

"So when *Are You Experienced?* came out in England, I got a copy way before anybody, from my publisher. Aaron had the US publishing for his company, Yameta. At Monterey I was totally conversant with that album, which was just coming out in America then.

So I knew all about him and used to read the English music papers like *Disc* and *Melody Maker*. I was into that. He was no stranger to me.

"When I was setting up Hendrix for sound, Jimi knew who I was; so when we met, it was quite nice. So he said, 'I'm gonna play "Like a Rolling Stone" tonight, do you want to sit in with us?' [Kooper is the organist on the 1965 original Bob Dylan "Like a Rolling Stone" recording.] I said, 'I would love to play with you, but I'm working here, I'm the assistant stage manager.'

"Can you imagine what kind of self-control it took to now do that? Another of my great career moves. I knew all his tunes. To play that song with him would have been great, which I later did at a club. I asked producer Lou Adler if I could have a little set on Saturday and they said okay."

**Top and above:** Jimi and friends offstage during Monterey Pop.

## PETE TOWNSHEND | The Who

"We were both of us competitive. He felt like something of a newcomer, and standard-bearer for black blues, I think—that he may have felt had been plundered by the British sixties bands. But he and I debated about who should go on first. I felt he was a master, a genius. I was not prepared to follow him, not because I was afraid to follow him but because in my old-fashioned show-biz mind the best artists go on latest in the set. In the end we tossed for it, and Jimi lost.

"We went on first; he then announced that if we preceded him, and set the crowd alight with our destruction act, he too would set them alight. So the crowd got two mind-fucking sets.

"A side issue was that we played at the Fillmore on this trip, and that was probably more important to us, because Bill Graham insisted we play a longer set than we were used to. It was around this time we began to include songs like 'Young Man Blues' and 'Summertime Blues.'"

Pete Townshend during the Who's performance at Monterey Pop, Sunday evening, June 18.

"**Everybody had dressing rooms. I knew the Who then and [was] very close to them. As a matter of fact, I went into their dressing room after the set and asked Townshend if everything was okay. There was some politics about who was going to go on first because they were both smashers of guitars. The Who went on first, and Hendrix said to himself, 'Let him bang his guitar. I'll set mine on fire!'**"

—**Al Kooper**, keyboardist, Blues Project

Contact sheet by photographer Henry Diltz of the Who's incendiary set at Monterey Pop.

## ROGER DALTREY | The Who

"I had seen him before loads of times in England. Yes, we'd seen how he copied our shows—not musically, but theatrically, a lot of it was stolen from Townshend.

"At Monterey there was a jam with Hendrix under the stage. Janis Joplin, all sorts of people all standing around— Buddy Miles, Brian Jones. . . . And Hendrix was playing 'Sgt. Pepper,' which had just been released, and he was doing all the top lines, all the bass notes, all in one. Just a fuckin' genius, you know."

Roger Daltrey onstage at Monterey Pop.

## JERRY WEXLER | record producer, Atlantic Records executive

"[I knew] Jimi Hendrix before the psychedelic phase, when he was playing with King Curtis and the Isley Brothers and around New York. He was a soul-circuit veteran.

"I'm in the wings when Jimi walked up to me just before he was going onstage, and now he is in full psychedelia regalia in feathers and a costume. And he looks at me, whispers in my ear, and almost apologetically, runs his hands all over himself and says, 'Hey man, this is just show business,' because of his outfit."

Jimi Hendrix at a tribute to Martin Luther King Jr. with Jerry Wexler, backstage at Madison Square Garden on June 28, 1968, in New York.

### LARRY TAYLOR | bassist, Canned Heat

"Monterey was our first festival. I was at Monterey for two days. I had heard of Jimi before the festival. I saw Hendrix when he was onstage, sitting right by Booker T.'s organ, watching him."

# Aftershock

Virtually unknown in the States, Jimi blew up any remnant of pop propriety, stalking the stage with a feral intensity, torching the village—literally—leav-

Canned Heat bassist Larry Taylor (left) and recording engineer Hank Cicalo at Monterey Pop. Canned Heat played Saturday afternoon, June 17.

ing the audience in a poleaxed state of shock and awe. (Don't believe it? Take a look at D. A. Pennebaker's documentary, *Monterey Pop*, to see the townspeople in abject fear.) For many present, it was a bridge too far; they quaked in their love beads and Nehru jackets. For others, though, it was an invitation to stand next to an artist's burning desire.

### CHRIS HILLMAN

"Jimi Hendrix . . . his playing. He was so out of left field—that's what got everybody. Not the burning of the guitar. That part was minimum. Here he was getting this tone on a guitar no one has heard before. My reaction at first was, 'That's a lot of noise.' Noel Redding was really loud, and the drummer [Mitch Mitchell] was playing nine million fills. But then that guitar tone comes in. He was such a good player."

Bassist Chris Hillman of the Byrds at Monterey Pop; the Byrds went onstage Saturday evening.

**PAUL BODY** | attendee, Monterey Festival

"There was something in the air—I could feel it. The world was changing. AM radio was slowly giving way to FM. Brian Jones appeared in a haze and introduced the Jimi Hendrix Experience, and Jimi, Mitch, and Noel took the stage in their hippie finery.

"It seemed like they were wearing all of the colors of the rainbow.

"I didn't know how three cats could make such a racket. It wasn't a minstrel show. It was a brother taking back the devil's music. He dressed the blues up in ruffles and bell bottoms. He took it off Highway 49 and took it to Monterey. Instead of a process, the blues had flowers in its hair.

"The show was pure Chitlin' Circuit, only louder. By the time they got to 'Wild Thing,' there was a chill in the night, but the stage was a burning red inferno. He said at the beginning of 'Wild Thing' that he was going to sacrifice something that he dearly loved, and we didn't know what the hell he was talking about. Then after beating his axe into submission, he kissed it, knelt in front of it, and set it on fire. Once again, the audience was stunned into silence."

Jimi Hendrix performing at Monterey Pop, Sunday evening, June 18.

### ROBERT MARCHESE | record producer/manager

"Jimi walked off; I shook his hand and said, 'You're the most psychedelic Negro I ever heard.' [Laughs.] That was my comment. And Jimi replied, 'That's right. I'm gonna make a lot of money.' 'Yes you are!'"

### MICHELLE PHILLIPS | actress, vocalist, the Mamas & the Papas

"Jimi Hendrix. I was so embarrassed and shocked. I had never seen anyone so sexually explicit on stage. I had never seen anybody treat their axe like that.

Festival coproducer and leader of the Mamas & the Papas, John Phillips, left, at Monterey Pop; at right, the "Mamas" Michelle Phillips and Mama Cass. The band went onstage Sunday evening after Hendrix.

"We were always so careful about our instruments and when we traveled we had the guitars in the plane with us. And then to see [him] set fire to the guitar and to slam it to bits on the stage was very upsetting to me. It was a form of expression that I was not prepared for."

### PETER LEWIS | singer/songwriter, cofounder of Moby Grape

"At Monterey we had some interactions in dressing rooms noodling before the Jimi Hendrix Experience set.

"I remember being backstage with Jimi Hendrix before he went on. At one point I asked him about his trip, and he replied with something like 'waking up in my own dream.' I really didn't get it at the time, but I sort of do now. His dream was not being a black guy who had to sit in the back of the bus, you know. His guitar was his weapon of choice. That's how he came off.

"All that stuff you can hear in Jimi Hendrix's music. It comes out. Like all that sublimated rage. It was on stage at Monterey. On behalf of all people, he was making a stand at Monterey.

"It was great. He did what he did, all self-explanatory. The hippie black movement was not around until Jimi Hendrix. He got everybody on that trip. He knew as long as they kept thinking about him on that level that he could turn into something like that. It reminded me more of voodoo. It was about music, and he could really play.

"Just before he went on at Monterey, I was wandering around and fell into his dressing room. I stared at him and he kind of looked at me. Jimi shows up in his feathers and shit and I wondered, 'What is gonna become of him?' America wasn't right on yet.

"Once we were in a hotel room and after Monterey I ran into him, Mitch, and Noel Redding in a motel [where] we were staying. He was very gregarious, a lonely genius type of guy. His whole thing was the guitar. He dedicated his life to it."

Guitarist Peter Lewis of Moby Grape at Shrine Exposition Hall, Los Angeles, 1967.

### DJINN RUFFNER | attendee, Monterey Festival

"I was at Monterey with a girlfriend named Candy. We went backstage. Jimi was a very shy person and in a corner by himself. I knew Jimmy James was Jimi Hendrix from reading the English music papers.

"He was so handsome and a beautiful man. Tall and slim. Big hands, and legs up to his ears. When his set started, I was sitting second row center. Brian Jones introduced him. It was FM radio music. First Jimi had sex with his guitar, and then he sacrificed it."

Paul Kantner of Jefferson Airplane, 1971.

### PAUL KANTNER | singer/songwriter, guitarist, Jefferson Airplane

"Monterey was just a booking. Another step; no one viewed it as some great momentous brouhaha. But it became more than that. As many things did in those days, because of what we did in San Francisco. No chains. And that was what was so glorious about San Francisco in those days. I enjoyed just the overall whole thing. There were great moments, like Jimi and Otis Redding. Jimi was impressive. He was Hendrix. You can't define it. You don't have to. If you saw it, you knew what it was."

## JERRY MILLER

"I saw Jimi and Otis [Redding] take over the show. Monterey was perfect. I was sitting right in front of Jimi at Monterey. It was wonderful. We sure had a good time. And Jimi got to see me, too. We were both left-handed guitarists. Here we are, a couple of schmucks from Seattle . . .

"What Jimi did was that he did the full-chord thing. Anybody can play lead a hundred miles an hour. But to do a full package with a three-piece, and have the P.A. and the lights. It was his day. It was beautiful. He had it. The sound was right, the color was right. And it was the chords and the Stratocaster and the Marshall amps. It came out with the full-body flavor. The Marshall amps gave the bottom, a nice hairy bottom, and a full six-string blend with meat and potatoes.

"After his show at Monterey, Jimi was signing girls' breasts. They would pull up their sweaters, hand him a tube of lipstick, and he'd sign his autograph. I said to him, 'That looks like a nice job.'"

## BARRY GOLDBERG | keyboardist and songwriter

"At Monterey I saw Jimi, and he called over to me, 'Hey Piano Man'– that's what he called me–'what's happening?' 'You are!' I replied. I remember that like it was yesterday.

"Shortly afterward, I wrote a tribute song with Michael Bloomfield about Hendrix, 'Jimi the Fox,' and we did it on my album *Two Jews Blues*. When Jimi and Buddy Miles did *Band of Gypsys*, Jimi told Buddy how much he really liked our song about him."

Drummer Buddy Miles of Electric Flag at Monterey Pop, Saturday afternoon.

## ALEX DEL ZOPPO | keyboardist, Sweetwater

"In the spring of 1967, in Los Angeles, my band Sweetwater was deep in rehearsals.

"Hearing [Hendrix] play for the first time was as if he was from another galaxy. Yes, his guitar chops were obviously informed by the blues and already sounding more powerful than any of my favorite guitarists, but way beyond other blues players that we'd heard.

"His most startling gift, though, was how astoundingly fluid he played, skipping between rhythm and lead, playing with jaw-dropping dexterity and ease, stretching notes into oblivion, then bringing it all back without missing a beat, as if we were hearing two or three guitarists!

> **"He played as if he had no restrictions—so confidently that he constantly took the chance of allowing the wheels of his barreling train to leave the tracks, while never fearing that they wouldn't return again just when they should. His playing was the perfect amalgamation of discipline and abandon."**
>
> —**Alex Del Zoppo**, keyboardist, Sweetwater

**MICKY DOLENZ** | vocalist and drummer, the Monkees

"I had seen Jimi as a backup guitarist for John Hammond Jr. in New York. I was singing on some recording sessions for our first LP at RCA. He was a sideman in 1966. Someone told me I had to go to this club to see this guitarist who played with his teeth. I didn't know his name. Hammond was pretty incredible.

"I'm sitting at Monterey and then Jimi, Noel, and Mitch come onstage.

"I didn't know Jimi had gone to England and Chas Chandler put a band together for him. Jimi walks out on stage, and I recognize him, because he's playing guitar with his teeth. 'Hey! That's the guy who plays guitar with his teeth.' I suggested him for our 1967 tour because we were looking for a great opening act and he was very theatrical. And the Monkees were theater. We were looking for a great opening act at the time, as the Monkees had a tour planned."

Monkee Micky Dolenz at Monterey Pop.

"I saw Jimi at Monterey, told our producers, who got in touch with Chas Chandler and then Jimi's booking agent. Everyone thought it was a great idea."

"I do remember after the Hendrix show that night, I ended up somehow as this sort of mascot to Jimi and God

Photographer Henry Diltz captured the scene at a club in San Francisco's North Beach on June 18, 1967. Jimi's explosive performance at Monterey Pop that night had made such an impact that the club's light show crew projected JHE's name in colored gels against the wall.

knows who else. I had acquired instruments, amps, guitars, and a generator for electricity, and long after the show was over and the event had essentially ended, everybody was so pumped up it was tough to go away. And there wasn't anybody who was forcing anyone out of the area."

### ABE JACOB | sound engineer

"In 1966, I was working for McCune Sound in San Francisco. I was on the sound crew at the Beatles' last concert in August '66, at Candlestick Park.

"I had gone to the Be-In in San Francisco and I was doing some work with Chet Helms at the Family Dog. McCune Sound had always done sound for the Monterey Jazz Festival. So it was a natural fit.

"I was mostly taking care of all the stage setup at Monterey and went out and mixed front of house for the Mamas & the Papas. I was onstage for almost all of it, and when I first saw the Jimi Hendrix Experience—wow! This guy plays guitar and puts on a show.

"I was primarily the guy that wanted to do the live event and make the audience that night very special and very unique. And go on to the next night. Not try to archive it or re-create it.

"In the live sound world, when you saw the guitar player come in for his solo, you wanted to bring that out, maybe more than it was necessary to do on the recording. Because you wanted the ear to follow what the eye was looking at as far as the performer was going.

"That was one of the first things I thought about in doing live sound. Not just re-creating a record. But to try and capture the performance that's going on the stage and make the event happen. I guess most of the acts that were traveling and playing in 1967 just stood there and played. Jimi gave it some kind of theatrical flair, which I guess really worked."

Monterey Pop coproducer Lou Adler (center) at the festival.

**LOU ADLER** | record and film producer, music executive, coproducer of Monterey Pop

"Everyone is now aware of what Jimi did at Monterey and what it meant to his career. It's an important moment of Jimi's career for a couple of reasons. One, obviously, was the size and the attention of the festival; but also, this was an American returning to America after being successful in England and parts of Europe. It's his homecoming, and he pulls it off amazingly. It's one of those things you dream about. It's going up to bat hitting the home run with the bases loaded, or throwing the touchdown pass to win the game. It's coming through after all of what you dream about."

Janis Joplin at the mike during Big Brother & the Holding Company's second set on Sunday evening (filmed for the D. A. Pennebaker documentary *Monterey Pop*).

**JANN WENNER** | publisher, *Rolling Stone* magazine

"The big stunners were the Who, Otis, and Jimi Hendrix. Otis was the one. I was familiar with the Who and they did a great job. Hendrix was dazzling, setting his guitar on fire. Jimi Hendrix, Janis Joplin, Otis Redding were so great."

"It was just one of those periods in the history of art where a dozen super important revolutionary artists are all around and on the stage at the same place or the world stage."

## JIM SALZER | concert promoter

"At Monterey, Jimi and I caught Ravi Shankar together and kind of bonded a bit.

"I told Jimi we were going to do some concerts together. Jimi is my favorite all-time entertainer. He was a gentleman and one of the best people I ever worked with. The Jimi I knew was a decent, wholesome kind of guy. Good friend with his word."

## KEITH ALTHAM | music journalist, *New Musical Express*

"Monterey to Jimi was like coming home. He knew that he had to live up to all the plaudits that he had from his peer group in England, you know. The prince of the rock guitar.

"Nothing like coming out to Monterey and playing to a large crowd. Probably the largest he'd ever played to. And seeing that kind of groundswell of interest in progressive rock music gave him hope for the future and an indication perhaps of the direction he might be able to take the music.

"I think, although there wasn't a road to Damascus at Monterey, I think he felt that it was yet another step up the ladder. He knew that was a foot in the door. I don't think it broke Jimi in America. I think it put a foot in the door and brought him to the attention of the mass media in America, and indeed to television and radio exposure, which he had not had yet. One guy in the press pit with me said after he finished, 'What the hell was that?'"

The crowd at Monterey Pop during one of the evening shows.

### JERRY HELLER | booking agent

"I worked for Associated Booking in Beverly Hills and [was] the agent for Canned Heat, Eric Burdon and the Animals, and Otis Redding at Monterey. . . .

"Jimi was beyond belief. Already there was a buzz about him, and he was just unbelievable. So much so, I beelined right after his set, I talked to him, because I had heard about him from some of my friends in England, and told him I was gonna arrange a tour for him. . . .

"So he said, 'Who you gonna have me play with?' and I wanted to put him in the biggest venues possible, and remember, I don't even know this guy, and had him then open for the Monkees.

"I booked the dates. I wanted to get him exposed to as many people possible. I liked Chas Chandler. He was a good guy. I knew the Animals and Eric. So I did have an entry and always had that kind of cachet."

### ERIC BURDON | lead singer, the Animals

"I had a blast at the festival. . . . It was truly a gathering of the tribes. It would be in California, so in a way it was like going home for me, and what helped me make up my mind was that Jimi was going to be there. It was his US homecoming, which, as he pointed out to the audience while onstage, he was not a homecoming queen. I have always felt that even though it was the launchpad for Jimi's career, it also heralded the end, because as I stood next to Ravi Shankar on the side of the stage as Jimi performed, a look of shock and horror came over Ravi's face that an artist was actually destroying his instrument, and that . . . no doubt is . . . bad karma.

"And all this—just to outdo the Brit boys, the Who. The question remains: how many times can you set your guitar on fire . . . and where do you go from there?"

Eric Burdon onstage during the Animals' performance, the first night of the show, Friday, June 16.

## HENRY DILTZ | photographer

"I was at Monterey. John Phillips asked me to be the official photographer.

"I never thought I was doing something historic. My job was to hang out and take photos of everybody doing what they did because I enjoyed doing it. And it got me around observing and watching.

"I was used to being with my friends and just documenting all the things that went on around them. The dressing rooms at Monterey were underneath the stage, on dirt floors in a basement.

"The Mamas & the Papas were backstage grabbing their tongues and doing various vocal exercises, like holding the tip of your tongue with your two fingers and sort of chanting sounds and making all these scales. OOO-AAAH.

Famed lensman Henry Diltz, official Monterey Pop photographer, at the festival.

"So the group is backstage, all holding their tongues, preparing to perform, and Jimi Hendrix, who had just finished playing, was on the other side of the room, sitting in a chair, eating a piece of fried chicken, people all around him, and checking out these other hippies, while the Mamas & Papas [are] doing their unique chant harmony."

## CLIVE DAVIS | former president of Columbia Records, founder of Arista, former CEO of RCA Music Group

"I really came to Monterey not knowing what to expect, but seeing a revolution before my eyes, that became evident. All of a sudden seeing Jimi Hendrix, Janis Joplin and Big Brother & the Holding Company, and the Electric Flag, and the artists that were there—no question there was a change in contemporary music. A definite hardening, edgier, rockier amplification that was taking place that truly was signaling a major revolution in rock music."

## ANDREW LOOG OLDHAM

"The fight in '67 was different. Even though the likes of Nancy and Frank Sinatra and Petula Clark dominated the charts—I'll tell you. Nancy and Frank, Sandie Shaw, Englebert Humperdinck, Harry Secombe, and the Monkees! That was the top five in England during April of '67. In the second half of the '67 charts come the Beatles, the Who, Jim Hendrix, and the rest.

"Anyway, along with an audience now pretty high on a regular basis that was going to be around for a while, that could be targeted and marketed to."

# 6
# On the Road Again

Monterey was a triumph for the Experience—first, they'd earned the admiration of their peers. Second, the band found itself the object of a near-worshipful following, which emboldened them to push their instincts to their outer limits. It would also prove to be a burden—all that adulation would eventually have its own toxic consequences.

**B**ut in the immediate aftermath of Monterey, there appeared to be one nagging problem—where was the next show?

Mitch Mitchell, in his memoir *Jimi Hendrix: Inside the Experience* (1990), explains: "We'd done incredibly well in Europe in a very short time; we'd got to America, gone down really well. We thought we'd arrived. Boy, were we wrong. In the long term, of course, it was the best PR we could have possibly had, but we came out of that gig with *nothing*. I'm not just talking financially—we had no gigs. We were saved basically by Bill Graham, who picked us up for the Fillmore in San Francisco and by John Phillips who booked us to open for the Mamas & the Papas at the Hollywood Bowl."

Los Angeles also welcomed the band at the Whisky a Go Go, where they opened for Sam & Dave. New York got the message too: Steve Paul's the Scene was ground zero for all the hippest bands to gather for many memorable really-late-night jams, and Jimi was right there, flashing his Strat before a small but influential audience of tastemakers who helped him go viral the old-fashioned way—by word-of-mouth.

**MARTY BALIN** | singer/songwriter, cofounder, Jefferson Airplane

"The light show was important. It was a lot of fun. I remember when the Jimi Hendrix Experience played the Fillmore on June 20, 1967, and we were playing with him for a few dates with Gábor Szabó. I went up and played the plates [with the Dan Bruhn Fillmore Lights] when Jimi was on and start[ed] working the light show."

**DENNIS LOREN** | graphic designer and art director

"The first time I saw the Jimi Hendrix Experience was on the evening of Saturday, June 24, at the Fillmore Auditorium, on a concert bill with Jefferson Airplane and jazz guitarist Gábor Szabó. I was amazed by the music this trio—of guitarist Jimi Hendrix, bass player Noel Redding, and drummer Mitch Mitchell—made together. So were my friends and fellow band members, Joe Toschi and David Green, who attended the concert with me. Both Joe and David were guitarists and truly fascinated by all the different sounds Hendrix got from his guitar.

"I would see the group perform again the following afternoon in the Panhandle of Golden Gate Park. Ace of Cups opened. This extension of the park was located between the streets Fell and Oak. At the intersection of Masonic was an area where the Diggers handed out free food to the growing

Noted rock graphic designer Dennis Loren, c. 1969.

population of hippies that poured into the Haight-Ashbury district of San Francisco during the summer of 1967.

"Since I had designed the poster for this concert, I thought it might [be] a good opportunity to have my Digger friends introduce me [to] Jimi Hendrix and the band, which they did. Behind the flatbed truck stage, I also met future Band of Gypsys drummer Buddy Miles."

Dennis Loren's poster design for a JHE concert on June 25, 1967, at the Golden Gate Park in San Francisco.

## JIM SALZER | concert promoter

"Eventually, I started booking my own shows at Santa Barbara's Earl Warren Showgrounds and the Starlight Ballroom in Oxnard.

"Two-dollar ticket price in advance for the Jimi Hendrix show. But I only paid him $1,200 each time. July 1, 1967. One thousand nine hundred people there. Captain Speed, Country Joe & the Fish, and the Strawberry Alarm Clock.

"One time at a show with Jimi, he dropped a belt, a chain thing with little stars. And I brought it to him after he got off stage. 'Here Jimi, you dropped this.' And he said, 'No, keep it.' Over the years it broke into pieces, and I've given pieces of it away to friends. I think I have four left.

"Whenever I worked with a band, I always looked to the lead guitar player as, you know, the guts of the group. Not that the singer wasn't important. The musicians are important, and the quality of the band has a lot to do with the skill of the guitar player. I think Jimi was the most unique and most talented."

Poster for promoter Jim Salzer's show of July 1, 1967, at the Earl Warren Showgrounds in Santa Barbara, featuring the Jimi Hendrix Experience, Country Joe & the Fish, the Strawberry Alarm Clock, and Captain Speed.

**JOHNNY ECHOLS** | songwriter and guitarist,
record producer, cofounder of Love

"Love was in San Francisco playing and a friend of ours said, 'You should see
this guy Jimi Hendrix play.' Now I didn't realize that Jimi Hendrix back then was
Jimmy James that we knew from before. I then saw Jimi play at the Whisky a Go
Go [July 2, 1967] right after Monterey '67.

"So when we get to the Whisky, we see him and he's totally different than
before. He is dressed differently. His hair is different. His attitude and everything
is totally different. He really has swagger with this confidence. 'Cause the guy I
knew was rather laid back and not all that confident. But this guy. . . . It was weird
to see the marked change in him. And then he started to play, and I thought,
'Fuck! This isn't the same guy.' But it was. And we talked about him playing on
Arthur's song.

"It was him. But he played entirely different. And the weird thing was, and it was
funny, I asked, 'Man, did you take a visit to the crossroads?' The difference was so
pronounced. And he replied, 'I've been in the woodshed.'"

The Whisky a Go Go on the Sunset Strip, with Love and Afro-Cuban
jazz percussionist Mongo Santamaría on the marquee, 1967.

### ROBBY KRIEGER | guitarist, the Doors

"I saw Hendrix at my favorite place—the Whisky—1967. Jimi at his best.

"I was in the second booth [near the front door]. The place was packed, so we couldn't see very well, so we ended up standing on the table. . . . Saw the whole show from that tabletop."

Robby Kreiger, left, and John Densmore, right, of the Doors, December 20, 1969.

### JOHN DENSMORE | drummer, the Doors

"I saw Hendrix in 1967 at the Whisky, just after the Monterey International Pop festival. God! We knew somebody was coming. A giant! It was just . . . I don't have the words.

"He was like Coltrane on guitar, playing it upside down, without changing the strings. Forget it. I saw Coltrane many times."

### SEYMOUR CASSEL | actor

"I met Jimi Hendrix at Monterey. I then saw Jimi at the Whisky and at the Laurel Canyon Country Store. He used to babysit my son Matt so my wife Elizabeth and I could go out. . . .

"I loved Jimi, man. I tried to get some of his music in *Faces,* a '68 movie I was doing with John Cassavetes where we did some filming at the Whisky a Go Go."

"Jimi was amazing to watch. I did see him play live a couple of times in Seattle, probably 1967, '68. Just blew my mind. Amazing. I think it was his technique, and the way he hardly ever looked at the neck of the guitar. It was like he was in another world and playing those things you shouldn't hear from a guitar. I think he was an innovator. I wore out his first album with 'Hey Joe,' 'Foxy Lady,' and 'Fire.' When the Ventures first started in 1960, songs were 2:20 minutes; 'Walk, Don't Run,' and 'Hawaii Five-O' is 1:50. In 1960 to 1965, if you played a song longer than 2:20, most disc jockeys wouldn't play it for a single. Then later, in 1967 and '68, Hendrix took it into a whole other world."

—**Don Wilson**, guitarist and cofounder, the Ventures

# Hendrix and the Monkees

The Jimi Hendrix Experience went out on the Monkees' July US 1967 tour in a deal made between Chas Chandler, Hendrix's comanager, and promoter Dick Clark of ABC-TV's *American Bandstand* and *Where the Action Is* fame.

Besides the Hendrix trio, on their 1967 Stateside concerts the Monkees championed R&B and soul stars for opening slots, including Jewel Akens, the Fifth Dimension, an all-female group called the Apollas, and, at the Hollywood Bowl, the Ike & Tina Turner Revue.

## STEPHEN STILLS | singer/songwriter, multi-instrumentalist, cofounder CSNY

"I met up with Jimi after he had been booked on the Monkees tour. I met him up at Peter [Tork]'s house after we had been in Monterey.

"Jimi was very much out of place because was a real musician in the midst of all these Hollywood showbiz types. He was just looking for friends, because he didn't know anybody. We just gravitated to each other. And Jimi was half the reason that I went to see the Monkees so much.

"I got back down and Jimi was at Peter's house and we decided to go out to my house at the beach. Peter lent me his car, a burgundy GTO hardtop that was given to him by Pontiac, and [we] drove out to the beach. I was driving along Pacific Coast Highway when, all of a sudden, smoke was everywhere. I started to pull over and some idiot creamed me in the back. Instead of stomping on the brakes, I floored it and got the car under control and then pulled over. And then the cops came, and all they did was get Jimi's bottle of whiskey away from him.

"We went down the street and bought another one. The cops gave us all a ride to my house. We plugged in the amps and equipment and I told the cops, 'Here's my lease. If there are any complaints, give me a call or just knock on the door.' There was a CHP [California Highway

Stephen Stills and Micky Dolenz in Chicago, June 1967.

Patrolman] and two sheriffs parked across the street. And they came and knocked on the door and said, 'We just wanted to tell you, in case you open the door and freak, right, that we're not after you. We're actually just kind of making sure that nobody else messes with you and listening, and it's great. You guys are great.'

"We played nonstop for fourteen hours straight. We went through two different rhythm sections and watched the sun come up on the beach, just me and 'The Fox.' And that was where Hendrix and I really got tight."

# Left-Handed, Upside-Down

**M**usician David Price, who was a friend of Monkee Michael Nesmith and became a stand-in on *The Monkees* TV series, worked on the 1967 summer tour as a roadie.

David Price photographed on the road during the Monkees/JHE summer 1967 tour.

## DAVID PRICE, 1967 SUMMER TOUR ROADIE

"We were in Greensboro, North Carolina, and it was during the day. Charlie Rockett and I were rooming together. We had gone out and cruised around some of the pawnshops in Greensboro, looking for good deals on guitars. Charlie bought a two-tone green Gretsch Country Gentleman. We went back to the room. We're sitting there with the door open.

"Suddenly there's a figure standing in the doorway, and we look up and it's Jimi Hendrix. He comes walking in and he goes, 'Hey, whatta you got? What's going on?' I was fiddling on the guitar. Jimi sat down on the end of one of the beds and I just handed him the guitar. He sits there and he was just going, 'That's a cool guitar.' We're just talking. He's noodling around on the guitar but he is holding it, it was a right-handed guitar, not a left-handed guitar, and he was playing it right-handed. I said, 'Well, wait a second. You're playing right-handed.' He said, 'Yeah, that's the way I originally learned, but then when I really realized that I'm a lefty [and] it would be better if I played lefty, I turned it over. At first I learned how to play it upside down, left-handed upside down. Then I switched over and strung it left-handed and been playing that way ever since.'

"While he's telling this story, he's playing right-handed. And then he flips it over left-handed but it's strung upside down 'cause it's strung right-handed, and he continues to just chit-chat and noodle left-handed upside down. Well, what happened is, people start hearing this and they start coming in. All of a sudden the motel room fills up with people.

"Mike is sitting on the corner of the bed right to next to him and he's leaning over and you can see he's looking at Jimi's hands trying to figure out what the hell he's doing. There's a bunch of girls and different people just hanging around.

"What cracks me up is Charlie and I are not in the photograph. We were the guys who he originally came to hang out with. That was a great afternoon. That's my bed that Jimi Hendrix is sitting on, and that's in Greensboro, North Carolina. And there he's playing Charlie's two-tone green Gretsch."

Jimi Hendrix demonstrating his upside-down technique (playing left-handed on a right-handed-strung guitar) while sitting on musician/roadie David Price's hotel-room bed in Greensboro, NC, July 1967. In both photographs Monkee Peter Tork is in the right foreground and Monkee Michael Nesmith is seated beside Hendrix on the bed.

# Touring and Segregation in America

The Jimi Hendrix Experience quickly left the tour after the gig in Forest Hills, New York. It just wasn't a good fit, owing to booing, racial taunts, and a barrage of avid

Teen idol Davy Jones of the Monkees, May 1967.

Monkees fans constantly screaming, "We want Davy!"

After that, Chas Chandler politely asked Clark to be let out of his contract, and they parted amicably. (Erroneous press reports have blamed the Daughters of the American Revolution for complaining that the Hendrix stage act was "too erotic.")

**DICK CLARK** | radio and television producer, host of *American Bandstand*

"When it came time to bring the English musicians over, they had no feel for the racism we had in this country. I used to have long conversations and discussions with Eric Burdon of the Animals.

"Eric and I sat and argued about this for years. He was such a fan of black music. I said to him, 'You have no idea what this country has been through.'

"His first introduction was on a rock 'n' roll tour. He found they couldn't eat with the black performers in public restaurants. They couldn't stay in the same hotels. It was a revelation.

"We'd run into posters like 'Don't Play Negro Music,' 'Don't Buy Negro Records.' It was a very bizarre experience. And if you are a young person, it's gonna make an indelible impression on you.

"The Penguins, the Crows, Little Richard, Chuck Berry, Fats Domino, and Bo Diddley all made their first appearances on *American Bandstand*."

**ANDREW LOOG OLDHAM** | Rolling Stones manager and record producer

"You have to remember we were still not long past there being 'Negro cinemas' in all your Southern major towns, and the attitude, the racism, had kept on going. It was very hard for America to tear away from the way it had been born."

> "Smokey Robinson and the Miracles used to tour with the Rolling Stones and Georgie Fame and the Blue Flames. Man, those early tours were a trip. Endless hours of bus rides and all these skinny English dudes asking us about the Tamla Motown sound. We also had some racial hassles years ago in the South. It's getting better now."

—**Bobby Rogers**, singer, the Miracles

## KHJ'S BOSS 30 RECORDS IN SOUTHERN CALIFORNIA

### PREVIEWED AUGUST 16, 1967

| LAST WEEK | THIS WEEK | TITLE | ARTIST | LABEL | WEEKS ON BOSS 30 |
|---|---|---|---|---|---|
| (3) | 1. | ODE TO BILLIE JOE | Bobbie Gentry | Capitol | 3 |
| (6) | 2. | GIMME LITTLE SIGN | Brenton Wood | Double Shot | 4 |
| (8) | 3. | REFLECTIONS | Diana Ross & The Supremes | Motown | 3 |
| (4) | 4. | SILENCE IS GOLDEN | The Tremeloes | Epic | 6 |
| (2) | 5. | ALL YOU NEED IS LOVE/ BABY YOU'RE A RICH MAN | The Beatles | Capitol | 5 |
| (1) | 6. | SAN FRANCISCAN NIGHTS | Eric Burdon & The Animals | MGM | 5 |
| (7) | 7. | MERCY, MERCY, MERCY | The Buckinghams | Columbia | 7 |
| (5) | 8. | HAPPY | The Sunshine Company | Imperial | 5 |
| (12) | 9. | BABY I LOVE YOU | Aretha Franklin | Atlantic | 5 |
| (14) | 10. | THERE IS A MOUNTAIN | Donovan | Epic | 3 |
| (23) | 11. | BROWN EYED GIRL | Van Morrison | Bang | 2 |
| (30) | 12. | THE LETTER | The Box Tops | Mala | 2 |
| (27) | 13. | THE LOOK OF LOVE | Dusty Springfield | Philips | 2 |
| (13) | 14. | WORDS/PLEASANT VALLEY SUNDAY | The Monkees | Colgems | 6 |
| (10) | 15. | IT'S THE LITTLE THINGS | Sonny & Cher | Atco | 4 |
| (16) | 16. | YOU'RE A VERY LOVELY WOMAN | The Merry-Go-Round | A & M | 4 |
| (11) | 17. | BLUEBIRD/MR. SOUL | The Buffalo Springfield | Atco | 7 |
| (20) | 18. | CARRIE ANNE | The Hollies | Epic | 4 |
| (22) | 19. | SOUL FINGER | The Bar-Kays | Volt | 3 |
| (9) | 20. | HEROES AND VILLAINS | The Beach Boys | Brother | 4 |
| (21) | 21. | I TAKE IT BACK | Sandy Posey | MGM | 4 |
| (25) | 22. | YOU'RE MY EVERYTHING | The Temptations | Gordy | 2 |
| (26) | 23. | FAKIN' IT | Simon & Garfunkel | Columbia | 3 |
| (24) | 24. | YOU KNOW WHAT I MEAN | The Turtles | White Whale | 2 |
| (28) | 25. | I DIG ROCK AND ROLL MUSIC | Peter, Paul & Mary | Warner Bros. | 2 |
| (29) | 26. | HYPNOTIZED | Linda Jones | Loma | 2 |
| (HB) | 27. | TWELVE THIRTY | The Mamas & The Papas | Dunhill | 1 |
| (HB) | 28. | MY MAMMY | The Happenings | B. T. Puppy | 1 |
| (HB) | 29. | COME BACK WHEN YOU GROW UP | Bobby Vee | Liberty | 1 |
| (—) | 30. | COLD SWEAT | James Brown | King | 1 |

**OFFICIAL**    **ISSUE NO. 111**

The popularity of records listed herein is the opinion of KHJ based on its survey of record sales in Southern California correlated with listener requests.

A KJH Boss Radio top 30 record survey from Southern California in August 1967; the Temptations, Aretha Franklin, and James Brown share the list with the Animals, the Monkees, and the Beatles.

# "We went through a few mind benders.

Some cats had to buy us food 'cause restaurants wouldn't serve us, mostly in the South. Things are much better today, but I can think of the times when I was driving independently of the group in my Cadillac and the police didn't like black people with money or any fame, made me get out of town. They wouldn't even let me stay overnight."

—**David Ruffin**, one of the lead singers of the Temptations

**ERNIE ISLEY** | singer/songwriter, multi-instrumentalist, the Isley Brothers

"My older brothers can tell you a lot of stories about the way it used to be. Things are different now for the black musician. You can't keep good music down. Eventually it will get heard."

**KEITH ALTHAM** | music journalist, *New Musical Express*

"Jimi was different after his success in America, but he was changing all the time. Jimi picked up things very fast and assimilated them and was looking to move forward the whole time.

"To change things, to get away from the essential pop publicity image that got him the attention to begin with and to get the music and the guitar playing out front and overcome the 'Black Savage of the rock guitar,' the image that he had to begin with. Which was hackneyed, and probably politically incorrect if not racist, which we were all kind of guilty in tabbin' on him. But it was a way to get people to pay attention, to notice. And he knew that.

"He was smart enough. He worked with Little Richard. He knew how it went. But he wanted to get away from that trap."

**ABE JACOB** | sound engineer

"After Jimi went out on the road with Dick Clark and the Monkees and left, Gerry Stickles, who was Jimi's tour manager, called and said, 'We want to take our own sound with us. Would you like to come?' 'Certainly.'"

# August 1967—
# Ambassador Theater
# and the Hollywood Bowl

In early August, the Experience departed from New York, the Monkees interregnum a distant memory and their triumphs around the Greenwich Village club circuit still ringing in the ears of their gobsmacked audience. Hit-and-run gigs in Washington, DC, and Ann Arbor, Michigan, served as tune-ups for their Hollywood Bowl debut on the eighteenth, opening for their Monterey cohorts, the Mamas & the Papas.

**NILS LOFGREN** | guitarist, songwriter

"We knew about Jimi Hendrix. I heard a couple of things from his debut LP, but I didn't understand it yet. We all bought tickets to see Jimi's show at the Ambassador Theater in Washington, DC, on August 13, 1967.

"But that night I first went to Constitution Hall to see the Blues Magoos, Herman's Hermits, and the Who, who finished with an extraordinary set and tore up their instruments. I was impressed by the music and the energy.

"It was a hobby and never entered my mind to be a professional musician, ever, in 1966, '67. After that show we all ran over to see Jimi Hendrix at the Ambassador.

"None of us knew what to expect. Jimi comes out with a power trio. And he said from the stage he was going to dedicate a song to Pete Townshend in the audience, 'Sgt. Pepper's Lonely Hearts Club Band' by the Beatles. Now we're all pretty young and square, and a lot of us thought, 'Well, it's a power trio, you can't do that. You need horns and strings—how can that happen?' As we wondered . . . Jimi counted it off, and literally, it was so loud and powerful. When the downbeat hit, Jimi disappeared. He fell to the ground, sat on his ass, rocking the guitar between his legs, and it was much like 'Foxy Lady.' And the whole room leapt to their feet. It was very hypnotizing, magical, powerful, strange, scary, and beautiful.

"After the Hendrix show when I left that night, I felt strangely possessed for the first time in my life with a notion I never thought of: I might need to try and be a professional rock musician. That never was a thought until that night, seeing the bands at Constitution Hall and then the late show with the Jimi Hendrix Experience at the Ambassador."

## JAN ALAN HENDERSON | writer and musician

"Watching the 2014 biopic *Jimi, All Is by My Side* took me back to my unorthodox introduction to Jimi Hendrix in 1967, the spring of the Summer of Love! Sprouting from the ashes of the movie studios, there was music in the air. The previous year the Beatles gave us the acid-soaked *Revolver*, the Stones sonically showed us what *Aftermath* would be like, and a Los Angeles band, Love, delivered the unsung classic *Da Capo* with the second jazz-tainted CD.

"I was a fixture at the Sunset Boulevard club Gazzarri's, sitting in the front row, watching my friends the Abstracts when a life-changing event took place. The band roared into a tune that was atypical of their repertoire, which was comprised of soul and pop tunes.

"From the opening guitar and drum riff, this didn't sound like my high school pals Tony Peluso and Hank Dandini. The song was 'Fire,' by a then unknown Jimi Hendrix, as Tony announced at the finish. After their set, I questioned them relentlessly about this Jimi Hendrix dude.

"It seems Tony Peluso had found the first English album at Lewin Record Paradise on Hollywood Boulevard.

"The kids who went to Hollywood High School had the inroads to sneaking into Hollywood Bowl shows. Our graduations were held there, so it was only natural for us to case the joint and memorize the terrain.

"In June of '67, 'Are You Experienced' was climbing up the UK charts, while 'Foxy Lady' and 'Purple Haze' filtered through American radio airwaves, and Jimi pulled out all the stops at Monterey.

"September saw the release of the Reprise version of Jimi's debut, and I was standing high above the Bowl, about to see Hendrix for the first time. Making my way down a coyote trail, careful not to tear up my new Sy Amber duds (a hippie-dippie clothes store), the crowd was screaming for the Mamas & Papas as the sun sank behind the Hollywood Hills.

"From the opening notes, the audience sat frozen, like a herd of zombies at a Mantan Moreland film festival, and the adults were catching flies in their astonished open mouths. It was like a Fellini film run at the wrong speed."

## ROBERT MARCHESE | record producer/manager

"When Jimi Hendrix opened for the Mamas & the Papas at the Hollywood Bowl on August 18, 1967, Mo Ostin and Joe Smith from Warner Bros. Records were sitting right in front of me. And besides them were two little white chicks. Like 'San Fernando Valley beach-bunny blondes.' . . . I leaned into Mo's ear and Joe's ear, and said, 'This is why you got millions of dollars staring you in your face.'"

Henry Diltz captured the scenes offstage and onstage at the Hollywood Bowl, August 18, 1967, when the JHE opened for the Mamas & the Papas. **Clockwise from top left:** Jimi Hendrix relaxes with Michelle Phillips and Mama Cass before the show; solo portrait of Hendrix; Hendrix plays the guitar with his teeth as Redding plays bass in the foreground; Hendrix at the mike; KHJ-AM "Boss Jock" Robert W. Morgan, Noel Redding, Mitch Mitchell, and tour manager Gerry Stickells, backstage.

Acclaimed photographer Guy Webster at Monterey Pop, June 1967.

**GUY WEBSTER** | photographer

"I saw Jimi Hendrix for the first time at Monterey, and then at the Hollywood Bowl.

"I loved his intelligence, his guitar riffs, and his backstage rhythm. His clothes were bad hippie clothes. I would have dressed him differently. The two white guys with him were kind of nerdy. I said to myself, 'How long are these guys gonna last?' They didn't look right."

**JOHN YORK** | bassist, the Byrds

"I was playing bass for the Mamas & the Papas in summer of 1967, including an August concert at the Hollywood Bowl."

"The drummer was Eddie Hoh and the guitar player was Eric 'Doctor' Hord in the Mamas & Papas.

"John Phillips, God bless him, had Jimi open the show. There was a middle act of a Beethoven string quartet.

"We all were at the sound check in Hollywood on a beautiful summer's day. What struck me was that Jimi was a very shy guy. Everything he had to do at the check was very gentlemanly. Every way he went he would be followed by half a dozen hippie chicks. If he was standing on one side of the stage, they would go sit over there. And if he had to get up and go over to the other side of the stage, they would—all of them—would stand up and go follow him there. They would never say anything, and sort of competing with each other. We all got a kick out of that.

"In the evening, Denny Doherty and I walked to the very back of the Hollywood Bowl, to look down over the audience and see the stage. All of a sudden Jimi went into his first song, 'Wild Thing.' 'Wow! What is this?' He starts playing single notes that are so loud and so clear that it is heaven in the air. It was like you could see the notes hanging in the air.

"So Denny and I went down immediately to the stage area; we had all-access passes, so we were able to go to the edge of the stage. And they had these tall trees on planters that were on wheels, one on each side.

"In one moment when the lights went dark between songs, we ran up onstage and hid behind one of these trees. So we were literally just a few yards from Jim, Mitch, and Noel. We stayed there for the whole set.

Webster's portrait of Hendrix at the Hollywood Bowl, August 18, 1967.

The Mamas & the Papas performing at the Hollywood Bowl, August 18, 1967.

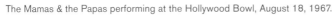

"We had never seen or heard anything like it. It was an amazing thing to experience. Jimi's rhythm section was incredible. Each one was highly innovative and playing the way they wanted to play. The drummer obviously came from a jazz background. The bassist, Noel Redding, was a converted guitarist. In a trio that worked, because there was no other guitar player. I mean, it was kind of the way Skip Battin played with the Byrds. Skip gave you a lot of information, and it was going against the way bass players were supposed to play. Bass players were supposed to be almost invisible. Both those guys impressed me.

"The thing about it was that they were able to give Jimi what he needed in order for him to float those notes, right? He needed these two guys who could make the background bubble and boil. They were on it every moment. They weren't kicking

back, being cool and letting him do everything. They were just churning under him so he was able to do whatever he needed to do without the energy dropping at all. It was remarkable. And at the time, 1967, this is new and very creative. The thing that touches me the deepest about Jimi is his guitar playing—a level of artistry that he was able to reach that was overwhelming.

"The night after the Hollywood Bowl, there was a big party at John and Michelle Phillips' house in Bel-Air, the old Jeanette MacDonald mansion. I had been there before. It was a party filled with people. There was a pool table, and Jimi was sitting right next to me."

Jimi playing pool at John and Michelle Phillips' house during the Hollywood Bowl after-party, August 18, 1967.

## JIM SALZER

"The second show I promoted was August 19, 1967 [Earl Warren Showgrounds, Santa Barbara; Jimi Hendrix headlined]. . . . 2,700 people. Moby Grape, Tim Buckley.

"I had first gotten together with him [Jimi]; he let me know where he was staying. I had overpaid him by $500 and I called him. And he said, 'Yes, I got it. Come get it.' I drove down to the Sunset Marquis, and we kind of partied all night.

"Jimi was a pretty straight guy back then when I knew him. I wasn't into the drug scene. I always used to worry about my customers and the people coming to my concerts being stoned and driving.

"Jimi was scheduled to do a third show, but he ended up doing it at UCSB [University of California Santa Barbara]. February 11, 1968. On the third one, Jimi called me and asked me if he could get out of it. And I said yes."

**Above:** A ticket to promoter Jim Salzer's July 1, 1967, show at the Earl Warren Showgrounds in Santa Barbara headlined by the Jimi Hendrix Experience.

**Right:** The poster for Salzer's August 19 show at the same venue, also headlined by the JHE.

# Back Across the Pond

Returning to England was, not surprisingly, a letdown. Old contracts had to be honored—playing the Boathouse Club in Nottingham after Monterey, the Fillmore, the Hollywood Bowl, well, it was a sobering reminder to take it all in stride. So they trundled on, with dates in Sweden, Paris, and an exhausting string of UK one-nighters and TV and radio spots, before concluding on December 22 with the Christmas on Earth Continued at the Olympia. This was another one of those grandly ambitious all-day/all-night spectacles that the Brits had perfected. Like its predecessor, the 14 Hour Technicolor Dream at the Alexandra Palace—Ally Pally—on April 29, these acid-addled jubilees set the stage for the big UK festivals to come, Glastonbury being the most famous.

**JON POVEY** | musician, Pretty Things

"I used to go to the Speakeasy Club in Margaret Street behind Oxford Street in London with Jimi and Noel Redding. I would drive him from his flat to the club. We would hang out and eat a meal together and generally get wasted. We used to mix Mandrax with booze, which seemed like a good idea at the time, but, of course, when we

English musician and Track Records label-mate Arthur Brown poses with the Jimi Hendrix Experience backstage at the Saville Theatre, London, October 8, 1967. Brown's band, the Crazy World of Arthur Brown, was opening for JHE along with the bands Eire Apparent and the Herd (with lead singer and guitarist Peter Frampton).

staggered out at six or seven in the morning, I was unable to get the car key into my car door successfully—a taxi was a better option.

"One day I did manage to open the door of the car and we all piled in. As we pulled out, I managed to bounce off about four parked cars on my way home! Misty and foggy days. Jimi was a quiet guy, and Noel was completely the opposite. Later on, after Jimi's sad and early departure, we toured Germany with Noel's band Fat Mattress. Needless to say, it was also slightly misty, but great fun! I believe that Jimi attended the only *S.F. Sorrow* live gig at the Roundhouse in 1968 by the Pretty Things."

### HOWARD KAYLAN | singer/songwriter, the Turtles

"On our first trip to England we met the Beatles. Graham Nash took us to the Speakeasy Club.

"John Lennon and Paul McCartney sang 'Happy Together' at the table. I met Jimi Hendrix. He got me so high on grass in a club that I puked on his suit. But Jimi did come to see our show that the Turtles did at the Speakeasy."

The American band the Turtles in 1969. Lead singer and founding member Howard Kaylan, second from right, later wrote a comedy film about his experience meeting the Beatles and having dinner with Hendrix in London, called *My Dinner with Jimi* (2007).

### MARSHALL CHESS | executive, Chess Records

"I met Hendrix when he came to London to play at the Scotch of St. James Club. He wasn't even playing psychedelic then. That's when I was setting up the Chess Records label in the UK. Jimi blew my mind when I saw him at the Olympia Theater in Paris. It was just an amazing thing and fuckin' overwhelming."

# 7
# Tilting the World Off Its Axis

Second albums have their own peculiar chemistry. Many artists stockpile all their best material for that elusive first album. It hits; then there's an avalanche of touring and promoting, leaving little time to prepare songs for the follow-up. Sometimes a band only comes into focus after its breakthrough, which may or may not be truly representative of what they're all about. Traffic's second, eponymous album (1968), is a great example of a group discovering its strengths after the initial flurry of interest. Procol Harum's *Shine On Brightly* (1968) and Brian Auger, Julie Driscoll and the Trinity's *Streetnoise* (1969) are also classic, late-sixties second efforts that revealed unexpected maturity.

**A**nd so it was with *Axis: Bold as Love*, released by Track Records in the UK on December 1, 1967, and by Reprise in America on January 15, 1968. The band squeezed in recording sessions between gigs in the manic month of October. The record is chockablock with sonic effects, including swirling guitars and a rigorous attention to detail that valued space and breath as much as clusters and layers. Eddie Kramer was back behind the board at Olympic, with Chas Chandler assuming his producer's hat.

It is remarkable that, despite the hurly-burly that consumed Jimi's time, he could still craft so much quality material. It reflected a deepening investment in learning the protocols of the recording process, discovering the studio as an instrument unto itself, hunching over the mixing console like a Merlin casting spells. And while the live shows gave him freedom to extend the pop song form into an epic journey, the album remained finely tuned to the strictures of telling a tall tale in two minutes and change. No matter how "far out" the arrangement, *Axis* was a testament to concision, a formal discipline in a field that rarely viewed that as a virtue.

A 1968 billboard in Los Angeles advertising the new album *Axis: Bold as Love.*

**JAMES CUSHING** | poet, English professor, deejay

"It was obvious from the first thirty seconds that Jimi Hendrix had gone beyond Mike Bloomfield—or George Harrison or Robby Krieger or Jorma Kaukonen—to become The Guitar Guy I Had Been Looking For, one who whose sound did things to me I had never imagined.

"I was aware of the music as a 'vibration from the world around and above and beneath me,' and please remember, I was fifteen and had never smoked pot or taken LSD. I knew this experience was completely real, and I felt that I had discovered something important about the world and what it contained.

"*Axis: Bold as Love* functions for me as a single thirteen-movement song-cycle that tells the tale of an extraterrestrial visitor's time observing life on our planet, where you can't believe everything you see and hear—the Spanish Castle isn't in Spain, six isn't really nine, and a gold-and-rose thousand-star vision was only a dream.

"In this aspect, the album anticipates *The Rise and Fall of Ziggy Stardust* by five years and marks an optimistic beginning to an era that ends with Bowie's bleak dystopia (1967 to 1972, the core years of classic rock?). The songs have a melodic originality and a depth of production that must have made them too hard to perform live, if the JHE set lists are any indication. Only 'Spanish Castle Magic' and 'Little Wing' show up with any regularity. But perhaps the unity of the album's sequence discouraged excerpting."

**EDDIE KRAMER** | recording engineer, producer

"There was always a bunch of instruments lying around the studio. Which of course, Jimi would take advantage of: the glockenspiel, for instance, on 'Little Wing.' It was there and Jimi picked it up. 'How does this work?' I showed him, and 'Great.' Five minutes later. Bang. There's the overdub."

# Second US Tour

The JHE returned to America for their second tour in February 1968. They began in San Francisco, at the Fillmore and the Winterland Ballroom. In total, they would perform in sixty cities over the course of sixty-six days, a grueling itinerary that pushed the band to its physical and psychic limits. Mike Jeffery was adding dates willy-nilly, happy to accept any promoter's offer that met his price, regardless of what logistical nightmare it unleashed.

Mike Jeffery was shrewd enough to fly the band from gig to gig, a rare luxury for musicians raised on the soul-sucking travails of life on the interstate, journeying by broken-down van, by befouled bus. Often, two shows were booked in one day, and then there'd be a 7:00 a.m. wake-up call to make the flight. The glamour was left to the fans who fantasized about the trappings of a star's life, but not the traps.

```
                        JIMI HENDRIX ITINERARY


February 1968

    1    Fillmore Auditorium - San Francisco        Buyer:  Bill Graham
    2         "             "              "                 415-567-3537
    3         "             "              "
    4         "             "
    5    Arizona State University - Tempe, Arizona (Gymnasium)
    6    University of Tucson - Tucson, Arizona
    7
    8    Sacramento State University - Sacramento, Calif. (Gymnasium)
    9    Anaheim Convention Center - Anaheim, Calif.
   10    Shrine Auditorium - Los Angeles
   11    University of California - Santa Barbara, Calif (Robertson Gym)
   12
   13    University of California at Los Angeles (Grand Ballroom)
   14
   15    Municipal Auditorium - San Antonio, Texas
   16    Will Rogers Auditorium - Fort Worth, Texas
   17    Music Hall - Dallas, Texas
   18    Music Hall - Houston, Texas
   19
   20
   21    Electric Factory, Philadelphia
   22        "         "        "
   23    Ford Auditorium - Detroit, Michigan
   24    Q. Eliz Bldg. - Toronto, Ontario
   25    Opera House - Chicago, Illinois
   26
   27    The Factory - Madison, Wisconsin
   28
   29

March 1968

   15    Clark University - Worester, Mass.
   16    Bates College - Lewiston, Maine
   30    UP Field House - University of Toledo
```

The Jimi Hendrix Experience tour itinerary for February and March 1968.

❝I was at Monterey in '67. I have this one photo of Jimi Hendrix. Shot at the Fillmore in 1968.

"Bill Graham let me into the show but said no photos. I violated his instructions and took one fleeting picture of Jimi. My mind was blown by his performance.❞

—Tom Gundelfinger O'Neal, Photographer

John Mayall (center) performing with the Turning Point at Fillmore West, 1969.

**JOHN MAYALL** | singer/songwriter, multi-instrumentalist, founder, the Bluesbreakers

"I did shows in America with Jimi, the Soft Machine, and Albert King the first week of February 1968 for Bill Graham at Winterland.

"Graham supported blues music and booked shows to have them with headliners.

"Bill was somebody who could really see the future of blues and rock and the first person in America to recognize that and put on these big shows at the Fillmores on the East and West Coast and Winterland venues where Jimi and I were on the calendar. Graham was very important in really giving a professional take on how to present artists. I did *Turning Point*, a live album, in 1969 at the Fillmore East."

**DENNIS LOREN** | graphic designer and art director

"The third time I saw the Jimi Hendrix Experience [was] at Winterland on February 3, 1968. Winterland was a larger venue that concert promoter Bill Graham used when he was sure the Fillmore would be too small on certain nights for some of the more popular bands of the era, such as the Doors, Pink Floyd, and Procol Harum.

"This time, I got in the ticket line early and was able to get very close to the stage. I knew this concert would be great, because I had seen artist Rick Griffin's terrific flying eyeball poster. The other two groups scheduled that night were John Mayall & the Bluesbreakers, featuring Mick Taylor, and blues guitarist Albert King and his band.

"When Jimi Hendrix came onstage I noticed that he had a second guitar, which he placed facing his amplifiers. These were the days before "guitar techs" who would be on hand with an extra guitar in case a guitarist broke a string. I already knew from reading in music magazines that Jimi used a Vox wah-wah pedal, a Fuzz Face distortion pedal, and an Octavia octave-splitting pedal—made especially for him by his friend and electronics wizard Roger Mayer—to achieve many of his special effects. Being left-handed already gave Jimi a different sound to begin with. I wasn't certain, though, how he controlled his use of feedback so well.

"I now firmly believe that this second guitar facing the amplifiers had something to do with it. Before the set began, I watched as he tuned the other guitar to a higher octave and turned up the volume control before setting it back down facing the amplifiers. During the set, Jimi never broke a string or used the other guitar."

**JOEL SELVIN** | author, music historian

"In the old days at the Winterland, every band played two sets, so the headliner's first set was followed a second time by the opening act, the middle act, and then the headliner's own final set. The first set the second night at Fillmore, Hendrix was kind of lame, never really got it going. He was followed by Albert King, who simply wiped the stage with him. He blew everybody in the place away. Mick Taylor in the John Mayall band didn't exactly suck, so when Hendrix took the stage for his second set, a gauntlet, so to speak, had been thrown down.

"He opened with a few pedestrian numbers and then walked back to his amps after one song, twisted a dial, and sent feedback screaming through the room—uncomfortable, shrieking feedback. He turned and walked back to the front of the stage, hands on hips, chewing gum and looking out in the audience like he was taunting them.

"People in the front rows covered their ears. Folks were screaming, 'Turn it down!' He simply stood there, arms crossed, slyly smiling. At some point, after the tension had built up suitably, he flinched, grabbed his guitar, and slammed into the introduction of 'Foxy Lady.' The place was his in a heartbeat."

**CAROL SCHOFIELD** | MsMusic Productions record-label owner

"Bill Graham presented Jimi Hendrix at both the Fillmore and Winterland. I went to one of them. 'Stone-y' times for sure! Quite a show! First time I heard 'Red House,' which I hadn't heard on Bay Area radio. Besides tearing it up on 'Foxy Lady' and 'Purple Haze,' it was really amazing when Mitch Mitchell invited drummer Buddy Miles to jam and they all did an instrumental version of Traffic's 'Dear Mr. Fantasy.'"

**ROBERT KNIGHT** | photographer

"I had just shot Jeff Beck in 1968 over multiple days, but when I heard Jimi Hendrix would be playing the Winterland Ballroom, I had to go and see for myself what he was about.

"Jimi had picked up [a] huge head of steam at this point, and I bought my ticket, brought my Nikon Camera and started to walk towards the stage, and when people saw my camera they got out of the way until I actually reach[ed] the front of the stage.

Photographer Robert Knight in Seattle, 1970.

"I brought one roll of film, as I thought thirty-six exposures would be a lot, and started to shoot when he came out. After several songs I stopped shooting and was just letting the sonic wave of music hit my solar plexus. I never had felt anything like that before. Not sure why I did not start shooting again, but just had to watch.

"It still blows my mind that in 1968, I walked into my first Hendrix concert at Winterland with a camera in hand and people would get out of my way until I reached the front of the stage. I only shot fourteen frames on one roll of film, as I was so blown away by Jimi I would just stand and watch. Years later, all fourteen frames were used in a CD package, *Live at Winterland*."

Knight's photograph of Hendrix at Winterland, 1968.

Jimi onstage at the Anaheim Convention Center. While in Southern California, the Jimi Hendrix Experience music machine made a pit stop there on February 9, 1968.

# Drawing Jimi

O n February 10, 1968, Hendrix scheduled a Pinnacle Dance Concert, produced and held in downtown Los Angeles at the Shrine Auditorium. One of the promoters of the visionary Pinnacle staff was legendary graphic artist and designer John Van Hamersveld, who drew the epic poster for the show.

In 1964, Van Hamersveld created the memorable *Endless Summer* surf art image, and then helmed the art department at Capitol Records from 1965 through 1968 in Hollywood. Here, he remembers the process of creating the Hendrix Pinnacle poster.

## JOHN VAN HAMERSVELD, GRAPHIC ARTIST AND DESIGNER

"Making the classic rock poster: I knew I had to get the drawing done. There were a couple of starts, but on the morning of December 28, 1967, as I sat down at the drawing table inside my second-story Coronado Street Studio, I started a new kind of drawing for the poster.

"The morning light came in through the large front window of the studio corner, casting the light across the table, spreading over the paper. With my black Pentel pen in hand, I began drawing from the image in my mind the portraiture of the head of Jimi Hendrix with wired hair, styled in his fashionable coiffure from London, like the Cream.

Graphic artist and designer John Van Hamersveld, 1968.

Van Hamersveld's poster for the Hendrix Pinnacle show at the Shrine Auditorium in LA on February 10, 1968.

"I put the drawing in a drawer for a week to think about it. My partners Sepp [Donahower] and Marc [Chase] had booked the Jimi Hendrix Experience for the Shrine Auditorium. The Single Wing Turquoise Bird did our multimedia light shows.

"My drawing was incorporated into the design of a Shrine Auditorium event. The poster was distributed locally and then nationally, and worldwide. "The Electric Flag was the [group] on the bill, and one of the band members was Buddy Miles.

"I was at one of the rehearsals that week. Hendrix was staying in the town at the Harry Houdini Mansion in Laurel Canyon. I was up on Sunset Boulevard at the De Voss clothing store where most in the rock scene, like the Doors, Beatles, and the Stones, bought suits, shirts, and shoes. I was in the hallway area of the store and ran into Jimi there face-to-face. I asked as a conversational question: 'How do you like LA?' And his answer came back: 'Confusing!'

"I had my Leica camera with me. They veered off into the room to look at jackets; there is where Jimi is looking into the mirror and picks out an Afghan jacket and put it on. I am at the back of the room and Buddy is staying behind him off to the side.

"I imagine Jimi would always have people and photographers chasing him every day. Buddy was big, as if he were the sideman, but maybe more often was like a bodyguard.

"Click . . . everything was history then in the moment, as the photo is now over fifty years old."

Van Hamersveld was able to capture this iconic photograph of Buddy Miles and Hendrix taking a break from rehearsals for the Pinnacle show at the trendy De Voss boutique on Sunset Boulevard.

## MARINA MUHLFRIEDEL | writer

"In August 1967, as *Are You Experienced?* cranked up the fervency of the Summer of Love, I had little sense of who Jimi Hendrix, the man—or god—might actually be. I'd seen photos, of course, but it was the records, not the persona, I was transfixed by. The Stones, Eric Clapton, Jim Morrison, Ray Davies, and so many others somehow seemed relatable. I'd hear stories about them, read interviews, and arbitrarily ascribe personalities to them. I never considered what it would be like to meet Jimi or see him perform, which, I suppose, made one particular evening in Beverly Hills even more surreal. A friend's family lived in an imposing mansion. The French Consulate would host soirées in my friend's sprawling basement/ballroom and we would sneak in, dressed as poshly as two fourteen-year-olds could manage, to sip champagne and smoke Gauloises—hippies flirting with men in suits.

Writer Marina Muhlfriedel, 1969.

"That night, though, entering the room, we spotted a reed-thin man, dressed in scarves and velvet, sprawled like a rag doll across a couch, head drooped to one side, baby sweet, blissed in dreamland. Watching someone, especially a stranger, sleep is an awkward and voyeuristic intrusion—but even odder when it's Jimi Hendrix.

"We assumed he was stoned, but it could have been jet lag. Other guests seemed to politely ignore the fact that Jimi Hendrix was out cold, but we were captivated. What, we wondered, does Jimi dream of? If we['d] had a camera, we would have posed with sleeping Jimi. We joked about carrying him to the back seat of a car and getting someone to take us on a drive around town. But instead, we just watched. Perched on the edge of the couch, I felt entrusted to guard him, protect his privacy. In some ulterior dimension, there was a bond of trust. So goes the self-important fancy of adolescence.

"We had to leave before he woke, and the next time I saw Jimi was one foggy February night in 1968 when he played the Los Angeles Shrine Auditorium.

"Given the odd fortune of our time together, I made the leap that I had miraculously acquired an intuitive understanding of Jimi. I thought I knew how he would jive with the audience and clutch his guitar, how his voice would careen as he played. Somewhere between genial conversation and electrifying vocal lines, though, he revealed his true intent—to seduce us, seduce me, into some rare cosmos where all else slipped away and he alone ruled. Like everyone else, I surrendered to his magic."

### DAVE PEARSON | musician and concert attendee

"I wasn't there at the Shrine just because our band members knew John Van Hamersveld. I was there because of Michael Bloomfield. Bloomfield had a longer, more familiar history with us, and he kept doing unexpected things. Seeing the Flag was a must.

"The Flag stole the show—even in the opinion of the Hendrix aficionados we knew. Their stage presence—with the spotlighted, windblown flag and Buddy in his American flag shirt performing various feats—seemed almost choreographed by someone like Gower Champion. When Michael played a solo, the spot was on him alone. It was very theatrical. It was so good, we were all exhausted by the time Jimi got out there.

"Noel Redding was duded up in psychedelic splendor, like the covers of *Are You Experienced?* or *Disraeli Gears*. Jimi and Mitch Mitchell looked pretty casual. The lighting remained the same throughout the Experience's set, and despite the amazing pyrotechnics of Jimi's music, the band looked ragged in comparison to the Electric Flag. The Flag-word that obtained for years among musicians I knew was 'professionalism.'

"Because the Electric Flag was so tightly organized, they made everyone else seem relatively sloppy—including Jimi Hendrix. It was Mitch Mitchell alone who held the Experience together."

### DENNY BRUCE | record producer, A&R manager

"I went with Jack Nitzsche. Blue Cheer were way too loud and my ears were ringing throughout Jimi's set, almost making it hard to appreciate anything subtle he was doing with his tone and sound. I knew Mike Bloomfield and dug the Flag. With his one Fender amp, Mike sounded like he was playing through a transistor radio!

"Jimi tuned up his guitar, or had a new one brought out, but he did strum a bit to check the tuning. Like a 'folkie,' he felt like he should say something while tuning. He says, 'This is from Nashville' and then does 'The Wind Cries Mary.'

"At the Shrine, he had his roadie standing behind the amps so he could go hump the amps. Watching Jimi at the Shrine. I never saw anybody [like that] since seeing Johnny 'Guitar' Watson at the Cinnamon Cinder do his thing in August of '63, when I hit LA and a homeboy took me there my first night in the City of Angels."

**The Jimi Hendrix Experience** galvanized UCLA in Westwood, California, on February 13, 1968, at Ackerman Union Grand Ballroom; the event was cosponsored by ASUCLA (Associated Students UCLA) and the Cultural Events Commission.

> **"I went to the Monterey festival in 1967.**
> Right after that I then started reading *Billboard* and
> *Rolling Stone* and wondered, 'How do I get into this
> world?' When Jimi Hendrix played at UCLA in the
> Ackerman Student Union ballroom, I was in the first
> row and could see everything. For free."
>
> —**Andrew Solt**, producer, director, screenwriter

### ED CARAEFF | photographer and art director

"The crowds were getting larger, and that's when all the worship really started. Jimi's management and people on the road were really nice to me, and I was always taken care of with backstage passes and dressing room access. My philosophy and job is to blend into the room and get out of the way. I usually shot behind the drums and amplifiers."

A.S.U.C.L.A. and BLUE KEY
PRESENT
**THE JIMI HENDRIX EXPERIENCE**
TUESDAY, 8:00 P.M.      GRAND BALLROOM
FEBRUARY 13, 1968      ACKERMAN UNION
$2.00 per person
College I.D. Required
N⁰ 619
A.T. Brugger
Executive Director

A ticket stub for the February 13, 1968 JHE concert at UCLA's Ackerman Union Grand Ballroom.

### MARK ROMAN | concertgoer

"I was a student at UCLA. Freshman year. I was living across the street from UCLA on Gayley Ave. Rates were cheap, $60 for four guys to live. Initially, the Hendrix sound was noise to me. I liked the Rolling Stones, the Byrds, and groups like that. But for $2.50, I could afford going to this on campus and investigate.

"At the time, the seating capacity for Ackerman was 1,200 people. I went in and, as they say, my mind was blown. I was unprepared. 'Cause I was wet behind the ears in so many ways at age eighteen, as many people are. I was knocked out. Jimi Hendrix was loud, but it was magnificent.

"But what was even more shocking was Soft Machine, which I was completely unprepared for. The drummer, Robert Wyatt, stood up at the end of the set wearing a light blue loincloth, not shorts, and that was it. I became a fan of Soft Machine. But it wasn't rock music, and that's why it was so much more dramatic in some subtle ways than Hendrix. That's why I was even less prepared for Soft Machine. It was because their sound was so different."

**Opposite:** View of Hendrix performing for students at UCLA's Ackerman Union Grand Ballroom, captured from the stage by noted photographer Ed Caraeff.

# Texas Bound

The Jimi Hendrix Experience, Soft Machine, and the Moving Sidewalks (with guitarist Billy Gibbons, a future ZZ Top member), did a handful of Texas bookings in Houston, Fort Worth, Dallas, and San Antonio in February 1968.

In a March 1, 2017, story by Danielle Sariyan published in the *Aquarian Weekly*, "An Interview with Billy Gibbons: Rockin' Around the World Aboard the ZZ Top Party Train," Gibbons reminisced about his week-long hang with Hendrix, who would gift him with a pink Stratocaster at the end of the tour:

> He was someone who was just great to hang out with and, of course, when we asked about how he accomplished what he did, he showed us whatever we wanted to know. Words really weren't adequate to explain it all, so we spoke thorough music. It was like being struck by lightning—but very gentle lightning that created a glow from the inside. Jimi Hendrix was a real inspiration; he was an innovator who changed the world, and we're fortunate to have spent significant time in his presence. He was an explorer who really discovered new worlds and was there to share them. What a privilege it was to have spent that precious time with him.

# Northern Territories

The Jimi Hendrix Experience had a devoted following in Michigan.

Detroit native and influential artist Gary Grimshaw had earlier witnessed, like Detroit deejay Russ Gibb, the 1966 psychedelic music world of San Francisco.

After both men returned from the Bay Area, Gibb hired Grimshaw to helm light shows at Gibb-promoted shows at his Grande Ballroom venue in Detroit. Grimshaw designed the debut poster for an MC5 performance in October 1966. He then created the February 23, 1968, poster for the Jimi Hendrix Experience's visit to the famed Masonic Temple, which was built in the 1920s and is the largest Masonic Temple in the world.

Grimshaw also did the graphics for their Toronto, Canada, appearance on February 24 at the CNE Coliseum Arena.

Two posters by graphic artist and lightshow designer Gary Grimshaw: above left, one for JHE's stint at the Masonic Temple in Detroit on February 23, 1968; and above right, one for the next night at the CNE Coliseum Arena in Toronto.

**Rochester, New York,** was always a hotbed for rock 'n' roll concerts. On March 21, 1968, WBBF 950 AM deejay Jack Palvino was instrumental in bringing Hendrix to the city, with the help make one local teenager named Jeff Gelb.

### JEFF GELB | former DJ and veteran radio executive

"I was a Brighton High School senior in Rochester, New York, in 1968. FM radio was still in its infancy. Hendrix had just brought out *Axis: Bold as Love*. I was listening to the local Top 40 radio station doing my homework one night and the deejay, Jack Palvino on WBBF, says, 'We have the chance to bring in Jimi Hendrix to Rochester! If enough of you tell us that you'll go, we'll bring him in.'

"That was all I needed to hear. So I had become a student reporter to the radio station and said to myself, 'I'm gonna bring Jimi Hendrix [to] Rochester.'

"I happened to own a mimeograph and ditto machine that I had in my basement because I used to produce a comic fanzine. Gene Simmons, before he was in KISS, wrote for my fanzine.

"And I worshiped *Axis: Bold as Love*. And the first song on the LP Jimi is getting off a spaceship and pretending he's coming off a flying saucer. 'This is my guy!' Remember: you can't be a comic book nerd, collector, or have a fanzine without loving science fiction.

"So I decided to create a petition to bring Jimi Hendrix to the Rochester War Memorial arena, a 10,000-seat room. I did a one-sheet and I pass[ed] it out to all the homeroom reps the next day. There were thousands of kids in my high school. And I wanted it all signed by the end of the next day. I was certainly a nerd, but determined to make this happen. And the homeroom reps had the kids sign it, and by the end of the day I had thousands of signatures.

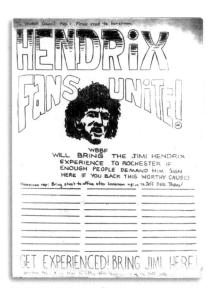

Rochester native Jeff Gelb's successful high school petition to bring Jimi Hendrix to the Rochester Community War Memorial arena (Blue Cross Arena) in 1968.

"I handed Jack Palvino the stack and said, 'I brought you 10,000 people who said they will come if you bring Jimi. So I hope you will bring him.'

"Two months later, on March 21 of '68, Jimi Hendrix comes to Rochester at the Community War Memorial. I was there with a buddy. We bought tickets for the show. The Soft Machine blew me away, 'cause they didn't have a record out. Soft Machine was incredible. 'This is exactly where I want to be, listening to music like this!' It was out there.

"Sure enough, after their set, I see Jack Palvino walking in front of the stage. I run up to him. 'Hey, remember me?' 'Yes, of course.'

"I boldly said, 'Listen, if it weren't for me, this concert wouldn't be happening. Do you think I can meet Jimi?' 'Let me check.' It was loose. He comes back in five minutes: 'Sure.'

"My buddy and I go down to the dressing [room] and there is Hendrix tuning up, getting ready. When I was introduced to him, I blurted out my story that I had something to do with him being booked for Rochester. 'Cool.' 'Mind if I take a couple of pictures?' 'Okay.'

"He was amused. He was twenty-five at the time and I was seventeen. Jimi asked how the sound was and about the audience. I told him where I was sitting, a third of the way back, it sounded fine and the crowd was very attentive. That was what he was interested in.

"He signed my *Axis: Bold as Love* album. 'Thanks for everything, Jimi Hendrix.' And it's signed by the whole band."

Scenes from Jeff Gelb's meeting with Hendrix in the dressing room at Rochester Community War Memorial arena before the show, March 21, 1968: **Clockwise from top left:** Gelb, left with Hendrix and another fan; Noel Redding; Hendrix with his guitar; Hendrix autographing an album for Gelb; and Mitch Mitchell.

Chaos in Cleveland as fans attempt to climb onstage during a performance at the Public Music Hall, March 26, 1968.

# 8
# Studio Daze, Those Hollywood Nights

The Record Plant in New York City was founded by Gary Kellgren and Chris Stone in 1968. Kellgren had previously been a sound engineer at Mayfair Recording Studios in New York, and Stone was the national sales manager for Revlon. They partnered with Ancky Revson, a model and the second wife of Charles Revson (founder of Revlon), and with record producer Tom Wilson, known for his work with Sun Ra, Bob Dylan, and the Velvet Underground. Acoustic designer Tom Hidley was brought in as well.

**J**ust before the Record Plant's 12-track studio opened on West 44th Street in March 1968, Wilson persuaded Hendrix and producer Chas Chandler to book time at the facility from mid-April to early July '68 for the recording of the Jimi Hendrix Experience's third album, *Electric Ladyland*.

### EDDIE KRAMER | recording engineer, producer

"Jimi had worked at Mayfair Studios in New York with Gary Kellgren and cut a side with Jimi. But he [Kellgren] was going to build a brand new studio called the Record Plant, which opened in the spring. He kept bugging me: 'You gotta come over to the US. It's a new studio, and since Jimi is coming to America,' which I didn't know, 'you should come over and finish your work with him and keep working with him.' And I did, arriving on April 17. Chas was working with Jimi. That's very short-lived because Jimi wanted to bring in all his friends and Chas didn't like that idea. Chas left the project and Jimi and I continued to work on *Electric Ladyland*."

### ALLAN ARKUSH | television and movie director

"When I was a film student at New York University, Martin Scorsese was my teacher and faculty adviser.

"I got tickets for Jimi Hendrix for his Friday night late show [at the Fillmore East]. The opening act was Sly & the Family Stone, May 10, 1968.

"Jimi was great. And then something happened onstage that made it transcendent and one of the amazing rock 'n' roll moments I had ever witnessed.

"He was playing the intro to 'Foxy Lady' in front of these giant Marshall amps with the big tops on them. And it just clicked off and overloaded. The roadies go crazy and then put two of 'em up there and now Jimi has twice as much power.

"And when he throws the switch to turn on his Fender, this buzz happened and he starts laughing, starts walking toward the amp with his back to the audience as this feedback thing starts building up into this electromagnetic happening. You feel it in your chest as this sound twists into the opening note of 'Foxy Lady,' slinging it at us, like he's playing lacrosse. You could hear it out on Second Avenue."

## PRESCOTT NILES | bassist, the Knack

"The first time I saw Jimi was in 1968, at the Fillmore East. I went with a bunch of guitar players from Brooklyn. I remember when he started 'Foxy Lady,' Jimi blew up three Marshall amps just by the feedback.

"As a bass player I was also checking out Noel, who overwhelmed me. I knew about Jack Bruce [bassist for Cream] and Jack Casady [bassist for Jefferson Airplane and Hot Tuna]. I was amazed at Jimi's sense of humor. He was shy but he could talk to the audience. He was cool, and it seemed like everything he did was improv. Mitch was one of my favorite drummers. I memorized his drum parts on the album, which were signature hooks. Very few drummers played like Mitch.

"I think Noel basically played the parts, which were not advanced parts, pretty fundamental. 'Manic Depression' had more movement. The biggest impression from that night was when Jimi did 'Red House'—a ten-minute version. Damn! The train ride back to Brooklyn was . . . we were all stunned."

Hendrix at Fillmore East, New York City, May 10, 1968.

# European Tour Take Two

JHE embarked on their second European tour in the summer of 1968 and it was relatively relaxed: a couple of dates in Zurich (for a Beat Monster Concert that featured Jimi sitting in with Traffic), Rome, and Bologna in May; a stop in London in June, for a guest shot on Dusty Springfield's *It Must Be Dusty* (those were the days!); the Woburn Festival in Bedfordshire in July; and two shows in Getafe, Spain, in July.

**ANYA WILSON** | music-business veteran

"My secretarial skills landed me a job with Peter Elderfield, one of the team in the international department of Pye Records. Pye was a very active record company representing many international labels that became major players. One of Pye's acts was Geno Washington & the Ram Jam Band, who would be performing directly before the Jimi Hendrix Experience at the Woburn Festival on July 6, 1968. A group of us from the record company made the trek.

"This was the first time I had ever been backstage at a music event. It was there that I was introduced to Jimi. The sun had come out that day. I was wearing one of my BIBA dresses and no coat, and although not cold, I was surprised to see Jimi in his much-photographed fur and suede jacket. I was introduced to him, and he gave me a hug and squeezed my hand and I kissed him on the cheek. We chatted for a while; then the hustle of the backstage crowd took over and my friends and I were herded toward Geno's camp.

> "The takeaway I have from that exchange with Jimi in my little fan's heart was how soft-spoken he was, almost shy, and how lovely and soft his skin was when I planted the kiss. What a night of incredible performances that was, to see the crowd revved up by Geno's set and lead-in to Jimi. It was a sequence that I've found hard to match."
>
> —Anya Wilson, music business veteran

# Roma
# and Jimi

**T**homas Harrison is a professor of Italian at UCLA; his brother, Robert, is a professor of literature at Stanford. But what really sets them apart from the sylvan groves of academia is their shared love of progressive music—"Prog Rock," that much-reviled but imperishable genre that speaks to the outré in many of us. Born to an American father and an Italian mother, they were impressionable adolescents living in Rome in 1968, feeling the cultural riptide of the sixties drawing them out to an inviting sea. Along with their older sister, Sandra, and a few other free-thinking friends, they ventured out to the Teatro Brancaccio on May 25 to hear an American guitarist whose dramatic entry into Italy echoed the Yanks landing in Anzio.

Jimi Hendrix played just this one time in Italy; Milan and Bologna made up the rest of this drive-by tour. His presence produced a mild form of mania, such was the level of interest he commanded from fans and media. The Harrison boys came home that night in a sonic stupor induced by the aural pummeling that Hendrix unleashed. They vowed then to start their own band and carve out a little piece of this magical mayhem for themselves. And they succeeded: their group—Sleepy Hollow—would eventually land prominent bookings, record original music, and allow them to experience just enough of the musician's hard road to let them know they preferred an ivory tower to castles made of sand.

## THOMAS HARRISON

"My photographs from the afternoon performance of Jimi Hendrix on May 25 in Rome show things I could not recall from memory: the airy lightness and breadth of Jimi's Afro . . . the nature of his medallion and crushed velvet pants. The pictures also evidence how close I got to the stage, within ten feet. . . . The best these pictures do today is signal an investment in that original experience, in 1968, and for decades to come. . . .

"Half American and half Italian, I and my siblings were well aware of the Beatles, the Yardbirds, and the Animals, and were fascinated by the mini-skirted English scene. We also knew something of California hippies and their beaches. But a black man who possessed that sound and their signifiers? And who instantly made the others appear affected and effeminate?

"The picture of me, my brother, and two friends of my sister was taken after the second performance of the day; my brother Robert and I attended both shows. I was probably the youngest person at either, and the throngs of smoking longhairs crowding the nighttime show made me sense my greenness. But I had been there before. I had 'been experienced.' I was now among the initiated and privileged.

Thomas Harrison, right, with his brother, sister, and their friends with a poster from the Hendrix concert they attended at the Teatro Brancaccio in Rome, May 25, 1968.

"I brought my Kodak Instamatic camera to the afternoon show and snapped some twenty pictures. The pictures say nothing of the searing performance, where guitar and voice cut straight through the forms that met the ear. The coolness of Jimi's demeanor acted as a harness, loosening itself only when an inner daemon proved impossible to contain. It is difficult for me to imagine any other performer ever compacting so tightly together sound, charisma, virtuosity, the erotic, mischief, and song.

"Following that intoxicating performance, we bought tickets for the night show as well, where the only seats available or affordable were in the gallery. The two of us sat close to the balcony rail, while my sister Sandy and her friends, who had bought their tickets earlier, were downstairs. . . . We all remember Jimi's antics with the amplifiers and how he singled out an attractive, embarrassed girl in the front row to receive the lyrics of 'Foxy Lady,' not to mention his playing with his teeth.

"On leaving the *teatro* after the second show, we were invited—or allowed—to take a concert poster from a very thick stack on the table. That is the one you see us holding in the photograph."

## ROBERT POGUE HARRISON

"Our sister's Italian boyfriend, Giovanni, who was a Hendrix fan and a few years older than us, got my brother Tom and me tickets to the early show. Tom and I had never heard of Hendrix before, and to this day we're grateful to Giovanni beyond measure for that initiation. I scarcely exaggerate when I say that, had I not attended that concert, I would not be the person I am today. By that I don't mean so much that I went on to become a musician and then a professor of literature. I mean that from that day onward, my inner selfhood and subjectivity has always been most at home in "electric ladyland." . . .

". . . Rome's electrical storms are among the most dramatic in the world. They typically approach from afar, with thunder rumbling faintly in the distance—an endless roll spreading from hill to hill—slowly getting nearer and more ominous.

"Having never been to a rock concert before, the only thing that even remotely prepared me for the experience of seeing and hearing Jimi Hendrix in concert at age fourteen were those Roman thunderstorms. The auditorium was only three-quarters full and we were sitting some twenty rows from the front. The first rumblings came with Noel and Mitch walking on to the stage like oneiric apparitions, Mitch rolling the drums, Noel striking a few low bass notes that pulsated through the hall. A few minutes later Jimi appears, like an extraterrestrial, tuning his white Fender and striking a few chords at enormous volume. I believe it was during the third song, 'Stone Free,' that Tom and I left our seats and went right up under the elevated stage. I vaguely recall Mitch Mitchell tapping his cowbell, which to an ex-altar boy like me sounded like a church bell's call to mass—the mass of some strange new religion.

"Tom had a Polaroid camera with him, and no one asked the two young boys . . . to go back to their seats, so we spent the rest of the concert right under Jimi, almost close enough to touch his velvet bell-bottoms and a few meters away from his thunderous Marshall amps, which he humped and slid his guitar strings against, provoking searing feedback effects. Add to that his other well-known rituals (but to us completely unheard-of), like playing with his teeth and behind his back and lighting up his guitar, and you can imagine what kind of electrification we underwent during that hour.

"Tom and I managed to get tickets to attend the second performance later that night. The concert still overwhelmed, yet it had more of an afterimage quality about it. It was the matinee session that had the kairotic, lifelong effect on us. I'm sure that many of the people in the auditorium went on with life as usual, yet for me the main goal in life after that experience was—and still is—to strive to remain true to the revelation."

## FILIPPO LA PORTA

"When on Saturday afternoon of May 25 I went to the Teatro Brancaccio with my friend Marco on a Vespa for the afternoon concert of Jimi Hendrix, I had no idea that I was about to see the most 'subversive' of all events in that fateful year of 1968. I was fifteen and was taking part in political demonstrations and sit-ins. . . . I was living in a sort of perennial state of ideological excitation. And yet the real revolution was not occurring there, in the protests and scorching debates about doctrine. Rather, it was occurring in the music of Hendrix.

"When I saw Hendrix in his pink shirt and heard him hammer the riff of 'Foxy Lady' . . . I had a kind of revelation . . .

"I'm not trying to say that Hendrix presented an example to follow, possessing the self-destructive fury and pained expression that he later showed in his famous performance at Woodstock. I just mean that on that warm and scented May evening in Rome, his music revealed an entire world, which belonged to me too, and about which I had had a vague intuition up to that time."

## SANDRA HARRISON

"It was certainly an exciting night for us. It was the first concert some of us had ever been to in our lives (I had already seen the Beatles but there is no comparison). Jimi Hendrix made us feel cool—not like screaming adolescents. We dressed up in outfits we'd planned weekends ahead. We wanted to look like glamorous groupies and we got our male escort to dress up like an Italian jet-setter.

"You have to know that at the time we were very young, and girls—even if we were sisters and cousins and not only girlfriends, socially we usually did what the boys wanted to do. If the boys wanted to sit around on a Saturday afternoon and listen to rock music by obscure bands, we used to do it too for a few hours. That is how we heard Jimi Hendrix for the first time, and we probably listened to his album a lot before going to the concert, because I remember recognizing the songs.

"We agree with each other that there was no guitar smashing or burning on the night we went. There were rumors that he was going to do that but I don't remember it happening. He did play with his teeth and his rear end to show off his virtuosity but also his disdain for whatever it was (us?). To him, the audience must have looked 'square,' to use a word of the day, or young bourgeois adults, not getting what he was all about but getting into the music."

## MARCO PERSICHETTI

"I remember that a Roman, on a high balcony in the gallery, with his arm around a column, towards the end of the evening concert, cried, '*Ahaa Giacomo, me pari Iddi* (Heeeey James, you seem like God!).' I'll remember it my whole life, for I agreed: He was and is the God of guitar."

**Above:** Photographs of Hendrix onstage at the Teatro Brancaccio taken by Thomas Harrison with his Kodak Instamatic, May 25, 1968.

# Back in the USA

Starting on July 30 in Shreveport, Louisiana, the JHE returned to America for yet another exhausting, exhaustive, Mike Jeffery–induced delirium. They played more than forty shows, concluding December 1 in Chicago.

**RICHARD BOSWORTH** | record producer, engineer

"Early evening, August 26, 1968. I arrived at Kennedy Stadium in Bridgeport, Connecticut, to see the Jimi Hendrix Experience for the first time.

"While opening acts Eire Apparent and Soft Machine performed . . . hordes of cops glared menacingly at the audience. After an interminable time, the Experience finally emerged from under the grandstand, headed for the stage.

"Even as Jimi walked out in a black velvet shirt with lime-green sharkskin trousers, I sensed something wrong. His shoulders were hunched, his gait stiff and uncomfortable.

"When they took the stage Jimi turned to Noel Redding, asking, 'What town are we in?' 'Bridgeport.' Hendrix angrily responded, 'Well, Bridgeport sucks!'

"Things went downhill from there. They opened up with an uninspiring 'Are You Experienced,' after which some in the audience were yelling for 'Purple Haze.' Without a word, the group jumped into a fairly good 'Foxy Lady.' Again came the calls for 'Purple Haze.' Obviously perturbed, Hendrix said, 'Hey! We're going to play "Purple Haze" for our last song so stop calling out for it!' Next up was 'Hey Joe.' The calls continued.

"Now Hendrix was really pissed off. 'Listen, you assholes! I told you I was going to play "Purple Haze" for my last song, so if you want this concert to end real quick, just keep calling for it!' They broke into 'Spanish Castle Magic,' which eventually devolved into a meandering, pointless jam. The calls continued. Jimi wearily walked to the microphone and said, 'Hey, my hands are getting cold up here so I'm going to play "Purple Haze" and go home.' And he did exactly that. A lot of booing commenced. Five songs and the entire set was only a half hour long.

"I read in the newspapers the next day that their manager/producer, Chas Chandler, had told the Bridgeport chief of police he wouldn't let the band go on unless they kept the lights off until they were on the stage. And if they refused, they would have a riot on their hands. Chandler was arrested for trying to incite a riot. No wonder Jimi was in a bad mood.

"At this time I've been in bands for several years, doing recording sessions in New York with top record producers and meeting major artists at their sessions. The studio reception areas had weekly music biz periodicals like

*Billboard* and *Cashbox*, which were a revelation to me. One had an advert for Manhattan-based Premier Talent Agency, headed by Frank Barcelona, declaring them the largest agency representing the most successful rock acts, including the Jimi Hendrix Experience.

"My high school had just built an auditorium that was very suited for music. So one day I got up the nerve to call Premier and asked to speak to Frank Barcelona. A woman who answered the phone requested my name and what I wanted. I explained I was inquiring about the possibility of booking the Jimi Hendrix Experience to play at my school.

She politely said, 'Well, Mr. Barcelona is in a meeting, but I will take your information and pass it on to him. In a few days you'll receive a tentative agreement stating the terms required to book the Jimi Hendrix Experience for a date yet to be determined.'

"When the official document arrived it was just incredible to read. The financial terms were $15,000 to book the group, $7,500 in advance to secure the date, another $3,750 two weeks before the gig, and final payment of $3,750 the night of the show before the performance.

"Jimi Hendrix did *not* play at my high school."

**There was a break in September**, when the band settled into a home in the Arcadian climes of Benedict Canyon, a popular retreat for Hollywood's haut monde. No less a personage than Cary Grant had been one of the property's previous occupants.

### CARMINE APPICE | drummer, Vanilla Fudge

"On that '68 West Coast tour the Vanilla Fudge did with the Jimi Hendrix Experience, I remember playing in San Diego at Balboa Stadium on September 3, 1968, and we played to maybe a third of capacity, 7,000 to 9,000 people in a racetrack-type setting, and Jimi started doing 'Voodoo Child.' It was echoing through all the empty seats as we were walking back into the dressing room after seeing him on stage, and to hear that wah-wah pedal traveling across those empty seats—it was fantastic. That was one of my vivid memories."

### ALEX DEL ZOPPO | keyboardist, Sweetwater

"On a night off during a week that Sweetwater spent in Phoenix, Arizona, the local Warner Bros. rep invited us to see Hendrix perform at the Memorial Coliseum on September 4, 1968.

"It was a truly unexpected gift. We were transported to the theater, greeted by the rep who escorted us to front-row-center seats! This would be a rare opportunity for anyone, but it gave us an opportunity to actually relax and even study Hendrix throughout the set.

"Watching him play, often with his eyes closed, even when moving his feet toward a fuzz switch or wah pedal, was nothing short of wondrous. Here, I captured in my mind the best glimpse of not only his slippery left-handed soul on the guitar, but also how passionate his voice was."

Keyboardist Alex Del Zoppo, center (in dark blue jacket), with his Sweetwater bandmates, c. 1969.

### CARMINE APPICE

"Another vivid memory of Jimi was when I think we were in Seattle, Jimi's hometown, at the Seattle Center Coliseum, on September 6, 1968.

"We were staying in a hotel and Jimi had just finished *Electric Ladyland* and had a test pressing, as they used to call it. We had a portable record player in the room with speakers. There was a bunch of us in the room, and he sat everybody down and said, 'Hey, I want to check out the new album.' He sat in the corner, very quietly, watching everyone's reaction. Then the album came out and it was legendary.

"Mitch Mitchell and Noel were at Jimi's side, playing their asses off. Mitch was like the rock that held it all together. Mitch and I come from jazz. I feel that back in those days, and I didn't include Charlie Watts, but I included four drummers that pioneered rock drumming back then as far as trying to taking it to another level: Mitch, Keith Moon, myself, and Ginger [Baker]. We were the four. Three of us were Ludwig guys. Keith wasn't.

"We were pioneering drum sets, playing, the jamming, incorporating jazz roots, coming up, in my case, with power rock drumming, you know, and in Mitch's case, jazz rock. And Ginger was kind of jazz rock, but Mitch was more traditional jazz, where Ginger was more like blues Afro, kind of blues jazz.

And Keith was just out of his mind and played whatever. He was so unique and so crazy. He was a tremendous innovator, and now I'm the only one left, unfortunately. Ringo is going, and Charlie is going, but they were different kinds. We were the powerhouse drummers."

**On September 14, 1968,** radio station KHJ in Los Angeles and Sight & Sound Productions promoted the Jimi Hendrix Experience at the Hollywood Bowl. Vanilla Fudge, the Soft Machine and Eire Apparent were also billed.

### ED CARAEFF | photographer and art director

"A beautiful day. Jimi was cool, calm, and confident at the Hollywood Bowl sound check. He was so pleased to see me. And when it got close to showtime, the road manager, Gerry Stickells, cleared everyone but let me stay. I'd go into the tune-up room. We knew Jimi and his crew, Jerry, and Michael Jeffery. Jimi knew me from Monterey and all his 1967 and '68 L.A. concerts. I loved shooting Jimi in the daylight with color film.

Ticket to the JHE show at the Hollywood Bowl, Saturday night, September 14, 1968.

"The sound check was wonderful and Jimi was in a great mood. I was embedded. Carmen Borrero, a girlfriend of Jimi's, was right there.

"When the show started, people began diving into the pool in front of the stage. We were all concerned that someone was going to jump onstage and grab Jimi and they both would be electrocuted. It was intense but Jimi was cool. It was an incredible show, and I'm glad nothing horrible happened. Cops were trying to pull the concertgoers out of the water."

### NANCY ROSE | concertgoer

"My friends Pat, Brian, and I went to the Hollywood Bowl, and we also attended the Jimi Hendrix autograph signing earlier that day at the Groove Company record shop on Crescent Heights and Sunset Boulevard. I touched the Buddha around Jimi's neck. Pat and I kissed him. . . .

"Loads of fans jumped in the pool before Pat, Brian, and I did. When Jimi started playing 'Fire' we couldn't contain ourselves! Then Brian lost his keys and we had to hitchhike home in wet clothes."

## LANNY WAGGONER | concertgoer

"In 1967, at the Monterey festival, it took a moment to realize the havoc Jimi was creating. He was absolutely on, as were Noel and Mitch. The music was like a tidal wave.

"At the Hollywood Bowl, by now a demigod, Jimi seemed to toy with us a bit, but played a good set despite the distraction of pool-divers who ignored everyone screaming 'you'll electrocute yourself!' I was not ushering at this show as I had for the Beatles and others years earlier. I do recall some members of the audience actually walking out because the scene had become so chaotic. Women were screaming all kinds of suggestive things at Jimi."

**Top and above:** JHE performs at the Hollywood Bowl on September 14, 1968, as fans dance in the reflecting pool in front of the stage (the pool was in place from 1952–72).

### JIM KELTNER | drummer

"My wife Cynthia and I saw Jimi at the Hollywood Bowl in 1968 with the Vanilla Fudge. Hendrix was incredible. And, of course, I loved the drummers Carmine Appice and Mitch Mitchell. I always like Carmine's feel and his approach.

"And as far as Mitch, everything musically has already been said. I got to know him really well when he came to L.A. We hung out a lot. We had a mutual fondness for the great drum teacher Freddie Gruber. I loved Mitch's stories about his days with Jimi."

### PETER PIPER | concertgoer

"I bought my tickets to see Jimi Hendrix at Wallichs Music City in Hollywood.

"I went with my girlfriend Carol. A guy I grew up with handed us these gigantic capsules of mescaline before the show. We took 'em and set off in my Ford Falcon station wagon.

"When we got to the Bowl, the parking attendant, for some reason, let us park at the very bottom of one of the lots near the back entrance, but near a hill. Our car blocked everyone who parked behind us.

Entrance to Wallichs Music City in Hollywood, which sold concert tickets as well as records.

"I paid twenty dollars each for tickets just above the box seats, a good location to see Jimi. I had my opera glasses. One guy in our row had a stack of fifty joints with a rubber band around them.

"Carol and I had not come on yet to the mescaline. Vanilla Fudge was incredible. That was the big toss-up—who would play better, them or Jimi. On their recordings they sounded tinny. But live, they sounded so much better. The sound mix was terrific. The organist sang lead and used his hands to signal the fellow musicians, like Carmen Dragon when he conducted the Hollywood Bowl Orchestra.

"And then Jimi comes out in a white suit, white boots, and a purple scarf. It was otherworldly. The roadies were adjusting all the amps when he was doing the first song. By the second song, the whole place really started feeling the vibe. Carol and I were really into the groove as people started going toward the front. And she started crying: 'If he tries to leave they are gonna riot.'

"Jimi dedicated 'Red House' 'to all the folks out there, including Buddy Miles and Carmen.' When he played 'Fire,' kids started to jump into the pool area just in front of the stage. Jimi wryly observed, 'Now we proudly present, Flipper!'

"Halfway into the set we came on to the mescaline. Carol and I left the concert just beaming. Then the real adventure started . . .

"We had no concept of where our car was. I was just flashing that we had to find this one long line of cars as we were the car at the entrance. We kept walking around the Hollywood Bowl and could not locate our wheels. It must have been ninety minutes. Basically, all the cars and buses were pretty much gone, and we're alone in front of the Hollywood Bowl marquee.

"I found one person with a flashlight and asked for some help. He told me there was a line of cars on the other side. He had a walkie-talkie. So we go to the other side and there [were] a few people who were angry as we needed to move our car to create a path for them to leave. And here is a van parked at the top of the hill by the back gate pretty close to us, and music was playing. It was the only vehicle near us.

A KHJ Boss 30 ad featuring a photo of Hendrix's September Hollywood Bowl show.

## BOSS HITBOUNDS

| | |
|---|---|
| MAGIC CARPET RIDE<br>Steppenwolf | Dunhill |
| DON'T LEAVE ME<br>Robert John | Columbia |
| PEACE OF MIND<br>Nancy Wilson | Capitol |

**93/KHJ BOSS 30**

KHJ AND THE BOSS JOCKS
THANK YOU
FOR MAKING THIS
SUMMER'S CONCERT SERIES
A SOLID SOLD-OUT SUCCESS!
WE HOPE YOU DUG THE
DOORS, THE RASCALS,
SIMON & GARFUNKEL AND
THE JIMI HENDRIX
EXPERIENCE!

## 93/KHJ
### BOSS RADIO
IN LOS ANGELES

JIMI HENDRIX soaks it to 'em at KHJ's concluding concert of Summer '68!

"We walked over and these two people come out—it's Jimi and this gorgeous girl. And they are heading in our direction. And Jimi is kind of half-hiding behind her. 'Hey, how did you like the show?' We didn't shake hands, but I exclaimed, 'You are the greatest, man, nobody like you.'"

**Jimi, Mitch, and Noel** then flew to San Francisco and played a Winterland engagement on October 10–12. Monterey International Pop Festival veteran sound engineers Wally Heider, Bill Halverson, and Abe Jacob documented the action.

### BILL HALVERSON | engineer

"Heider and I had recorded Chuck Berry in late '67, Hendrix and Cream at Winterland. In these recordings, when I first opened up the mike on the amps, it was distorting. And I finally found this place by accident in between the four speakers of a Marshall stack where it was just up against the grill cloth. And it was clean."

**On October 19, Jimi Hendrix** and Mitch Mitchell, along with George Harrison and Pattie Boyd, attended Cream's last LA show at the "Fabulous Forum" [the Forum] in Inglewood. Later that same night, Jimi jammed at the Whisky a Go Go with organist/vocalist Lee Michaels and drummer Barry "Frosty" Smith.

### ED CARAEFF | photographer and art director

"Jimi jumped onstage at the Whisky after he saw Cream at the Forum. Mitch Mitchell and George Harrison were there. I was with Rodney [Bingenheimer]. We'd always go to the Whisky, and Mario [Maglieri] would always let us in. And I would always bring my camera.

"As far as shooting, the Whisky had low light, but I got some shots. He [Hendrix] played solo. Jimi was a professional and at ease in [a] public setting.

> **"Jimi could play the guitar like no one had ever seen, behind the back, with his teeth, and so effortlessly. His fingers seemed to be twice as long as anyone and he could wrap them around the guitar."**
>
> —Ed Caraeff

MAGIC CARPET RIDE
Steppenwolf                    Dunhill
DON'T LEAVE ME
Robert John                    Columbia

**RODNEY BINGENHEIMER** | radio host, SiriusXM, *Rodney on the ROQ*

"Ed Caraeff and I were walking on Sunset Boulevard and Chas Chandler saw us, waved and invited us in. After Jimi did a few solo numbers, Jimi jumped into Ed's car and we all went to John and Michelle Phillips' house in Bel-Air. Ed and Jimi played pool.

"I cruised with Jimi a couple of times in his yellow Corvette Stingray to Gold Star recording studio from Peter Tork's house when the Cake was recording at Gold Star Studios. Jimi's girlfriend was Jeannette Jacobs [singer, the Cake]. He knew her in New York and she was at Monterey in 1967."

**Muddy Waters' album *Electric Mud*,** released in October 1968, was produced by Marshall Chess and Charles Stepney for the Cadet Concept label, a subsidiary of Chess Records. The album, which was a brew of electric blues with psychedelic elements, made an indelible impression on Jimi Hendrix.

**MARSHALL CHESS** | executive, Chess Records

"It was the biggest album Muddy had ever had. For half a century I've been noshing on the road and people have come up to me saying, it's the greatest and I love it.

"Miles Davis said it blew his mind. The guitarist on it, Pete Cosey, told me, and because of that album became Miles' electric guitar player during 1973–75.

"Peter told me that Miles just loved it and also mentioned that Miles had a hair dresser, who was also Jimi Hendrix's hairdresser in 1968 and '69, and they all played another cut from Muddy's May '69 *After the Rain* album. That was my second album with the same band, and that Hendrix would play it before he went onstage. The hairdresser told Pete and he told me."

**Opposite:** Hendrix with Rodney Bingenheimer, the unofficial "Mayor of Sunset Strip" and later, renowned KROQ deejay.
**Above:** Muddy Waters live at the Country Club, London, December 1, 1970.

# TTG Studios

TTG Studios was founded in LA in 1965 by sound engineers Ami Hadini and Tom Hidley. In the fifties and early sixties, the building that housed the studio on North McCadden had been Radio Recorders, and later Conway Recorders, before TTG obtained the property license. TTG installed a 16-track machine, one of the first in town.

The Mothers of Invention cut *Freak Out!* (1966) and *Absolutely Free* (1967) at TTG with producer Tom Wilson. *The Velvet Underground & Nico*, along with *Winds of Change* by Eric Burdon and the Animals, was also recorded with Wilson during 1967.

Hendrix took up residency there in October, but the sessions were plagued by a litany of technical glitches. Jams with Jack Bruce, Graham Bond, Jack Casady, Robert Wyatt (whose own studio musings finally surfaced in 2013 on the album '68 on Cuneiform Records), Lee Michaels, and Stephen Stills remain mere vapor trails, beyond the reach of even the most determined bootleggers. Jimi added producer chores and some guitar parts for an Eire Apparent album recorded during this period, but it was weak tea by everyone's reckoning, and faded promptly into obscurity—a footnote for Hendrix scholars. Jimi was also flagging in his personal life; nasty potions were escalating in and around the Experience camp.

**KIM FOWLEY** | songwriter, record producer

"I was [at TTG] in 1966 and '67. TTG Studios was a giant cheeseburger box with high ceilings. I worked with [a] coowner and sound engineer, an Israeli named Ami Hadani. "Bill Parr was formerly with Conway studios, built and designed the custom TTG board in the big film-scoring room upstairs. Bill was one of the engineers on 'Alley-Oop,' [a] hit that we did at American Recorders in 1960.

"Jimi Hendrix recorded at TTG and cut one of my songs, 'Fluffy Turkeys.' Jimi sang, played guitar, and did the bass. Robert Wyatt of Soft Machine was the drummer. Never has been released."

**RODNEY BINGENHEIMER** | radio host, SiriusXM, *Rodney on the ROQ*

"During October 1968, I would see Jimi around Hollywood. Once at TTG studios, when I was with the photographer Chuck Boyd. Jimi did some recording sessions there with Mitch and Noel, Cream's Jack Bruce, Buddy Miles, Jim McCarty, and Lee Michaels."

# On the Road Yet Again

By November, it was time to decamp from LA and hit the road, where a semblance of sanity returned.

**RICHARD BOSWORTH** | record producer, engineer

"On Sunday, November 17, 1968, I was driving west on the Connecticut Turnpike on my way to see the Jimi Hendrix Experience at Yale University's Woolsey Hall. I had tickets to the late show but decided to get there early, as anything could happen.

"We were also told the doors of the hall would open, allowing us to hear the band's first set, which had just begun. I was able to position myself by the open door and could see a bit of stage right, which was Jimi's side of the stage. Every now and then Hendrix came into view wearing buckskin with fringe and black velvet pants with knee-high white leather boots. He was in a great mood, laughing and joking with the crowd. Jimi was an emotional player and at his best when happy.

"After performances by Terry Reid and Cat Mother and the All Night Newsboys, the Experience took the stage, opening up with a short but sweet 'Sgt. Pepper's Lonely Hearts Club Band.' The band only played the first verse and chorus then jammed to a quick ending. Next up was a blazing 'Fire,' and then a spectacular take on 'Red House.'

"Hendrix was still in a cheerful mood, cracking jokes, making funny off-the-wall comments between songs. As usual, people were calling out requests, and one particularly obnoxious voice in the balcony kept yelling for for 'Hey Joe.' The familiar sound of feedback signaled the beginning of an awesome 'Foxy Lady,' followed by 'Hey Joe,' after which that same voice shouted, 'Play guitar with your teeth!'

"Hendrix had enough: 'Hey man, pull down your pants and I'll play guitar with my teeth.' The audience roared in laughter, and that shut the loudmouth up for the rest of the night.

"*Electric Ladyland* had just been released October 16, so it was thrilling to hear the iconic wah-wah guitar intro to 'Voodoo Chile,' arguably the high point of the set. It morphed into 'Sunshine of Your Love' with a drum solo from Mitch. They ended with an extended 'Purple Haze' where Jimi pulled out all his showman moves, slamming his body and guitar into the already tattered Marshall amps.

Poster designed by Dennis Loren for the JHE concert at the Cobo Arena, Detroit, Saturday, November 30, 1968.

**DENNIS LOREN** | graphic designer and art director

"I happened to be in Detroit for my brother David's wedding. While I was [in] town, I spent some time with musician friends and went to the Grande Ballroom. One of the people I met there was Matthew Rock (né Rokofsky) who was one of the Grande Ballroom poster artists. We bonded over music, art, and concert posters. Matt told me that he had begun work on a poster for the upcoming November 30, 1968, Jimi Hendrix Experience concert at Cobo Hall, or as it was sometimes called, Cobo Arena.

"He asked if I would help him with the final mechanical layout and color the poster. Matt had already finished the hand lettering (that you see in red and yellow) and had positioned the poster image of Hendrix in the center.

"I added the bolder display lettering using Letraset rub-down letters, and the smaller text information using regular Compugraphic typesetting. I hand-cut the green and purple floral background using Rubylith film, and then I used a tissue overlay to indicate the color separations for the printer. Ironically, I wasn't able to attend the concert because I had returned to San Francisco by the time it was held."

The Knack bassist Prescott Niles in 1968.

Hendrix protégé Velvert Turner, c. 1970.

## PRESCOTT NILES | bassist, the Knack

"I was playing in a blues band when Velvert Turner comes in to audition. He was six foot three and hunched over like Jimi. He kind of looked like Jimi and wore a chiffon belly shirt. He picked up a guitar and played 'Foxy Lady,' and at the time not many people in Brooklyn could do that. And I asked him where he got his shirt. 'Jimi gave it to me.' We kept in touch.

"Around Thanksgiving on November 28, Velvert telephoned. 'Do you want to see Jimi at Philharmonic Hall?' It's a classical place. 'Yes!' We go to the concert. The band was brilliant that night. The acoustics were incredible. And they debuted some songs like 'Spanish Castle Magic' from *Axis: Bold As Love*. I saw the growth of the band and heard the difference.

"I'm recovering from the show and Velvert said, 'Let's take a train and go uptown for a party to celebrate Jimi's twenty-fifth birthday.' I believe we went to the Cheetah. It was a very diverse crowd with lots of beautiful women. I'm ten feet away from Jimi when Velvert introduced me. Jimi's persona—he was so not what you think he was—was shy, intellectual, and sometimes he had his outbursts, of course.

"A little later in I met Jimi again with Velvert at a restaurant called Nobody's in Greenwich Village. Velvert knew Jimi and around that time had taken some guitar lessons, or instruction, mentorship advice from Jimi at his apartment at 302 West 12th Street. And Velvert knew Eric Barrett, from Jimi's road crew, so we got to see his equipment, pedals, and knew what he was using."

"In the beginning Velvert was a pain in the ass, and he admitted that later on. He was just a hanger-on, you know. However, my opinion of him changed as he became a very sweet guy. And as he grew up in maturity, he was a dear friend of Jimi's. Jimi really liked him an awful lot. And the family, Janie Hendrix, John McDermott, and I really liked him a lot."

—Eddie Kramer, recording engineer, producer

# On Tour with the Jimi Hendrix Experience

**H**ugh Hopper was, like his fabled American counterpart, James Jamerson, an idiosyncratic master of the Fender bass guitar. His tone, touch, and, most importantly, "feel," showcased a virtuosic command of understatement; he let the bass breathe, allowing the space between each note to resonate with an airy elegance, occasionally fractured by the impertinent outburst of a fuzzy embellishment.

Hugh Hopper, Soft Machine bassist, at the Amougies Festival in Belgium, October 24 to 28, 1969.

Hugh earned his greatest renown for his work with the whimsically demanding British band, Soft Machine, whom he joined in 1969. The year previous was spent in the memorable if thankless role as their tour manager during the group's Lewis and Clark–like expedition across America, opening for Jimi Hendrix and the Experience.

The Softs were an inspired choice to share the bill. Described by Hugh as "a freaky trio whose music combined elements of Thelonious Monk, Beatles, and Stravinsky"—nothing immodest about their ambitions—they were held in high esteem by Jimi who had already shared some bills with them in England. They were also represented by the same management—the Anim Agency—run by Mike Jeffery and Chas Chandler.

Hugh, who passed away in 2009, gathered his reminiscences about this epochal tour in an unpublished manuscript that he shared with co-author, Ken Kubernik, following their collaboration on a Soft Machine tribute album in the early 2000s. They are excerpted here for the first time.

## HUGH HOPPER, BASSIST, SOFT MACHINE

"The tour almost ended at the first gig. [Our] drummer objected to the way [concert promoter] Bill Graham ran his Fillmore Ballroom like a military operation, and called him a Fascist. This was not tactful, we were told, as some of Graham's family died in Auschwitz. We were packed off to wait in the next town. . . .

"For the next five weeks we were working every day—either a concert or driving to the next concert, usually overnight grabbing what sleep we could in dressing rooms or in the cab of the truck. It had to be done by truck; we had lost or had damaged too much equipment flying it between gigs. Amplifiers would come off the plane with their innards hanging out, drum cases crushed. It looked like the loading crew held an Olympic meet with equipment-destruction as the favorite event.

"The worst thing was the disorientation; finding yourself driving off in the middle of the night to the next gig, having driven overnight to this one, and the one before and the one before that. . . . Checking into the same Holiday Inn that you checked into the afternoon before except that that one was three hundred miles back down the road . . . wasn't it?

"That was if all went well on the road. Usually something happened to cause us to arrive at the gig with minus time to spare. The miracle about the Jimi Hendrix Tour of 1968 was not that he brought wonderful music to people all over the States and became a legend within two months: it was that any single one of the concerts happened at all. If you're sitting in a theatre waiting for the show to start and it's ten minutes late, you grumble and grouse, don't you? I do myself. But you try making it from Philly to Detroit overnight, in winter (minus 23 degrees), then Toronto the next day, then back to Chicago for an afternoon performance, en route bluffing your way through US/Canadian Customs and Immigration twice. And how would you feel if, having survived all this and seen the signs for Chicago coming up, the gas gauge suddenly started dropping at the rate of a gallon a mile? And it was Sunday?

"It was *survival*. We had two gigs in Canada; Montreal and Ottawa, and then had to drive down to Rochester. Not a bad drive, really. Except that the beautiful Thousand Islands area of the St. Lawrence River was in the solid grip of winter, and south of that as evening fell a fog surrounded us, so dense that we could see no further than ten feet ahead. I really got the horrors. I told Oscar [another roadie] to slow down, told him to let me drive, lasted about five minutes behind the wheel and then had to pull over. We tried blanking off part of the headlights to cut down the reflected glare, tried driving lights on and lights off; it made no difference. And all the while, Greyhound buses and giant trucks were sweeping past us in the fast lane a steady seventy. Horrifying. We limped into Rochester and collapsed onto hour hotel beds, drained.

"Crossing the border [from Canada] back into the States could be interesting too. The US Customs guy would brighten visibly when he caught sight of our disreputable truck trying to sneak in. And when he found out we were carrying musical instruments. . . . 'I'm not going to pretend—what I'm looking for is drugs.'

"The Experience received a visit from the Plaster Casters in Chicago [on February 25, 1968]. These industrious ladies were making a collection of musicians' penises, by cornering 'em in their rooms, forcibly stimulating 'em (using very unfair methods) and then slapping quick-setting plaster of Paris on the erect prick. Noel announced that his turned out bent—he'd collapsed, probably from laughter before it had set.

"We were pleased to see that the dirty icebergs in the streets of Newark were at last receding as spring approached. What could go wrong? Martin Luther King could get shot that very day, that's what. [Hendrix equipment manager] Gerry Stickells met us at the theatre and told us to set up the gear, but that most probably the gig would be cancelled. People were nervous and shaky; you could feel it, and the promoter figured no one would step outside the door, let alone come to the show. We unloaded the truck in silence in the back street behind the aged theatre. I checked all the truck doors and picked up the last piece of equipment, a chrome microphone stand, and turned to follow [the crew]. The stage door was locked fast and no outside handle. I pounded and shouted to no effect. So, great—here I am in Newark, New Jersey, on the night that one of the world's best-loved black men has been shot, and I've got to walk around to the front doors of the theatre (nearly half a mile, it's in the middle of a block), by way of some very dark back streets, with only my pale British face showing.

"I looked down at the shiny mike-stand in my hand, thinking that if anything happened it might be some defense. . . . Then: Christ! I suddenly realized what it would look like from a distance in the semi-darkness, either to a prowling cop or a lunatic sniper—the quick flash they'd get would be enough like a rifle on a night like this.

"Of course, nothing happened, and my other fear, that they wouldn't let me in at the front, was unfounded. 'What kept you?' I could think of no words equal to what I'd been through. I set about working in silence.

"Most days Jimi would lock himself in his room, usually with a willing new female friend. He was given the nickname 'The Bat' because of his routine of staying put, with all the curtains tightly closed until evening.

"Most of the violence in Jimi's act was confined to the last song, and was completely controlled. Jimi would strap on his most elderly Strat and would attack an equally old speaker cabinet. From the audience it looked like a savage animal attack or a rape. He would never damage his favorite guitar—the Gibson Flying V—unless he was really pissed off. Gerry Stickells was always standing behind the speaker, steadying it against Jimi's attacks. It was all worked out and very controlled."

**Opposite:** Jimi "attacking" his guitar during a show at the Star-Club in Hamburg, Germany, March 17, 1967.

# 9
# Electric Ladyland

The third and last album recorded by the Jimi Hendrix Experience—*Electric Ladyland*—was the culmination of their wild ride from precocious upstarts to unrivaled superstars. In just eighteen months, Jimi had become this alluring, illusive visionary, whose benign, ecumenical practice of Black Power was at odds with the disaffected outrage expressed by other young African Americans. Jimi's message seeped into the listener's consciousness with the hypnotic charge of a snake charmer. Because he resisted political affiliations, and because his audience was overwhelmingly white, he had a reach that was unmatched.

*E*lectric Ladyland arrived then, as a new-fangled book of common prayer. It connected all the disparate threads of his life—a childhood adrift in fantasy, the rapture he found in the blues, the tough love he gleaned from his mentors, and an insatiable desire to create with any and every tool at his disposal—into a lustrous tapestry, resolute in Jimi's talent, confidence, and clarity. He felt, not surprisingly, that it only approximated the sounds he was hearing in his head. But it was close enough for immortality.

*Electric Ladyland* went to No. 1 on the *Billboard* chart, confirmation that Hendrix's ambition did not exceed his ability. Like his two previous albums, it was produced in fits and starts between grueling tours. Sessions began in earnest in April at Olympic Studios. Most of the songs, though, were cut at the Record Plant in Manhattan. Jimi would jam at the Scene until the wee small hours before returning to the studio with a motley posse of newfound friends who delighted in their access to rock royalty. It became a constant struggle; Chandler was driven to his wits' end by all the distractions, the need for continual retakes, songs shifting in focus befitting Jimi's many moods.

Halfway through, Chas had had enough. With his wife pregnant and progress grindingly slow, he left for the relative sanity of London. Noel Redding, too, was pissed off by all the foofaraw. The Experience bassist was already the designated mumbling grumbler in the group, scornful of Hendrix's need for attention. It was "unprofessional." Jimi, for his part, seized the opportunity to take more control, assuming producer responsibilities, enlisting a glittering cast of guest musicians to compensate for the growing limitations of the trio format. He had finally put the puzzle together, but the pieces remained subject to forces beyond his control. He was a genius walking a razor's edge.

That "edge" cut in a variety of unexpected, exhilarating ways. *Sgt. Pepper's* had just liberated the conventions of pop music; Hendrix, fine-tuned to both the Beatles' innovations and his own febrile imagination, wantonly embraced this new music and cultural aesthetic. Like fashion and the visual arts, music was drawing from a combustible, irresistible mix of the high and low. Ian MacDonald, in his 1994 book *Revolution in the Head*, described it as "casually voracious 'nowness.'" The Beatles, he said, "*felt* their way through life." There could be no better description of what *Electric Ladyland* represented to Jimi, the most intuitive of artists, an adventurer with keen survival instincts who exalted in uncertainty.

**JAMES CUSHING** | poet, English professor, deejay

"*Electric Ladyland* is in the elite category with [Dylan's] *Blonde on Blonde*, the Beatles' *White Album*, [Captain Beefheart's] *Trout Mask Replica*, [the Stone's] *Exile on Main Street*, and no more than two or three other seventy-plus-minute double LPs from the core years with no fat and an overall atmospheric coherence that leaves one feeling that a whole emotional world has been brought into being.

"The release of the UK edition was complicated by pointless controversy over a girly-skin cover Hendrix hated, a sign that control was slipping away, as was the Experience itself; Noel Redding is absent on many tracks, and Jimi's prose-poem liner notes express loneliness and a sense of loss. The last two tracks on side four were the hits. 'All Along the Watchtower' and 'Voodoo Child (Slight Return)'—has any album ended with a more indelible one-two punch than this? Side three offered a cinematic journey from Hammond B3 blues into outer space. Isn't this Sun Ra territory?"

Jimi in London at his Mayfair apartment, displaying the infamous European album cover of *Electric Ladyland*.

# Hendrix and Dylan

As a result of the growing tension between Hendrix and Redding (who parted ways the following year), Hendrix took it upon himself to play bass on most of the songs, including on the cover of Bob Dylan's "All Along the Watchtower," the only Jimi Hendrix Experience single to reach *Billboard*'s top 20.

Guitarist Larry Coryell was present during the sessions and shared his recollection in *Guitar Player* magazine's September 1975 tribute edition to Jimi:

> I watched him work in the studio while he was doing *Electric Ladyland*. He turned his amps up—he had a couple of Marshalls stacked up all by themselves. The basic tracks were already down, and it was amazing to watch him work. I learned a lot about how to work in a studio myself from that experience.
>
> Specifically, he was working on vocal and guitar overdubs for "House Burning Down," and that same night he also jammed with Traffic's Stevie Winwood, with Stevie at the organ. The result was that long blues thing, "Voodoo Chile." The stream of energy just went back and forth between them. I wanted to get in there and play but Jimi was saying it all, and another guitarist would have been in his way.

Jimi's interpretation of "All Along the Watchtower" has achieved emeritus status among the legions of Dylan obsessives. It became a crossover hit on both AM and FM radio—the only single of Hendrix's to go Top 20. The song was an acknowledgment of Jimi's preoccupation with Bob.

Everyone in his orbit—friends, lovers, players, eavesdroppers—confirms that the mere mention of Dylan would command Jimi's undivided attention. Linda Keith has described the fascination in terms of a love affair; Eddie Kramer observed that Jimi kept a Dylan songbook in his flight bag and would refer to it on a daily basis.

Mitch Mitchell remembered the session as typical; he'd never heard the original, so Jimi ran the chord changes down—just strumming the guitar, this is how it goes—and a couple of takes later (with crucial overdubs), we have the pop music version of a Rembrandt self-portrait.

The Record Plant's taping log for the "All Along the Watchtower" recording session, July 3, 1968.

**JAMES CUSHING** | poet, English professor, deejay

"The Jimi Hendrix Experience recorded Dylan's 1965 single '[Can You] Please Crawl Out Your Window?' at an October 17, 1967, BBC Radio taping and included it in their May 1968 Fillmore East appearance.

"They play it live in the studio. There was a rider in the contract that said whenever a performer [appeared] on the BBC, they had to perform at least one song they had not recorded or released in any other form, which is why the group did 'Hound Dog,' 'Day Tripper,' and 'Sgt. Pepper.' There was even a session with Stevie Wonder on drums, which is pretty crazy. There's a cover of Wonder's 'I Was Made to Love Her.'

"As far as Dylan's lyrical influence on Hendrix, it might have begun with the song 'Foxy Lady' and the reference to 'precious time,' owing to 'Don't Think Twice, It's All Right.'

"Hendrix and Dylan, both born in the early forties, are two examples of people who grew up without television, which might have informed their wild imagination. These men, in terms of originality, I think they are the two individuals who stand out more than anyone else from the entire rock generation, including Elvis Presley.

> "Dylan and Hendrix together justify the entire existence of rock. Because with Dylan you have a genuine poetic sensibility that enters the music and flourishes, and with Hendrix you have a genuinely original take of the blues. In terms of timbre, in terms of rhythm, harmony, and the fact that Dylan's journey continues and the fact that Hendrix's journey was hideously cut off at age 27."

—James Cushing

# A Pilgrim's Progress

TEOFILO F. RUIZ, Professor of History, UCLA, Recipient of the
2011 National Humanities Medal from President Obama

" **H**aving been asked to describe my own personal reaction
to and to compare the music of Jimmy Hendrix and Bob
Dylan, I find myself facing the quandary of choosing
between my jumbled memories of more than fifty years ago and the
need, as a historian, to explain the popularity and impact of these
two gifted musicians on an entire generation and beyond. Having
come from Cuba in the early sixties, living and working in New York,
American music was almost entirely new for me. The majority of my
Cuban friends still embraced our homeland music. I did, and still
do, too, but I worked in a can manufacturing plant in Queens. All
my fellow workers were Americans, and they introduced me very
early on to their music. During smoke and lunch breaks, I sat in awe
seeing how passionately they argued about the virtues of one singer
over another or glossed over the meaning of certain songs. Each one
had its favorites, but one of them introduced me to Dylan early on.
Hendrix, I got to know only much later.

"I attended City College in the evening and became even more deeply involved in the politics and the music of the age. I also did so because music and politics were two faces of an ideology. It was a growing awareness that the music and lyrics, besides being beautiful, also loudly proclaimed an ideological message. It was not dissimilar to the music associated with the Cuban revolution in my teens, or with the Spanish Republican songs (which was part of my family's experience).

"For me, personally, Bob Dylan defined the period. Although less mercurial than Hendrix, less of a stage presence, and not having a great singing voice, Dylan's lyrics were, and remain, powerful evocations of resistance, sexual passion, and a call to a better future. His yearning for a different America, articulated in numerous songs, spoke powerfully to many of the young people who were the standard bearers of the sixties' revolution or its failed hopes for change.

"Hendrix's importance should, of course, not be underestimated. African American musicians, from Ray Charles, James Brown, and others, stood somewhat at the fringe of 'white music' which, although deeply influenced by Afro-American singers and songwriters and 'crossing over' as Louis Armstrong, Nat King Cole, or Johnny Mathis did, remain tied to other musical traditions. Hendrix, because of his talent and fierceness, always fully belonged to all: blacks and whites alike.

"What Hendrix did was to address the grievances of African Americans against the country's

Professor Teofilo F. Ruiz in Havana, Cuba, March 2012.

social injustice. In that sense, his music had also a direct impact on many of us. It made us learn. His songs, while making a more direct call to change, lacked Dylan's kind of poetry and universality (as recognized recently by the Nobel Prize). Hendrix and Dylan's music remains relevant today. It is a call, a reminder that we must resist those nefarious forces at work in our culture today."

## DAVE MASON | singer/songwriter, cofounder, Traffic

"Jimi and I heard an advance copy of [Dylan's] *John Wesley Harding* at his girlfriend, Kathy Etchingham's, apartment. We went over to Olympic Studios for a session. A couple of other people were present, two of the guys in the Pretty Things. I played acoustic guitar with Jimi on 'All Along the Watchtower,' and then there were three or four tracks with him where I played bass and sitar. I also added background vocals on 'Crosstown Traffic.'

"Olympic was a great room. It was a huge studio that had a large room to record in. Traffic recorded there with Jimmy Miller producing. It's an easy song and cool lyrics. It lends itself to interpretation—three chords. That's all it is. I later did my version of it because it was a great vehicle to play guitar.

"There was a point when I wasn't with Traffic and Jimi wasn't working with Noel Redding. Jimi and I talked seriously about me taking Noel Redding's place on bass. I believe Mike Jeffery put a stop to it."

**Left to right:** Jimi Hendrix, Noel Redding, Dave Mason of Traffic, and Mitch Mitchell, in Hollywood, 1968.

## JIM KELTNER | drummer

"I also really liked the way [drummer, songwriter and vocalist] Jim Capaldi played with Dave Mason in Traffic. In 1970 I played on Dave Mason's *Alone Together* LP on Blue Thumb Records. The producer was Tommy Li Puma.

"'All Along the Watchtower' was always one of my favorite songs to play with Neil Young. It's an amazing song.

"Playing it with Neil was always a huge amount of fun because of the way he plays. The song just allowed him to soar, completely fly. And it allows for a big, massive, wide beat. It has so many powerful elements. Playing it with Bob Dylan was the ultimate, of course."

## MICHAEL HACKER | filmmaker

"Hendrix made it plain to all around him that he believed he 'couldn't sing,' and his shyness about recording vocals is well known. But something about Dylan's lyrics set his voice free, and Jimi's vocals on the five Dylan tunes he covered bring shades of emotion and insight that were barely hinted at in Dylan's versions.

"When Jimi released his version of 'All Along the Watchtower' on September 21, 1968, this record, much as 'Like a Rolling Stone' did three years earlier, pushed a conglomeration of sounds out of the transistor radio and the hi-fi console that had not been heard before. No one but Jimi had the expansive consciousness to even imagine this kind of sonic landscape, much less apply it to a mysteriously sparse tune like 'Watchtower.'"

"All Along the Watchtower" hit No. 5 on the KHJ Boss 30 survey, October 16, 1968.

### KHJ'S BOSS 30 RECORDS IN SOUTHERN CALIFORNIA

PREVIEWED OCTOBER 16, 1968

| LAST WEEK | THIS WEEK | TITLE | ARTIST | LABEL | WEEKS ON BOSS 30 |
|---|---|---|---|---|---|
| (2) | 1. | THOSE WERE THE DAYS | Mary Hopkin | Apple | 5 |
| (8) | 2. | MAGIC CARPET RIDE | Steppenwolf | Dunhill | 3 |
| (1) | 3. | GIRL WATCHER | The O'Kaysions | ABC | 8 |
| (10) | 4. | SWEET BLINDNESS | The 5th Dimension | Soul City | 4 |
| (13) | 5. | ALL ALONG THE WATCHTOWER | Jimi Hendrix | Reprise | 3 |
| (12) | 6. | HEY, WESTERN UNION MAN | Jerry Butler | Mercury | 4 |
| (3) | 7. | ELENORE | The Turtles | White Whale | 6 |
| (19) | 8. | ABRAHAM, MARTIN AND JOHN | Dion | Laurie | 2 |
| (28) | 9. | LOVE CHILD | Diana Ross & The Supremes | Motown | 2 |
| (14) | 10. | LITTLE GREEN APPLES | O. C. Smith | Columbia | 5 |
| (16) | 11. | HI-HEEL SNEAKERS | Jose Feliciano | RCA | 3 |
| (4) | 12. | HEY JUDE | The Beatles | Apple | 7 |
| (17) | 13. | POOR BABY | The Cowsills | MGM | 4 |
| (7) | 14. | OVER YOU | The Union Gap | Columbia | 5 |
| (6) | 15. | PIECE OF MY HEART | Big Brother & The Holding Co. | Columbia | 6 |
| (23) | 16. | ON THE WAY HOME | Buffalo Springfield | Atco | 3 |
| (27) | 17. | DON'T LEAVE ME | Robert John | Columbia | 3 |
| (18) | 18. | JESSE BRADY | The McCoys | Mercury | 5 |
| (25) | 19. | CYCLES | Frank Sinatra | Reprise | 2 |
| (11) | 20. | SUZIE Q | Creedence Clearwater | Fantasy | 8 |
| (9) | 21. | LALENA | Donovan | Epic | 5 |
| (24) | 22. | CHAINED | Marvin Gaye | Tamla | 3 |
| (29) | 23. | PEACE OF MIND | Nancy Wilson | Capitol | 2 |
| (30) | 24. | WHITE ROOM | Cream | Atco | 2 |
| (5) | 25. | MY SPECIAL ANGEL | The Vogues | Reprise | 6 |
| (26) | 26. | FOOL FOR YOU | The Impressions | Curtom | 3 |
| (HB) | 27. | RIDE MY SEE-SAW | The Moody Blues | Deram | 1 |
| (HB) | 28. | PEACE BROTHER PEACE | Bill Medley | MGM | 1 |
| (HB) | 29. | KEEP ON LOVIN' ME, HONEY | Marvin Gaye & Tammi Terrell | Tamla | 1 |
| (HB) | 30. | SHAME, SHAME | The Magic Lanterns | Atlantic | 1 |

**OFFICIAL** ISSUE NO. **172**

The listing of records herein is the opinion of KHJ based on its survey of record sales, listener requests, and KHJ's judgment of the record's appeal.

"I play a lot of *Highway 61 Revisited* and *Blonde on Blonde* on my Outlaw Country Sirius XM radio channel. I've programmed Rod Stewart and the Faces covering 'The Wicked Messenger' from *John Wesley Harding* and Jimi Hendrix doing 'All Along the Watchtower.'

"Jimi Hendrix did more to promote *John Wesley Harding* than anybody. It was one of the most remarkable records ever made, of course. And the fact that Jimi picked up on that, from that unusual and not very popular Bob Dylan album, made everybody go back to it. And I'm telling you, that's how powerful that record was. Everybody went back to *John Wesley Harding* after hearing Hendrix, thinking, 'You know, maybe I missed something? Look what Jimi Hendrix did with it. Look what the Faces did with it.' It's a terrific album but sort of subtle compared to *Blonde on Blonde* that most people consider Bob's peak."

—Steven Van Zandt, guitarist, deejay, actor

**DANIEL WEIZMANN** | writer, music historian

"It's a funny thing—for a guy who's been covered as often as Dylan has, most of those covers fall in his shadow. Maybe the Byrds, Johnny Cash and June Carter, Richie Havens took his words somewhere new, but nobody ever *interpreted* Dylan with quite the daring that Jimi did. The secret is in the plaintive vocals.

Jimi could've taken Dylan's lyrical maze in so many directions. What he does is totally counterintuitive. Between explosions, he deploys Homeric trance-inducing parataxis—short, even phrases to mount tension. The effect is apocalyptic."

**By 1974, Dylan demonstrated** the ultimate show of respect when he began using Hendrix's template to perform his own song. On a February 9, 1974, tour stop at the Seattle Center Coliseum with the Band, Dylan, in a rare stage comment, proclaimed, "Great to be in Seattle, birthplace of Jimi Hendrix!"

**JANIE HENDRIX** | Jimi's sister; CEO
and President of Experience Hendrix

"He really loved the lyrics of Bob Dylan. And he was one person who I met who really admired Jimi.

"Years after Jimi died, my dad got a phone call. I had come home from college and he said, 'You'll never believe who called today.' 'Who?' I asked. 'Bob Zimmerman. Bob Dylan.' 'What did he want?' I wondered. 'Well, he called, and said, "First of all, I want to give you my condolences for Jimi passing. And I know you'll find this odd that it's ten years later and I'm finally calling, but I've picked up the phone so many times in the last decade and I just couldn't bring myself to call you and talk to you. But Jimi was more than somebody that admired my music. I admired him. He was a friend. And it just hurt extremely when he died. And just wanted to pick up the phone to call you and give my condolences."'

"Wow! Of course my dad was very emotional and it made him cry. 'Why thank you for calling.' And Dylan said, 'The next time I am in Seattle, I'd like you to come to the concert.'

"So a few years later, Bob Dylan came to town and he invited us to the show and we went backstage. And here is my dad, late seventies, and a little camera on his wrist, and he's got arthritis and not walking very well. But we get backstage at the Paramount in the green room. And he's reaching for his camera, and Bob Dylan doesn't like to take pictures, so his bodyguards almost attack my dad. 'I'm sorry. I would like to have a picture with you.' And Bob Dylan had on his slip-up hoodie and pulled the hood off and said, 'It's okay. Come on.' So I took some pictures of them. I mentioned, 'Jimi always said he loved your lyrics.' And he said, 'I loved his guitar playing.'

"At the concert we also had been given seats and chairs at the side of the stage, and the guitar player nods at me and I nudged my dad as they were getting ready to play 'All Along the Watchtower.' And Bob Dylan made it a point to say, 'I do it the way Jimi did it to honor Jimi. Even though it was a song I wrote.'"

# Two Meditations on Jimi and NAM

ROGER STEFFENS, SSG US ARMY, RET.

"**D**uring my two years in Vietnam, from '67 to '69, it became very apparent to me that Jimi Hendrix was writing the soundtrack to the war. 'All Along the Watchtower' blared constantly.

"It's spring 1969 and I'm in the Central Highlands, flying out of Pleiku's stiflingly hot red-dust airfield, over endless parched iron sandscapes, muted and spooky.

"Johnny Pissoff, the pilot, wants to scare me, so he dives to within fifty feet of the thatched rooftops of the first Yard hooches we come upon, pulling up steeply and grinning as I try and fail to lift my arms, struggling against the Gs. His face is contorted into a lascivious leer of certain death, but suddenly he levels off.

"Something has caught his eye. 'Look,' he commands. 'Eleven o'clock low.' There, about eight clicks off, I see a medium-sized American base. Far off to its right screams a rocket, its trail fiery clear in the shimmering yellow light. The missile describes a lethal arc. 'No!' breathes Pissoff.

"Soundlessly, we see a huge two-story barracks blow a hundred feet straight up into the air. Bodies tumble akimbo, smoke and fire shoot out in every direction as our tiny craft shudders slightly several seconds later. As we shift course, AFVN comes over our headsets. It's Jimi, singing about sweet angels flying on through the sky.

Photograph of a US army watchtower (right) in South Vietnam, taken by Roger Steffens during the Vietnam War.

"'Jimi Hendrix in Nam? That's affirmative, bro! Hell, he wrote the fuckin' soundtrack!' says anti-war vet Buddy Roche. 'But, hey, we were into Hendrix before we went over. In October 1967, near the Alamo in San Antonio, Texas, Jimi used to play the Pink Pussycat every Wednesday, Friday, Saturday, and then on Sunday afternoon. We'd take peyote and mescaline and watch him burn his guitar every day.'

"The day Buddy nearly bought the farm was when his unit was taking shelter in a bomb crater whose base was several feet deep in rank water.

Roger Steffens, SSG US Army, Ret., in South Vietnam, 1968.

Steffen's photograph of flaming skies during the war.

"'Guys were dyin' all around me, screamin' "Medic! Medic!" But I had a spinal cord concussion, shrapnel in my right foot, and then I got shot in my left knee. I seen 'em comin' in. I still do.'"

"Despite his own desperate wounds, he still managed to pull four other injured men to safety. For his actions he was awarded America's third-highest military decoration, the Silver Star, for bravery under hostile fire.

"In rehab, Buddy heard Jimi playing in Camp Drake Evac Hospital in Tokyo: 'I was in the spinal cord neurosurgery ward. That place was without a doubt the most terrible experience I've ever endured. We played Hendrix as we drag raced all night on motorized wheelchairs. We got thoroughly fucked up and listened to Hendrix all night long. For me, that was like medicine. That was the cure. Back in the world every place I went, every head's house, crash pad, and every place had Hendrix posters and albums. See that guy? That's who we are. That's where we're goin'. That's us there.'"

# Monterey Pop: The Film

The documentary *Monterey Pop* by D. A. Pennebaker was originally commissioned as the very first ABC-TV Movie of the Week by network president Tom Moore. When he saw a director's cut, though, he flipped out over Jimi's performance—not in a good way. The film never aired on ABC.

On December 26, 1968, the groundbreaking film made its West Coast theatrical premiere at the Fine Arts Theatre in Beverly Hills on Wilshire Boulevard.

I [Kenneth Kubernik] wasn't there opening night but went the following weekend, joined by my friend, Jim Katz, who was just getting into playing electric guitar.

We were fourteen, ravenous for new music, and a little too young to be let loose on the Sunset Strip or any of the concert arenas (without adult supervision). So seeing Jimi on the big screen was the closest we could get to sharing in the buzz. I vividly remember leaving the theater in an agitated state, just pounding the air with excitement over what we had just seen. I now understood that the key to Kubrick's mysterious monolith from his *2001: A Space Odyssey* (1968)—that unearthly whine—wasn't emanating from the moon or Jupiter or a London sound stage but from within Jimi's amps, taking us on a journey through his own wondrous cosmology.

## D. A. PENNEBAKER | director/filmmaker

"Lou Adler, John Phillips, Cass Elliot, and I initially flew up to Monterey to see the place, and I looked at it and it was this tiny place. I had no idea what was going to happen there. I had never seen a music festival at all, and I loved Monterey. And I sort of thought, 'Well, these guys know what they are doing.'

"I knew Lou and John were hatching a real interesting game. Which was from the beginning: get rid of the money. [It was established as a nonprofit endeavor.] That was the big thing. Get rid of the money. And I could see that was gonna make it work. It was a very Zen thing.

"We had no idea about Jimi Hendrix going in. John Phillips had said, 'Listen, this guy will kill you. He sets himself on fire.' And he comes out and he's chewing on his flat pick. I thought he was chewing gum, and I thought, 'This is blues?' I mean, I didn't know what to expect.

"We had thought we would save film a little bit and shoot one song for every group. So we had this lamp with a little red light. Bob Neuwirth, John Cooke, and

*Monterey Pop* filmmaker D. A. Pennebaker, c. 1968.

myself were gonna figure out what songs to do and end. Neuwirth kind of mostly figured it out—he was like the music director. And when Hendrix came on, I think the light was on for the first song. I don't why, but I remember that light went on very soon and never went off for all the Hendrix thing and we shot everything. They had film for it.

"Lou Adler and I showed some Hendrix footage bumping his amp to Tom Moore, instead of the Association, and it didn't take him long to say, 'Take it back. Not on my network.'

"In my mind, I remember thinking, 'If we can have this Southern gentleman Tom Moore not take it, we're better off because we've seen it and it's too much for television.' They owned the film and all they had to do was sign some shit and they would have taken it free, but they let it go. Because they knew it couldn't play on their network.

"One of the producers of Woodstock saw *Monterey Pop* and wanted to do a festival.

"*Monterey Pop* has a certain kind of history people want to examine over and over again. And I think it's like Hendrix. Nobody expected that he'd be history in the beginning—you couldn't give him away."

**DEL BRECKENFELD** | former director, entertainment marketing, Fender

"Fender was planning to discontinue the Stratocasters until Jimi played at Monterey in 1967 and the *Monterey Pop* documentary movie Pennebaker did came out in 1969. A whole new generation of guitarists and consumers really saw the Stratocaster, which is a testament to Jimi's influence. Because the Strat was designed way before Jimi played it, by guys like Buddy Holly back in the Fifties. Jimi took the Stratocaster and put the cool factor on the Strat."

**Opposite**: A still of Hendrix from *Monterey Pop*.

# 10
# '69 Turned Out to Be Fine

Jimi returned to London on January 2, his first time back in six months. His long-time (long-suffering) girlfriend, Kathy Etchingham, met him at Heathrow, hoping to ease his return to some place resembling home. But there was no time—there never was—to unwind by lazing by the Serpentine lake in Hyde Park, to wander blissfully along the ins and outs of thrumming Portobello Road. Mike Jeffery had other plans for him, another rasher of European one-nighters. But not before Jimi slipped a mickey into his manager's well-laid plans.

**J**anuary 4, 1969. The JHE is booked on *Happening for Lulu*, a popular variety program on the BBC. Lulu, a pop idol with a surprisingly bluesy voice, would regularly duet with that week's guest star. Jimi was cool with it—"Hey Joe" was bandied about as a possible choice. But come show time, he ripped up the script, tearing into Cream's "Sunshine of Your Love" as a tribute following that band's recent breakup, sending the show's producers into a conniption. "You'll never work for the Beeb again, yada yada . . ." "Whatever, dude." Lulu, to her credit, just laughed it off.

The clip has ascended into pop music infamy, joining a long line of rock stars taking the piss out of TV's stiff upper lip. Two years earlier, the Stones had caused a national furor in Britain when they refused to join the carousel at the end of the venerable show Sunday Night at the London Palladium. Across the pond, the Who's Keith Moon almost ended the band—literally—on CBS' *The Smothers Brothers Comedy Hour* when he packed his drums with explosives that nearly took out their leader, Pete Townshend.

### BARRIE WENTZELL | photographer

"I saw Jimi with Chris Welch on the *Happening for Lulu* BBC show and went around for an afternoon rehearsal. We saw Jimi at the bar and did some pictures of him. The BBC bar was notorious for drunken producers. There was a sound check, and suddenly I heard a couple of radio techs or engineers yell out some horrible racial stuff.

"We went back to the dressing room afterwards, and Chris said, 'Fuck them.' And Jimi said, 'I'm treated better here than I'm treated back home. No big deal. It's love and peace.'

Scottish singer Lulu on the set of her BBC show *Happening for Lulu,* 1969. Hendrix appeared on the show that year, on January 4.

"It was like he was way beyond any of that. Jimi was humble and talented. And he was always incredibly well dressed. . . .

"You can take pictures and be transported at the same time. Jimi Hendrix told me that. I remember asking him [about when] 'sometimes I see you play and the guitar is playing you.'

"'Yeah . . . Sometimes when you're in the groove, as they call it, I'm not playing the guitar. It's the guitar playing me.'

"It's like being inspired by a different dimension or a different aspect of yourself to do that. It's infectious. And people get it. You're really into it. Not out of it. It's a magical bliss I guess, like sex. That's what music can bring to life."

**Meanwhile, six weeks of numbing one-nighters** throughout Europe awaited Jimi, Mitch, and Noel.

George Varga is the long-standing pop music critic for the *San Diego Union-Tribune.* He attended the January 17, 1969, JHE concert at the Jahrhunderthalle in Frankfurt, Germany.

### GEORGE VARGA | music critic

"The earth may not have moved when the Jimi Hendrix Experience performed in early 1969 in Frankfurt, Germany. But the enormous curtains at the rear of the dome-shaped venue certainly did.

"Of course, by today's standards, the volume Hendrix and his band produced was nothing excessive. At the time, though, it was loud enough to make the Jahrhunderthalle's nearly two-story-high curtains gently sway.

"The concert was not the Experience's first Frankfurt area concert. In May 1967, Hendrix, Mitch Mitchell, and Noel Redding appeared at Stadthalle Offenbach, where their performance was filmed in black-and-white for the memorably named TV series *Beat! Beat! Beat!* The audience for that show, as a readily available YouTube clip now attests, appeared largely bewildered by what they heard and saw.

"Hendrix's attentive audience that night was comprised of German hippies, American GIs (Frankfurt's US military community at the time numbered 50,000), and a fair number of young people who aspired to be hippies, myself included. At the time, it was almost mandatory for German and American cover bands in Frankfurt to include at least one song popularized by Hendrix ('Hey Joe' and 'Stone Free' seemed to be the favorites). One band, whose members were students at Frankfurt American High School, was named Crosstown Traffic.

"For their 1969 Jahrhunderthalle appearance, the real Experience was booked for an early show and a late show, both of which were sellouts. I attended the first. I was only twelve at the time and it was the second concert of my young life, following a Frankfurt double bill by the Doors and Canned Heat a few months earlier.

Hendrix arrives in Hamburg, Germany, January 11, 1969, during JHE's tour.

"It was also my first time at the Jahrhunderthalle, where I would happily attend dozens more concerts over the next four years. What struck me that night—and still remains firm in my memory now—is not how wild Hendrix and his band were that evening, but how focused and disciplined.

"The Experience took to the stage following a brief opening set by Eire Apparent, the short-lived Irish band whose sole album, *Sunrise*, Hendrix played on and produced. With Redding to his left and Mitchell behind him, Hendrix zipped through his opening show with what, in hindsight, strikes me as a no-nonsense, taking-care-of-business approach.

"If memory serves, no guitars or amplifiers were ignited, destroyed, or even jostled. Instead, the three musicians performed with poise and polish, led by a legend in the making who—at least at this show—was neither wild nor mild.

"That doesn't mean Hendrix wasn't playful. I recall him injecting a snippet of the Beatles' 'Day Tripper' into 'Hey Joe.' He also threw in a memorable vocal ad-lib during 'Purple Haze' . . . 'Excuse me while I kiss . . . Noel Redding!'"

"It was the first and, alas, last time I saw Hendrix perform live, a fact that has given me a certain amount of bragging rights ever since. But the concert did make an enduring impression on me, albeit for a visual reason rather than an aural one.

"Lippmann + Rau, the top German concert company which produced all the dates on Hendrix's early 1969 tour of the country, had commissioned Gunther Kieser to design a poster for the tour. Kieser memorably did so, producing [a] 35 × 25 inch work of art in which a multicolored Hendrix appeared, Medusa-like, sporting a huge Afro, out of which came a panoply of bright, seemingly neon-colored tubes.

"I bought one of the posters at the concert for three German marks (which, at the time, was all of 75 cents). Last time I checked, original copies were fetching thousands of dollars."

# The Royal Albert Hall February 1969 Shows

The six-week European tour concluded at London's Royal Albert Hall with two shows—February 18 and 24. The first concert, which was filmed, caught them on an off night.

However the second night, which featured a breakout performance from opening act Van der Graaf Generator, found JHE at their peak, a performance that still has fans talking about it, particularly those who weren't there.

**HUGH BANTON** | organist, Van der Graaf Generator

"JHE had sold out the Albert Hall the previous week (8,000 seats)—to the usual acclaim—and upon discovering the venue was free exactly a week later, they decided to book a reprise show. Noel Redding had insisted (I have read) that his new parallel venture Fat Mattress could appear, but that still left space for another act.

"Our manager, Tony Stratton-Smith, no doubt at his nightly watering hole in Soho, got into a conversation with the promoter about the upcoming event and

**Opposite**: Hendrix performing at Royal Albert Hall, London, February 24, 1969.

put our name forward. We only had three or four days' notice. As well as the album and single, we'd recently been on deejay John Peel's show on BBC Radio 1 and so on, so things were starting to move for us. That was literally all there was to it!

"I don't recall much. . . . Our roadie was well up for it, scrounging extra amplifiers and so on so that we'd be loud enough. Some hope. In those days you couldn't rely on a big PA for audio support; stage gear alone was always expected to fill any venue. (There's something to be said for that, but that's a whole different subject.) I remember the day before the gig we collectively took a decision to blow the expenses budget and go clothes shopping, which didn't go down well at the Charisma office."

### FRED SHUSTER | writer/guitarist

"I remember that on the first of the two 1969 Royal Albert Hall shows—on February 18—Jimi pulled out all the stops—humping the amps, swinging the guitar around and playing it behind his back, playing it with his teeth, etc., and I think there was some grumbling in the press that . . . he was such a superb musician that he didn't need to do anything more than stand there and play the damn thing.

"On the second show a week later, on February 24, he did just that—standing still on his side of the stage, playing incredibly well with none of the showmanship. You know, I always felt that 'Red House' was Jimi's 'My Favorite Things'—it was the tune that he made his own each time, changing it around and really making the connection with his guitar and the audience. His blues that night was stunning.

"Another amazing memory from the second concert was Jimi's cover of Cream's 'Sunshine of Your Love'—which we'd seen him do on the *Lulu* show in a famous moment of live TV theatrics—and a show-closing 'Star-Spangled Banner' in the style of the Woodstock performance which was to come six months later back in the States."

# Spring Haze

In April, the band returned for yet another slog through the States, two months of mostly forgettable shows—the crowds demanding a smash-up on stage, the sacrifice of a beloved Stratocaster. It was a shambolic bore, from the interchangeable arenas to the processed cheese on the room service menus. Noel had badgered

A pensive portrait of Hendrix, c. 1969.

Jimi into allowing his side project, Fat Mattress, the invaluable opening slot. Jimi was dismissive—"Thin Pillow" was his assessment of them. But that was the least of Redding's problems. After their last US date in June, in Denver, he left the Experience; Redding was said to have been unhappy with Hendrix's decision to expand the group without consulting him first. Then Fat Mattress disintegrated in late December among personal tension between members of the group.

# Pop Expo '69—Teen-Age Fair

On April 4, 1969, drummer Jim Keltner recalled a memorable night at the Hollywood Palladium: "I was playing with Delaney & Bonnie at the Thee Experience club on Sunset, and Jimi Hendrix came in two different nights to jam. Jimi also stepped onstage [April 4, 1969] with us at the Teen-Age Fair at

The Aquarius Theatre, across the street from the Hollywood Palladium on Sunset Boulevard; its exterior, shown here in May 1969, had been recently painted by the Dutch artists known as the Fool.

the Hollywood Palladium on Sunset Boulevard." The Teen-Age Fair, described as a mini world's fair for teenagers, dated back to 1962, and had been held at the Palladium since 1964. The fair that took place from March 28 to April 6, 1969 was recast as Pop Expo '69.

At that '69 Teen-Age Fair appearance, Hendrix had politely asked Bonnie if he could play with them during the set, having known their repertoire. Jimi was in the neighborhood as a customer of West Coast Organ & Amp Service in Hollywood, which had developed and installed Super Lead heads and big cabinets for speakers on his '69 tour.

The Palladium was located directly across the street from the recently painted Aquarius Theatre, courtesy of the Fool, the Dutch artists who had created the colorful graphics on the building of the Beatles' Apple Boutique (see pages 45–46).

Robert Kushner, a blues harmonica player and Beverly Hills High School student at the time, caught the scene. "Jimi came out, started to play a Delaney & Bonnie tune, or maybe 'Red House,' and everyone started yelling 'Purple Haze!' He was pissed off. And after a number or two, he said 'Fuck off, teenyboppers.'"

# Stalking the Razor's Edge

KIRK SILSBEE, MUSIC JOURNALIST

"Glowing reviews for *Electric Ladyland* greeted 1969, but Hendrix felt trapped. Recording in Los Angeles at TTG Studios amounted to time-wasting marathons as he struggled to create in a circus of scenesters, drug connections, and 'friends.' Noel Redding and Mitch Mitchell spent long, boring hours waiting to play.

"Hangers-on and fair-weather friends were everywhere, but Hendrix wondered who was listening, and who really cared about his music. For a black musician who came up through the ranks of R&B, the overwhelming whiteness of his audience was a source of chagrin. Black acceptance and pressure from representatives of the increasingly violent Black Power movement were concerns for Hendrix. He also had a drug bust in Toronto that was coming to trial.

"Soul stations across the country ignored Hendrix, and it bothered him. He told *TeenSet*'s Jacoba Atlas about his frustration, adding that he was working on a song dedicated to the Black Panthers. After a rambling discourse on America and race, Hendrix called for some kind of action, but didn't articulate precisely what—aside from 'to scare' some people. In February, he told London's *New Music Express* of plans to retire for a year.

"When he was in Los Angeles that year, Hendrix stayed in a rented home in Coldwater Canyon. If he wanted nightlife, he had an invisible gold card to all the clubs. Nowhere did he have more entrée than at Thee Experience, Marshall Brevetz's psychedelic club on Sunset Boulevard. It sat at Sierra Bonita Avenue, over a mile from the gold-standard Strip, with none of the star power of West Hollywood. Transplanted Miamian Brevetz booked second-tier bands, but bent over backwards to make the room a clubhouse for musicians to sit in, get high, and gorge on his wife Marsha's kitchen delicacies.

"Thee Experience opened in late March, and by May Hendrix had dropped in and jammed. That gave the room cachet, and Brevetz had a giant Hendrix head painted on the outside of the club. Its giant mouth was thrown open—right around the double front doors. More than a few people presumed that Hendrix was the actual owner. By later December, the room had closed for good.

"At the Whisky a Go Go, Hendrix was polite, asking for no special attention, though occasionally he would jam. At Thee Experience, he could relax, play, or just goof. Former waitress Wendy Weatherford recalls, 'Marshall's son Michael told me, "I have the weirdest recollection of hanging out under a staircase, coloring in my coloring book with Jimi Hendrix." I said, "Well, that's what you used to do; Jimi used to love to go under there and draw with you." The place was about soulfulness.'

"John Kale was a music student when he went to the club in June. 'I went to hear Larry Coryell, but my girlfriend wasn't feeling well,' Kale says. 'I got up to take her home, and through the front door came Jorma and Jack from the Jefferson Airplane. There was this pregnant vibe, and I really hated to leave. But we got out onto the sidewalk and there was a limousine, with Hendrix getting out with a guitar case!'

"The impressive Miami band Blues Image had moved to LA, and used Thee Experience as home base. The late drummer Joe Lala had some long talks with Hendrix, and found him 'the sweetest man you'd ever want to meet. He didn't like where he was at that time. The managers had him dressed in all of those flashy clothes, burning his guitar and sticking out his tongue—but that's not who he was. When he came into the club, he didn't do any of that stuff. He just sat on an amplifier and played. It was way different than what you saw on the concert stage. He was a blues guy, an R&B guy, but a genius and an innovator—real smart, but soft-spoken.'

An ad for the opening of Thee Experience in March 1969. The club, owned by Marshall Brevetz (sometimes spelled "Brevitz"), was one of Hendrix's favorite LA hangouts.

"Seventeen-year-old guitarist Mark Rodney was a Hollywood kid and knew Hendrix by sight. Before he was in Batdorf & Rodney, the guitar duo on Atlantic Records, Mark got to know Hendrix. 'He loved to hear me play classical guitar,' Rodney says. 'He was a very mellow guy, almost effeminate. He hated all those antics he had to do onstage.'

"Waitress Jaki Read recalls that Hendrix 'moved through the crowd like a leopard. It was the most elegant thing you've ever seen. People tried to touch him and sometimes paw at him in the club but he'd just quietly look at them and say, "That's not cool." He wasn't "onstage" all the time, unless he wanted to be.'

"Rodney jammed with Blues Image guitarist Mike Pinera and Hendrix at the club, but recalls that it wasn't magic. 'No one took the lead that night,' Rodney recalls. 'Jimi was dope sick; he didn't play too well.' Rodney also watched as Hendrix reluctantly jammed one night. 'I could tell he didn't want to be there,' Rodney says. 'Whenever they saw him, they tried to pull him onstage, but he didn't want that. He'd see me, come over and say, "Let's get out of here."'

"'The last time I saw Jimi at Thee Experience,' Rodney remembers, 'he had a real sad look. He was on a big downer for a long time. I was only a casual acquaintance, but I was looking at a lonely man. He was warm-hearted, but he was sure down-hearted.'"

"If you saw Jimi, you often saw Buddy Miles. Not a great drummer but an enthusiastic one, Hendrix dutifully sat in when the Buddy Miles Express played the club in August. Rockin Foo roadie Phil Hartman—long before his comedy career—saw the bass drum moving ever-forward one night. On his hands and knees, Phil held it from moving while Miles bashed. 'You're earning your money now, Mr. Roadie Man!' shouted the self-important Miles.

"Mike Pinera shared the bandstand with Hendrix several times—once when they accompanied a bearded Jim Morrison, who just wanted to sing blues. 'That was some pretty cosmic stuff,' Pinera reckons. He contends, 'Jimi had to have some jazz in his background to play what he did. He could play real spacey. But he could also take a Sly Stone riff and build a funk thing off of that.' Pinera was invited to follow Hendrix home one night. At the early-morning party, one of the girlfriends quietly presented Pinera with a guitar case. 'Here's a gift from Jimi,' she offered. Inside was the Chet Atkins model guitar that Hendrix had played on 'All Along the Watchtower.'"

—Kirk Silsbee

"During 1969, I went to Michael Jeffery's office to take some pictures of Jimi. I get to the office and [the] secretary points me in and Jimi is sitting in Mike Jeffery's desk looking down, rather unhappy with all this paperwork in front of him. He had just had a meeting. 'I guess it's time.' Took a few pictures at the desk and asked if I could do some snaps by the window—better light. 'Sure, man.' He didn't look happy. 'What's up?' 'Pressure of business. . . . It was like you gotta be here or there. All I wanna do is write songs and record . . .'

"He wasn't happy with that huge business sort of thing. Which was exhausting I guess, and rather painful, too."

—Barrie Wentzell, photographer

**JAMES WILLIAMSON** | guitarist, songwriter, the Stooges

"It's so hard to separate Jimi Hendrix from my late teenage years. I heard Hendrix's first album, *Are You Experienced?* and knew there had been a sea change. Our world would never be the same. Of course, it was also very hard to separate Jimi Hendrix from our own drug consumption and progression.

"From there on out until his death, I was a fanatical listener of Jimi Hendrix's work. I wore out my copies of all three of his studio albums and all the singles I could find.

"While I never really styled my guitar playing after his, I could do a reasonable facsimile from time to time since I loved how he played so much. I even, as did so many others, bought a Stratocaster guitar at one point. Frankly, he was just the coolest dude I had ever run across on guitar. He was right there with James Dean and Elvis.

"One of the only live shows I saw of Jimi's in Detroit was at Cobo Hall, May 2, 1969. I took my girlfriend to see him and at one point I asked her if she would fuck him if given the chance. She said she wouldn't, that he didn't appeal to her. I knew right then that there must be something wrong with her. That was the kind of effect he had on me."

# LA—Where It Was At

Los Angeles was now the epicenter of youth culture. The confluence of mass media—TV, film, and the music industries centering their production and, increasingly, decision-making in and around Hollywood—colliding with the unshackled appetites of kids with time and money, gave the Southland a sun-kissed glaze that proved boundlessly inviting to those in search of the starry lights.

Music was everywhere; driving through the canyons the chime of Martin 12-strings, the errant chording on a blistered baby grand, bespoke a creative community striving to unravel the DNA of a magical middle eight. And there were no shortage of premier showcases for your efforts: the Whisky commandeered the Sunset Strip, hosting all the hottest new British bands; the Troubadour on Santa Monica Boulevard cultivated folkies with Stratocasters; the Ash Grove harbored the blues, both Southside and Delta. Driving north on the Pacific Coast Highway you'd eventually tumble into the Topanga Corral, a haven for the buckskinned fringe, the native habitat for Neil Young and his kind. Clubs opened and closed like pop-up bazaars, a fabled jam bestowing a glimmer of historical significance to their fleeting presences. If it wasn't Berlin in the '20s, it sure as hell had a better soundtrack.

**KIM SIMMONDS** | guitarist and cofounder of Savoy Brown

"Los Angeles was a city that always supported the blues. I was in Los Angeles in 1969. I heard Jimi was living in LA. I had a jam with him. It was ships passing through the night, really, at Thee Experience on Sunset Boulevard. We were all hanging out. Suddenly Jimi gets up and walks on stage and starts playing guitar. And I'm watchin' this. 'Wow!' I wasn't as shy as I thought I was because, okay, I had already done a lot of jamming with different artists that year, Bobby Bland, and I took the guitar off the other guitar player. And I joined. Fantastic time. I'm pretty sure Eric Burdon was there.

"We played and after the show I went up to Jimi; there were booths and he was sitting with a girl. I sat down and talked with him. And then I was astounded with his humility. It reminded me of all the blues guys I had met. They were all incredibly humble and can't remember any of 'em having an attitude. I assumed that Hendrix hadn't a clue who I was. I was age twenty-one. We spent the night chatting a bit."

Hendrix fan Elizabeth Darrow, c. 1970.

## ELIZABETH DARROW JONES | fan and singer

"In 1969, I remember a trip to Hollywood with friends. Hollywood was fueled with excitement and wonderment in the sixties and early seventies, and the streets were filled with hippies, musicians, actors, and artists.

"Eventually, I wandered off by myself on the Sunset Strip, lured by the sound of an amplified guitar. It was coming from a slightly open door. I saw a guy on his knees (his back was facing the sidewalk) with his head bent forward, playing guitar at a place called Thee Experience.

"I was captivated by his guitar playing and the clothes he was wearing. He stopped playing to cheers and loud applause. Covered in sweat, he stood up and turned to the open door, still holding his guitar, and looked me square in the eyes—it was Jimi Hendrix. I did not say a word. He kept looking at me. We were wearing almost the same clothing: white hats, white Levi jackets, white Levis . . . uncanny.

"I just remember turning around and walking away completely numb. I will never forget this. This was my first encounter with Jimi Hendrix."

# JHE at the Forum

On April 26, 1969, the Jimi Hendrix Experience slayed their audience in Inglewood California at the "Fabulous Forum." It was their first and only performance in Los Angeles in 1969.

**PAUL DIAMOND** | screenwriter/ television writer

"Walked out of the Forum into the Inglewood mist (half fog, half unburned jet fuel from LAX), having just fixed the worst mistake I made in the sixties. Seven months earlier I'd given away a couple of tickets to see Jimi at the Hollywood Bowl—not to a friend, or relative, or perfect stranger as you'd expect, but to a girl who knew two things: she didn't care about Jimi, and she didn't want to go *anywhere* with me.

"That girl wasn't even the one I wanted to go with. *She* was in New York that week. So, poof, two tenth-row tickets, gone forever. But Jimi'll come back, won't he? Bands always come back.

"He did, the next April, and so did my now-girlfriend, and I snagged tickets at one of three Beverly Hills record stores and then, Friday evening, April 26, 1969, put the girl in the '67 Camaro, got on the 405 South, and put my favorite bootlegged tape in the Muntz 4-track player.

Ticket stub for the April 26, 1969, JHE concert in Inglewood, California at the "Fabulous Forum." Price: $6.50.

Nighttime view of the Fabulous Forum in January 1968, a year after it opened in Inglewood, California, as a premier music venue and as the home of the L.A. Lakers and the L.A. Kings. The Experience tore up the stage there on April 26, 1969.

"It was Iron Butterfly. I loved Iron Butterfly. I hadn't listened to Hendrix in forever.

"Traffic made us miss most of Cat Mother and the All Night Newsboys' set. Nothing great. Then some horn band called Chicago Transit Authority. Amusing. Didn't think the guitarist was any good.

"Finally, Jimi's backline was onstage, usual mike check, then nothing. Eventually Jimi, Mitch, and Noel wandered out. Don't remember much of an ovation, don't remember *any* attempt to connect with us other than Jimi's perfunctory standard, 'Give us a second to tune up here, because we really care for your ears—that's why we don't play so loud.'

"When they started, they played *loud*. But they were playing a song nobody knew—the Swedish jazz duo Hansson and Karlsson's 'Tax Free.'

"The crowd was puzzled. The crowd called for 'Purple Haze' until the second song, 'Foxy Lady.' The crowd, at the first hint of feedback, was hooked.

"But then Jimi threw the crowd back in the lake. 'Damn, you want to hear all that old stuff?' And he took off his Strat, spent a good three minutes tuning his Flying V, and then started playing 'Red House.' A slow blues. With his back to us.

"In hindsight, naturally he was making a point: that we couldn't have him on our terms, we couldn't force him to play what he didn't want to, no matter if we thought that's what we were paying him for. It was *his* stage.

"Only it wasn't, and that's part of what killed him.

"The rest of the show was actually pretty good. He chatted, did his tongue-flicking, guitar-behind-the-back schtick, played the oldies, dedicated several songs 'to the little girl over there with the red underwear.' (It was more graphic than that, but I'll spare you.) Something odd at the time—Jimi might go and have a chat with Mitch from time to time (particularly when a Marshall blew and had to be swapped out), but I don't remember him going anywhere near Noel. I guess by then Noel was already rolling down the exit ramp.

"So it was over. Ears buzzing, we walked back to the Camaro. I took the Iron Butterfly tape out of the player, tossed it in the back seat. It was never seen again."

### GENE AGUILERA | author/music historian

"Getting in to see the Jimi Hendrix Experience at the Forum on April 26, 1969, was icing on the cake for this fifteen-year-old Chicano kid out of East L.A. But gone was Jimi's wild electric hair and hip Carnaby Street psychedelic garb. From my $5.50 loge seat, uneasiness kicked in watching Hendrix dressed in soft pink and purple pastels along with a short-cropped 'fro. It was adios to the sixties as we knew it. Nevertheless, Jimi hypnotized us with his Stratocaster magic, reducing our ears to mere mush by the end of the evening. Hendrix's opening acts were Chicago Transit Authority (later Chicago) and Cat Mother and the All Night Newsboys, a side project of his. Soon after, the Experience would be gone, and a year and a half later, the light of Hendrix's short, fast life would be gone too."

### TOULOUSE ENGELHARDT | guitarist, composer

"I had the chance to see Jimi Hendrix back in 1969 at the Fabulous Forum in LA. He was 'One Step Beyond.' To say he was a major influence over me as a young and up-and-coming guitar junkie and now a composer is an understatement. He taught me not to be afraid to explore the 'Event Horizon' of the guitar. To not settle for mediocrity, to use the whammy bar and chart out undiscovered territory and master the use of feedback as a vehicle to accent his melodic lines. He had the balls to go anywhere!

"As far as Jimi's guitar, his setup: there might have been some advantages of the high strings where they were closest to his chest versus the other way around, where the thicker strings are down and facing us. He had it the other way around, playing upside down and left-handed. I imagine he had a difficult time with some of those octave chords trying to do that, because he was doing it upside down, essentially. That double-octave was the signature sound of jazz great Wes Montgomery."

### KEN RESSER | concert attendee

"On April 26, 1969, I saw the Experience for the second time, this one at the Forum with Cat Mother and the All Night Newsboys opening ($6.50). I saw them with my twin sister, sitting in the loge about twenty rows up on the right side at about a forty-degree angle. The sound was bigger than at the Hollywood Bowl (indoor vs. outdoor). I distinctly remember in an attempt at alerting my sister when Jimi first ran his arm and hand all over the guitar (the flash) that I jammed my elbow into the armrest and was in pain for days after. But it didn't dampen my enthusiasm and [I] was once again thoroughly amazed at what I was hearing and seeing."

# O Canada

And then . . . there was the matter of the drug bust in Toronto on May 3, an increasingly routine occurrence for touring rock stars. Jimi was nabbed by the do-right Canadian authorities with a small bag of heroin, which, he insisted, was handed to him by a fan somewhere on the road (he had been feeling sick to his stomach, and a young woman had handed him what he said he thought was Bromo-Seltzer antacid) and tossed it innocently into his suitcase.

After being processed, he was escorted to the Maple Leaf Gardens for the show that night—the Mounties got their man *and* backstage passes! On December 7, Jimi returned to Toronto for trial. "Not guilty" was the jury's verdict after eight hours of deliberation. It was a relief, no doubt, but also a sobering reminder that it was all becoming too much—the monstrous demands of constant touring, the unnerving idolatry—and there wasn't enough time to relax, reflect, to gather the splinters of a very public life and reassemble them into a privately revivified whole.

## LARRY LEBLANC | writer and author

"I have a clear image in my mind of seeing Jimi live at Maple Leaf Gardens the evening that he was busted for drugs at the Malton Airport in Mississauga (since renamed the Toronto Pearson International Airport in 1984).

"I remember that the show started quite late, maybe by a half hour, and there was speculation that Jimi would not be performing. Nobody knew anything about his arrest or that he had been arrested by the RCMP, who were really clamping down on musicians at the airport, which is outside Toronto.

"Finally, Jimi came on and he was really brilliant. Didn't say a word to the audience. We thought he'd comment slyly about the bust. He played all the well-known tracks of the Experience and even did the playing guitar behind his head, which was a surprise, because in an interview around that time he said he hated that type of theatrical stuff.

Jimi Hendrix's mugshot after his arrest at the Toronto airport on May 3, 1969, for heroin possession (he was found not guilty at the December trial).

"The one surprise for me was he played B. B. King's 'Rock Me, Baby' near the end of the show, and he played it exactly like B. B. No sound effects or added bits whatsoever. Note for note what B. B. played back then. He sang it as if he was B. B. too. That's when I realized that his roots truly were in American blues and more so, he knew the genre well."

## GARY PIG GOLD | singer-songwriter, record producer, author

"If I can just get my mind together, the first 'real' concert I ever attended as a wee Canadian tyke was the Jimi Hendrix Experience at Toronto's Maple Leaf Gardens, May 3, 1969. I'd already been a fervent fan for a couple of years, having spent most of my Grade 8 art class making swirly sketches of Jimi in charcoal. Plus the *Are You Experienced?* album was right up there—almost—with *Monkees Headquarters* on my 1967 Most-Played List.

"My most-trusted pal, Ric, scored two tickets in the Gardens' nosebleed section and I fibbed to my parents that we were off to a hootenanny for the evening. Yet no sooner did we approach the venue than word began a-buzzin' that our hero had just been busted for carrying a batch of nonpharmaceutical mood enhancers into Toronto Airport. Hmmm . . .

"Undaunted, we climbed skyward to our seats and sat on sonic needles and pins all through the opening act (the pretty cool Cat Mother and the All Night Newsboys, whose big hit 'Good Old Rock 'n' Roll' my little band was already struggling to learn . . . and if Noel's Fat Mattress was rolled out as well that evening, it would be news to me) until, *finally*, the one and only Jimi Himself sauntered on stage. Seemingly very cool, quite calm, and perhaps even collected.

"Now considering all the man had already been through that day, I guess it should have been no real surprise the evening's set ran quite downcasted through a severely blue 'Red House'—with lyrics duly modified to include a plaintive 'soon as I get out of jail I'm gonna see her' . . . though Jimi did graciously treat our teenaged throng with occasional bursts of that fabled, fiery Foxy Purpleness of yore.

"And then, suddenly, he was gone. Experience over.

"However, James Marshall Hendrix returned to town briefly that December—just long enough to be completely exonerated of all narco charges ('Canada has given me the best Christmas present I ever had!' he exclaimed to the *Toronto Daily Star*), but I suppose one could question if,

Gary Pig Gold's ticket stub to the May 3, 1969, show at the Toronto Maple Leaf Gardens.

or why, that life lesson ultimately went unheeded. And I suppose it does say something that out of all the delicately detailed minutiae forever etched upon my grey matter concerning that momentous concert many long, long Toronto Mays ago, I can still most vividly recall *exactly* what Jimi was wearing (all Harlem–Ashbury chic all the way), what I was wearing even (don't ask), the appropriately brilliant weather, the commuter train Ric and I snuck on after we told our parental units we'd just be folking around."

# Surf's Up

In late May of 1969, Hendrix and Co. arrived in Hawaii. They played at the Waikiki Shell in Honolulu three nights, from Friday, May 30 to Sunday, June 1, backed by Fat Mattress. The first night, Friday, the performance was cut short due to amplifier issues, so a third night was added.

"Jimi and I talked about the idea of an 'Electric Church.' He saw concerts as a worship service and felt connected to the Universe as he played.

"The Otani House in Honolulu was where promoter Tom Moffatt would put high-level bands, right at the foot of Diamond Head Road. But I did not shoot Jimi there, as he was always in a bathing suit and that wasn't the vibe he wanted to promote around his concert on May 31 at the Waikiki Shell.

"Hawaii was the place he could hang out and not be bothered. He came many times and spent a long period on Maui. When he was at the Otani House I would go down and hang out with the band and talk about very strange things. When I first met Janie Hendrix, she asked me what Jimi was like, as she was a very young girl when he was alive. We talked a lot about UFOs, which Hawaii had a lot of."

—Robert Knight, photographer

# Newport '69

Hendrix and his bandmates headlined the Newport '69 music festival held in Devonshire Downs, California, June 20–22. More than 150,000 people attended, although the peace and love setting was somewhat ruined by violence, riots, and injuries to approximately three hundred people.

Lost in the press reports were stellar performances by the Ike & Tina Turner Revue, Spirit, Joe Cocker, the Edwin Hawkins Singers, the Don Ellis Orchestra, Jethro Tull, the Byrds, Sweetwater, Booker T. and the M.G.'s, the Chambers Brothers, Johnny Winter, and the Rascals. Marvin Gaye was a no-show, having missed his flight. Janis Joplin took a surprise stage bow.

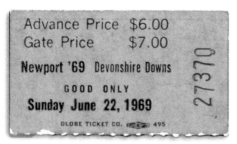

Advance Price  $6.00
Gate Price      $7.00

Newport '69  Devonshire Downs

GOOD ONLY

Sunday June 22, 1969

GLOBE TICKET CO.  495

27370

Ticket stub for the Sunday, June 22, 1969, lineup at the Newport '69 music festival held in Northridge, California, at Devonshire Downs, from June 20–22. JHE performed on June 20; Jimi jammed with Buddy Miles on June 22.

**GLENN ARCHAMBAULT |**
Newport '69 crewmember

"There was a big issue onstage. We hauled in all this state-of-the-art Fender amps, got a truckload a day before the concert. We struggled with the sound system, and we had Jimi coming up. Panic time. I'm working on the equipment when a guy called to me, 'Hey, I'm Jimi's personal chef.' He wanted in the stage gate. I got too close and he grabbed me by the neck and tried to get my badge. We struggled. I was terrified. People were obsessed with Jimi, and I realized we needed to get our act together. When Jimi was onstage we had people trying to get onstage, all around us. I tried very hard to keep the stage appearance professional.

"Friday was panic time for us—something was wrong with Jimi, and we couldn't fix it . . . he was just *off*. But we also were struggling with equipment, and had been earlier in the day. People couldn't hear: lots of background noise, engine noises, really loud people; we had not cleared the stage yet. A big basic problem. We weren't up to the task.

"Jimi played hard. Up close, you could tell this guy was strong and had stamina. Very important in outdoor concerts to have the strength to sing to a vast audience and play at the same time. All of us onstage worked to get the PA and equipment up to catch Jimi's performance."

**On Friday night**, Hendrix, who was allegedly paid a fee of a hundred grand, couldn't find his groove. He dismissed the audience from his platform as a "teenybopper crowd."

I [Harvey Kubernik] went to the festival. It was the weekend after I graduated from Fairfax High School and two weeks before I was to start summer school at West Los Angeles College and work in the school's library. Until July 5, I was truly "Stone Free."

Jimi's set was ragged and listless. I'd been so looking forward to seeing him for the first time, and it was disappointing. But my world was transformed during his slow, hypnotic, revealing *Twilight Zone*–inspired "Red House" travelogue. Sometimes all you get is a moment, and it was well worth it for that.

The Edwin Hawkins Singers were marvelous, gospel music in the California sunshine. The Don Ellis Orchestra made me now listen to KBCA-FM, our local jazz station. Joe Cocker and his band were terrific. But Spirit stole the show.

For some founding members of Spirit, it was also a reunion with Hendrix that day. In 1966, as a fifteen-year-old, guitarist Randy Wolfe met Jimi Hendrix at Manny's Music in New York, and that summer he'd played in Jimmy James and the Blue Flames. It was Hendrix who gave him the name "Randy California."

### ED CASSIDY | drummer, Spirit

"We were exploring new ways of improvisation. Randy and I were keen on that. The thing that was successful about Spirit was that we didn't try to contrive any of the elements that appeared in the music. We weren't rock and rollers, and we weren't jazz. The band had to be seen to be believed. Our LPs were pale by comparison."

**Jimi also shared the Newport '69 platform** with his old employers, Ike & Tina Turner. Hendrix did return for a Sunday afternoon guest set and redeemed himself, participating in a jam session with Buddy Miles, Tracy Nelson of Mother Earth, and Eric Burdon.

### GLENN ARCHAMBAULT

"A lot changed on stage by Jimi's second set on Sunday. We were doing better with the equipment and we had some experience with other bands. By the time Jimi came on the second time, the crowd had also learned that this was a huge event, and they accepted some of the defects in sound and got into the idea that they were at the biggest rock concert ever."

**Opposite, above, and left:** Hendrix tearing up the stage at Newport '69, June 22, 1969.

## MARK ROMAN | concertgoer

"I saw Jimi at Newport in '69 at Devonshire Downs on Sunday. I missed the Friday night Hendrix because I was working at the May Company department store and couldn't get off, so I felt bad because I couldn't see Jimi.

"I read later that Jimi was dissatisfied by his Friday performance. This was a festival. On Sunday I was with a woman from my high school and we sat on my grandmother's quilt in the back on the sand. And I said to her, 'You'll have to excuse me.'

"So I ran to the front of the stage and immediately I was surrounded by hundreds of people. I couldn't budge if I wanted to, and I didn't want to budge.

"I took some photos. The Byrds played on Sunday. Clarence White was the guitarist, along with Roger McGuinn."

Clarence White, the bassist for the Byrds, at Newport '69, June 22, 1969.

## ROGER MCGUINN | lead singer and guitarist, cofounder, the Byrds

"Clarence was a brilliant musician. I mean, it was like working with Hendrix. He was just a triple A-plus musician and over the line every time. I see this imaginary line and some musicians come up to it and they just hit it and everything is fine. It's in tune and it's in time. But Clarence was way over. He'd just fly over the line."

## JOHN YORK | bassist, the Byrds, 1968–69

"That day Clarence and Jimi were on the same stage. They had a very unique connection in that they both found their own language. They both had listened to what had been done before, and they knew there was another way they wanted to do it. You could hear where Jimi came from. You could hear where Clarence came from."

# Smash Hits

Reprise Records in the United States released the compilation album *Smash Hits* on July 30, 1969, with additional tracks that weren't on the UK Track edition , including "All Along the Watchtower," "Crosstown Traffic," and "Red House." The UK configuration (released on April 12, 1968, by Track Records) had "51st Anniversary" and the utterly mad "The Stars That Play with Laughing Sam's Dice," a guided tour to outer space that threatens to be a one-way ticket. Its blend of extreme distortion and vaudeville remains startling.

> "I was in a group, the Cherry People, and went to Steve Paul's the Scene. Jimi Hendrix used to hang out there and they jammed with Jimi. Hendrix invited our whole crew, and Buddy Miles was there, over to the Record Plant. That's where I met Gary Kellgren, one of the owners. Some of the US versions of the Jimi Hendrix Experience *Smash Hits*, including 'Red House' and 'Remember,' were put together by engineer Jack Adams.
>
> "I'm hanging big time with Jimi and trying to keep my mouth shut and listen to what's goin' on. Biggest lesson I learned. When Gary was working with Jimi, it was cool for me to come to the studio. We would discuss electronics."
>
> —**Jimmy Robinson**, recording engineer

# 11
# Woodstock and Them Changes

Denver, Colorado, was the site of the last concert performed by the Jimi Hendrix Experience. Everyone in and around the organization was flatlining, the musicians most of all. Noel was out; Mitch bailed back to England, to his newly acquired house in Sussex. And Jimi? Management had relocated him to Upstate New York, to horse country, where he could take stock and consider his options.

**I**n early August, Mitch was summoned back into action. Jimi had got something cooking—Gypsy Sun and Rainbows—more of an idea than a prospective working band. He'd drafted in two percussionists, a rhythm guitarist, and his old comrade from the 101st Airborne, Billy Cox, on Fender bass. Mitch would handle the traps.

Mitchell remembers that the rehearsals were grim, like the ostentatious property Mike Jeffery had leased. The musicians weren't jelling; Hendrix was frustrated and distracted. It was, Mitch felt, that it was his only experience of a group not getting better over time.

But there was a big festival date looming, and by the time they got to Woodstock, the weather had taken over with a vengeance.

# Woodstock

Few pop cultural events have shimmied into mythic stature quite like Woodstock, held from August 15–18, 1969, on Max Yasgur's farm in Bethel, New York. Reasonable people can agree to disagree about its legacy: a monument to peace, love, and tie-dye accessorizing, or, more derisively, a breakthrough in the commodification of the baby boomers' latent narcissism. What isn't subject to debate is that early on Monday morning, long after he was scheduled to go on, beneath a torrent of yuck, mud, and misery, before the hardiest of souls (or, more likely, those unfortunates who'd missed their rides), Jimi brought the festival to its sodden conclusion, gutting the "Aquarian Exposition" by plunging a shiv into America's national anthem. Contrary to the conventional wisdom, the Experience had been performing "The Star-Spangled Banner" intermittently for months. It wasn't rehearsed for this engagement, but Jimi lit it up as they were winding down and it ignited like the USS *Maine* in Havana harbor.

A cottage industry has flourished in the parsing of Jimi's performance, so visceral was (and remains) its impact. It has withstood the weight of scholarly sociological analyses, arch metaphorical appropriation, and the wincing embarrassment of air guitarists flailing to corral its ferocious bite. Jimi was nonplussed by all the fuss. He told TV talk show host Dick Cavett that it was simply a song he liked from childhood.

Hendrix at Woodstock; the last performance of the festival, the morning of Monday, August 18, 1969.

Musicologist Samuel Floyd Jr., in his book *The Power of Black Music* (1995), takes a more emphatic position: "Hendrix inserts 'calls' at 'the rocket's red glare' and 'comments' appropriately at 'the bombs bursting in air' and other 'telling' points. Here, Hendrix is a musical teller of the narrative using his instrument in a manner similar to that of African callers and the tone painters of the European classical tradition."

Pop music critic emeritus Robert Christgau, dismissive of Jimi at Monterey, has moved to a more nuanced appreciation of his contributions. Writing in the August 15, 2019, edition of the *Los Angeles Times* and reflecting on Jimi at

Woodstock, Christgau declares that Hendrix "meant to claim the national anthem for his white, groovy, long-haired, spaced-out tribe. So he tore it down and built it back up into something so avant and anarchic that peaceniks and radicals have taken it for their own ever since. . . . What matters about this 'Star-Spangled Banner' isn't what Hendrix thought it was, if he even knew exactly. Rather, it's what he meant to leave us free to think it was."

In his own searing, transformative, graceful way, Jimi recalibrated the meaning of patriotism, delivering a new emancipation proclamation for those ready to answer the call.

### MEL LAWRENCE | director of operations, Woodstock

"I saw the new world in June 1967 at the KFRC Fantasy Fair and Magic Mountain Music Festival [on Mount Tamalpais] in Marin County, California, and at the Monterey International Pop Festival.

"I thought it was recognition that you weren't alone. Those events set the tone. That there was this group consciousness that you didn't know of before these festivals. I then worked at the Miami Pop Festival, a major festival in between Monterey and Woodstock.

"When Woodstock happened, we were able to handle it pretty good. Woodstock gets the attention. It's the matter of scale and time. Woodstock was different than the wide-eyed innocence of Monterey, even though many of the artists, the Who, Ravi Shankar, Hendrix, Jefferson Airplane, Country Joe & the Fish, and Canned Heat played Monterey and then Woodstock.

"The legacy of Mount Tam and Monterey was flashing on me, just to know how people have to operate with huge crowds of people and how to operate in circumstances with a show going on. That kind of experience and knowledge makes the system better."

Woodstock operations director Mel Lawrence, photographed by Henry Diltz at the festival.

## HENRY DILTZ | photographer

"I did see the impact of Monterey. But at Monterey there was a lot of hanging out and people and the artists being together. At Woodstock the groups flew in on helicopters, and didn't stay and hang out.

"There was a lot of love at Monterey, and people performing for their peers. Monterey was a closed venue, a contained little group in an outdoor festival, with bleachers on the side. At Woodstock, the massive sea of faces went on forever."

An entry page from the journal of official Woodstock photographer Henry Diltz; on Monday, August 18, he notes that he "woke in his station wagon (about 9) to Jimi Hendrix music" playing.

## EDDIE KRAMER | recording engineer, producer

"You do get a different Jimi on tape if the venue is indoors. The live festival stuff is tricky, because there is very little coming back to you as an artist other than the speakers, if you are so fortunate. But he was lucky at Woodstock because the PA system was pretty damn good.

"We all know about the personality differences Jimi had with Noel, and there were plenty. But musically, I think Noel Redding is very underrated, and I think he did a tremendous job. I think Noel has been much maligned, putting aside his personality quirks. His playing and his understanding of what it took to support Jimi was remarkable.

"Mitch, being the ex-jazz drummer, was the perfect foil for Jimi. I don't think any other drummer kept up with him."

Diltz's photograph of the Hendrix entourage at Woodstock, August 18,1969.

**BILLY COX** | bassist for Jimi Hendrix at Woodstock,
Gypsy Sun and Rainbows

"At Woodstock—I had never played to as many people. In a way it was frightening.
But you know, Jimi had this uniqueness about him. His thought patterns were
unique. In the way he spoke. Mitch and I looked out at the audience. Jimi looked
out and with all his knowledge and his wisdom, 'You know what? Those people
are sending an awful lot of energy up to the bandstand. What we will do is take
that energy and utilize it and send it right back to them.' With that in mind, we
stayed up on that stage for almost two hours."

**The feature-length movie *Woodstock*,** distributed by Warner Bros. and directed
by Michael Wadleigh, was released on March 26, 1970.

Portions of Hendrix's performance set are in the movie and on the sound-track: "The
Star-Spangled Banner," "Purple Haze," an item called "Woodstock Improvisation,"
an instrumental solo later titled "Villanova Junction," and "Voodoo Child."

**JERRY WEXLER** | record producer, Atlantic Records executive

"After Monterey International Pop Festival in 1967, I later got the music rights to Woodstock. The soundtrack albums came out on our Atlantic Records/Cotillion label.

"There was a lawyer named Paul Marshall—he used to be our in-house council. He called me up: 'Listen. Are you interested in Woodstock?' It was going to take place in two weeks. Who the hell knew what Woodstock was going to be? He said I could have the rights for seven thousand dollars. I thought about [it], and bought it for seven grand. I figured, seven grand? Let me take a shot. And that was it. I should have grabbed the film rights, but Warner Bros. got them. Thank God that I bought Woodstock."

Hendrix onstage at Woodstock.

**JANIE HENDRIX** | Jimi's sister; CEO and President of Experience Hendrix

"To actually watch it now after living a little more life, and realizing, 'How did you wrap your hand around the neck of the guitar like that? How do you stretch your fingers on the neck?' All of what he did with the guitar and music."

# Harlem Benefit

This Woodstock lineup was short-lived; a few weeks after Woodstock, on September 5, 1969, the Hendrix and Gypsy Sun and Rainbows band played again, along with Maxine Brown and Big Maybelle, in a New York area date for a Harlem United Block Association benefit concert in a community center.

**JAMES WILLIAMSON** | guitarist, songwriter, the Stooges

"I had driven all night with some friends to see him perform in Harlem and had slept on the banks of the Harlem River with the rats in order to hear him live. [They performed outside 139th Street and Lenox Avenue.]

"Recently, I toured the Rock and Roll Hall of Fame in Cleveland, since I had donated my *Raw Power* album guitar to them since I had been inducted with the Stooges.

"They took me into the back where they had many of the obscure artifacts from the various artists' collections. . . . There they showed me Jimi's moccasin boots, explaining that he was part Cherokee Indian, and some letters that he had written. Of all the exhibits I saw there, that was one of the most meaningful to me, due to the lasting impression he had made on me."

# Band of Gypsys

Long before he was famous, Hendrix had signed what he thought was a release for appearing as a studio musician in October 1965. The one-page artist agreement drafted by PPX Industries bound his services for a period of three years.

Hendrix agreed to a 1968 legal settlement whereby Capitol Records would be granted the distribution rights for his next album. By the autumn of 1969, Capitol and PPX were demanding an album delivery, and Hendrix decided to provide them with a live recording for the spring of 1970.

After Woodstock, a new trio emerged in October that Hendrix dubbed Band of Gypsys, consisting of Hendrix, Cox, and Electric Flag drummer Buddy Miles, who would also contribute occasional lead vocals. They were to do a series of four concerts over the course of two evenings.

It took place at the Fillmore East in Manhattan—two on New Year's Eve 1969 and two on New Year's Day 1970, each of which was professionally recorded. Hendrix had sold out Madison Square Garden just nine months prior, but the Fillmore East was chosen as the setting for a live recording.

### EDDIE KRAMER | recording engineer, producer

"Jimi owed a record for Capitol. Now, in my summation, yes, he knows, and his management knows, he has to do this. So at Woodstock there's the first inkling of what's coming up. Jimi says very clearly, 'We're nothing but a band of gypsys.' And that's the first key that one can draw back to.

"But not only that, but Billy Cox is in the band. And that's a big part of it. Noel is no longer there. That changes the aspect of the band. And when they reach Woodstock, which he has all these musicians with him, Larry Lee, which was a wonderful thing, 'cause Larry had just come out from Vietnam and Jimi was very generous, an incredible, generous human being. And he loved his friends and always wanted to do something for his buddies. So here he is at Woodstock, and if you use that as the marker, I think that's the start of it. August 1969.

"They go to Baggy's rehearsal rooms in New York to start rehearsals. I popped down there for one or two of them. It sounded pretty amazing. And you have Buddy Miles in the band. All of a sudden you got this power trio, this amazing force of nature, and Buddy is a perfect choice for Jimi because he is the master of fatback. In coming into the Fillmore East with a very tight band in spite of the fact that these are new songs, the band was bloody tight."

### ALLAN ARKUSH | film producer and director

"I'm working at the Fillmore East as an usher in the stage crew. At some point we were told the Band of Gypsys wanted to rehearse and they would be coming in every day.

"Bill Graham did not just care about the sound. We took pride in having the best sound and lights in the world.

Film producer and director Allan Arkush, shown here as a Fillmore East stagehand, c. 1969.

"Six inches from the Fillmore East was the NYU theater school, right next door. Those people are the newest and the finest of the people who are starting to make the conversion to concert production. Bill wanted good sound and sound engineer Bill Hanley, because there was nobody doing sound for rock concerts.

"So Bill took Hanley and he installed a sound system at the Fillmore East. And as time went on, he started understanding the building and what was possible. And it was not unusual to come in on a Sunday night and help him and his team set up the most advanced sound tracking equipment you can get.

"Every afternoon, Jimi would have the theater for two or three hours. And because our crew knew Jimi was recording live and because Eddie Kramer was someone who always hung at the Fillmore, the microphone placement was figured out pretty much over the course of two or three days of rehearsal. Jimi would stand up there on stage.

"And picture this: there is nobody in the theater but us on the stage crew, and it's four hours before the early show. And I would sit in the third row, put my feet up on a chair, and watch Jimi Hendrix figure out these songs with Buddy Miles and Billy Cox. That's how I spent two afternoons and maybe one more. At rehearsal in the afternoon there were no theatrics—just three musicians facing each other, working out the arrangements on this stuff and jamming on different blues songs."

### JIMMY ROBINSON | recording engineer

"I worked on the *Band of Gypsys* recording, assisting Wally Heider, who supervised it. Gary Kellgren needed some representation from the Record Plant at the Fillmore and asked me to assist Wally for two nights.

"Wally arrived in a 1961 Cadillac with a huge trunk, with a portable 8-track machine, microphones, cables, tapes, speakers. He drove the Caddy from California to New York with the gear. At the Fillmore, there was no alleyway. Underneath the stage at the Fillmore East were three or four rooms that were isolated, stage floors that would rise up and drop through. We took a room and put some carpet and set up Wally's recording studio with heavy Sony mikes that he brought."

### BILLY COX | bassist, Gypsy Sun and Rainbows, and Band of Gypsys

"We decided that we couldn't do any songs that had already been released. We wanted to give them something different. So we went at the project in a joyous, creative posture and ultimately developed the repertoire of the *Band of Gypsys*.

"We had rehearsed 'Changes' and a few others for Buddy. All of the songs we performed had been rehearsed. We didn't look at it as Buddy's part of the show. We were all there to give. We were all there to help, and material went on whether it was written by Jimi or not."

Velvert Turner, center, with Buddy Miles and Billy Cox of the Band of Gypsys, 1999.

### PRESCOTT NILES | bassist, the Knack

"One day Velvert Turner and I were hanging out and we wanted to see Band of Gypsys. He could talk like Jimi if he wanted to sound like him. A number of times before, Velvert would telephone Kip Cohen the managing director: "Hey, I'm with a friend, can I come over and enter backstage?'

"So we did that a few times. One afternoon Velvert called, and Kip said, 'Hold on a second. I've got Jimi here. Who are you?' And over the telephone we heard Bill Graham scream, 'Listen, if you ever fuckin' call again I'll break your fuckin' legs!'"

### ALLAN ARKUSH | film producer and director

"And then we had the sound check on New Year's Eve. We were told to not let anybody backstage to see Jimi. This was really important and they didn't want a whole scene, and only five people were allowed backstage: the three members of Band of Gypsys, the father of Billy Cox, and the manager, Michael Jeffery. And besides working stage crew that night, I had to go out and get fried chicken for one hundred people, along with Cold Duck wine. Because we're gonna have a little New Year's Eve party. Part of my job was to bring food to everybody."

**True to his unpredictability**, Hendrix opened his four-show stint with eleven songs that had not been commercially released. New tunes such as "Izabella," "Ezy Ryder," and "Burning Desire" were well received.

Jimi peppered the remaining three sets with favorites such as "Stone Free," "Purple Haze," and "Fire." Also included were Howard Tate's "Stop," "Steal Away" by Jimmy Hughes, and "Bleeding Heart" from Elmore James.

### ALLAN ARKUSH

"The first show, I was in the wings on the side of the stage, and Jimi stretched out and played with his teeth and all that stuff. And as he stood on the side of the stage after encore, he went up to Bill and said, 'Wasn't that great!' And that's when I heard Bill [Graham] give him a speech: 'You're Jimi Hendrix. You're better than this. And it's one thing to be doing this stuff when you're on tour, but you're playing songs about Vietnam ["Machine Gun"] tonight. And you should be showing the world.'

"So Bill tells him off and now comes the late show. And Hendrix comes on and plays the show, just magnificent and amazing. And he does one encore. And I think a second encore. Bill had gone up to the dressing room each time and gotten him. And so Bill said [to me], 'I don't want to go up there and beg them for another encore. But I will. But first you go up and ask them if they will go back down, and hold the door open so they can hear all the screaming.'

"Bill was very good at this stuff, me as the human sacrifice. Jimi said no to me. 'We don't know any more songs. That's it. And we played everything we rehearsed.'

"Jimi looks at Buddy and Billy and says, 'Do you guys know the chords to "Purple Haze"?' And they run through it standing there, and they go out and do an encore. Jimi sees Bill watching him. He then takes the guitar and goes down on it, licking the strings, and behind his head just laughing and pointing at Bill the whole time, and the audience."

### BILL GRAHAM |

rock impresario and promoter

"Jimi Hendrix once came late for a show. I'm pacing in front of the Fillmore, and he gets out of the cab, and I'm yelling at him, and he looked at me and said, 'There was this great movie on in the motel . . .'

"I finally realized that after the gig I could do the yelling."

Famed rock impresario Bill Graham at Woodstock, August 1969.

## BILLY COX

"After we were finished, Jimi was quite relieved. We were on, big time. After the first set, when we walked off, I remember Jimi, who was smiling, telling me and Buddy, 'It's gonna be all right now.'

"We felt the concerts went well. I might add that in previous gigs with the Experience, Jimi had used a Fuzz Face [tone-control pedal] and a wah-wah pedal, then at Woodstock he used a Fuzz Face, wah-wah pedal, and Uni-Vibe; but at the Fillmore East he used a Fuzz Face, wah-wah pedal, Uni-Vibe, and Octavia, and it was incredible. In fact you could hear all of it kicking in on 'Machine Gun.' It was incredible. There were people in the audience with their mouths open.

"The *Band of Gypsys* turned the world upside down. He had done [earlier] albums, and then I came on board with a lot of the things we had. He called them 'patterns,' but they're just riffs. We played around with them, and a lot of times he'd say, 'If people heard us play this stuff they'd lock us up.' But we were completely free musically.

"So with the Band of Gypsys, Jimi was at his peak. Buddy Miles! Oh man! What a guy. No restraint. The Band of Gypsys was a trend-setting group. We didn't know that. But it has been said that the Band of Gypsys inspired reggae, free-form rock, portions of rap. Jimi wrote about 90 percent of that stuff. And Buddy had 'Them Changes.' We did some stuff that we put together that we enjoyed which had a rhythm feel to it."

## MICHAEL SIMMONS | musician and journalist

"I was fourteen going on fifteen when I caught Jimi and the Band of Gypsys at the early show at the Fillmore East on January 1, 1970.

"A kids' choir called the Voices of East Harlem opened. Their soaring voices were the perfect way to greet the new decade, and I thought it was cool that Jimi embraced the notion of community here in New York—one of his hometowns, along with Seattle and London. He emphasized his guitar playing that night and disregarded stage shtick. We—the audience—were witnesses to Jimi's evolution as an artist, and it was thrilling. Personally, I was glad—picking with his teeth or with his axe draped behind his back was getting old.

"I later learned that Fillmore boss Bill Graham had encouraged him to just play. And yet he was very personable and relaxed and yapping about that New Year's Day's football scores. Most importantly, I've never seen a guitarist—or any musician—who could equal him in technique or feel or presence. I have friends who got to see Coltrane and Monk. My mother—a jazz singer who dated Charlie Parker's pianist Al

Haig—saw Bird. But I saw Hendrix, and he set a standard in rock that, for my taste, has never been surpassed. Awww, Jimi—though we hardly knew ye, you remain the greatest."

**The live album *Band of Gypsys*** was released on March 25, 1970. Culled from both nights at the Fillmore East, it fulfilled the terms of that onerous contract that had dogged Jimi for years.

## EDDIE KRAMER

"I didn't record it. I did all the mixing subsequently. After the four shows, the pressure was on us to deliver the record. I seem to remember Jimi and I started sifting and mixing the multitrack recordings at Juggy Sound in New York. January 1970.

"If you can imagine Jimi and I sitting at the board when we mixed. He knew what he wanted and cherry-picked what songs he wanted. And then we assembled it and started mixing.

"During the mixing, there is one moment I will always remember because it points to what happens afterwards. Jimi is listening and here goes Buddy, launching into one of his long vocal jams, if you will, scatting and doing his thing, and Jimi puts his head in his hands, his hat dipped down and he's on the console, and I could hear him say, 'Aw . . . I wish Buddy would shut the fuck up.' And it points to what happened later, because we all know the BOG is short-lived.

"It served its purpose. It had dramatic impact, of course, for many years to come. It's part of Jimi's arsenal of great songs, great performances, very R&B based, very funky. It showed the new shift. It showed the direction he was going in. And then he re-forms the experience but with a 'newly minted Mitch Mitchell.' And I say that in quotes because Mitch has obviously been seriously looking at the shift and he had adopted and adapted some of Buddy Miles's technique.

"One can make a case for Buddy Miles being the best fatback drummer, which he was, and able to keep a tremendously steady beat, which he did, ridiculously; but Mitch was the little-known genius, you know, who just sort of fiddled around the kit and did the most spectacular thing that would spark Jimi's imagination. And he was able to stay with Jimi and always land on the downbeat, even though he would do the most outrageous fills. You'd think, 'There's no way in hell he's gonna land on one.' But he did."

"Not his most important album, it nonetheless is my personal favorite of them all because his lead guitar improvisations are at the center of the songs, and they continue to amaze in the way solos by Parker or Coltrane continue to amaze. I use the phrase 'stealth jazz' to describe music like 'Machine Gun' or 'Power of Soul,' or 'Flute Thing' or 'Do What You Like,' high-level improvisation successfully marketed as rock because of timbre—loud lead guitar/funky bass guitar/fatback drums—and cultural association (Fillmore East).

"*Band of Gypsys* was the first time a major rock act had released a live album of all-new material, a familiar jazz practice. Given the material and the personnel, it's Jimi's second 'debut' album. Are you still experienced?"

—James Cushing, poet, English professor, deejay

# 12
# Walkin' on Gilded Splinters

What next? In March, after taking time in London to sit in with some friends and consider his future (Kathy Etchingham had just married, putting paid to his longest, most-committed relationship), Jimi returned to his old stomping grounds, Greenwich Village, hoping to find inspiration in comforting haunts, familiar streets. His passion project, a custom-built recording studio he dubbed Electric Lady, was consuming time and ungodly sums of money. The refurbishment of the nearby property was a money pit, and Jimi's creditors—Warner Bros., his management—were anxious for him to generate income to defray these outlays.

A t one point Jimi considered reuniting the Experience. Mitch Mitchell was in New York, working with ex-Cream bassist Jack Bruce and guitarist Larry Coryell. He was excited to get it going again. But the question of inviting Noel lingered; no one was prepared to commit either way, and so the cruelest outcome prevailed. At one point Noel was contacted and flew to New York, filled with high hopes, only to be met by an associate of Mike Jeffery, who pulled the plug on him. Billy Cox got the gig instead.

Three months of dates were booked, beginning at the "Fabulous Forum" in Los Angeles on April 25.

## KEN RESSER | concert attendee

"On April 25, 1970, I saw Jimi at the Forum ($6.50), sitting in almost identical seats as the previous time. I don't know who I attended the show with. Billy Cox had replaced Noel Redding on bass. He was much less flashy than in the two previous concerts I saw, but played great. No opening act as I recall.

"A loud (Marshall stacks), intensely powerful sound assaulted my ears and awed my eyes at all three concerts, though Jimi's music was changing—evolving—by the time of the last show I saw. It's hard to compare the live sound with Noel Redding as bassist to Billy Cox as bassist for that reason. In all of the shows, the rhythm section seemed to be challenged to keep up with Jimi. They were never a tight band—didn't need to be—many times on the edge of being out of control."

Ticket stub to the Hendrix show at the "Fabulous Forum," April 25, 1970.

## PAT BAKER | concert attendee

"Jimi took the stage at the Forum and gone were the flashy multicolored clothes. Dressed mostly in black, he seemed serious and ready to play.

"The opener, 'Spanish Castle Magic,' lit up the venue and had the audience fully engaged from the first chords. Billy Cox and Mitch Mitchell held down a solid bottom that allowed Hendrix the space to explore and improvise. Hendrix resorted to few gimmicks—just straight-ahead incendiary and soulful guitar throughout the entire performance. Truly fantastic."

"Jack Nitzsche and I went to see Jimi in 1970 at the Forum. Jack yelled to Buddy Miles, 'You suck!' when he sang a super long version of Neil Young's 'Down By the River.'

"At the Forum I remember when Jimi surveyed the crowd and said, 'This is for the soul sister in aisle eighteen!' Everybody looked around, trying to see her. There were no black faces there. . . . The song was 'Foxy Lady.'"

—Denny Bruce, record producer, A&R manager

**JIMI HENDRIX LIVE AT THE LOS ANGELES FORUM 4-25-70**

Album sleeve for a bootleg record of the Hendrix show at the Forum.

# Electric Lady Studios

In September 1969, Jimi and Mike Jeffery hired engineer Eddie Kramer and architect/acoustician John Storyk to design and build a state-of-the-art studio in New York City. After thirteen months, Electric Lady Studios was completed. Eddie Kramer served as its director of engineering from 1970 to 1974.

John Storyk received his architectural training from Princeton and Columbia Universities. He is a founding partner of WSDG, and has provided design and construction supervision services for the professional audio and video recording community since 1969 with the opening of Jimi Hendrix's Electric Lady Studios in New York City. Storyk, a fan of John Cage, studied with Buckminster Fuller, whose anticipatory design philosophy came to define the creative aesthetic that distinguishes Electric Lady's unique character.

Led Zeppelin, Stevie Wonder, David Bowie, and the Rolling Stones have produced some of their most acclaimed work here, undeniably inspired by the musician whose vision permeates the room like a spirit guide.

On August 26, 1970, Jimi Hendrix hosted the grand opening of his psychedelic-themed studio to friends and fellow musicians. Attendees included Stevie Winwood, Eric Clapton, Ron Wood, and rock 'n' roll scribe/poet Patti Smith.

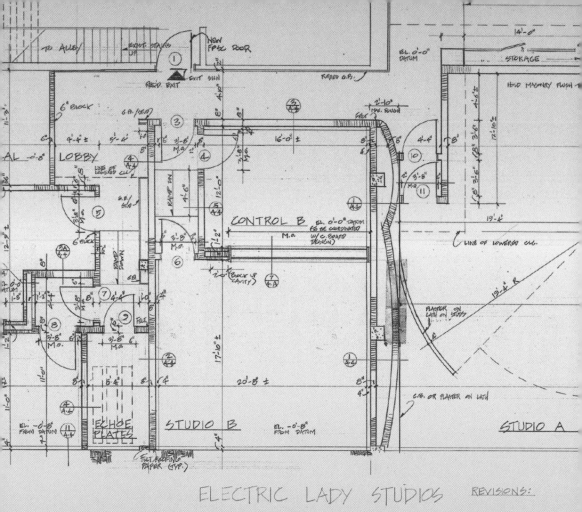

ELECTRIC LADY STUDIOS     REVISIONS:

## JOHN STORYK, ARCHITECT AND ACOUSTICIAN, COFOUNDER OF WSDG

"1968. I was in a band, and my then wife was also in an all-girls band, the Untouchables. I'm going to the Fillmore every Friday night when I answered a classified ad in the *Village Voice* newspaper: 'Wanted: Carpenters to work for free on an experimental nightclub.' The Cerebrum club opens, and life changes. It's in *Time* magazine and on the cover of *Life* magazine by April '69. Jimi went one night.

"At the same time Jimi is playing a lot at the Generation club in Greenwich Village, which was the basement of the 8th Street Cinema [52 West 8th Street]. Imagine how surprised I was when I went to the New York City Building Department to get the drawings for that building, only to find that this was the Film Guild Cinema that

NOTES:

1. MASONRY ↕ DRY WALL PART DIMENSIONS ARE ROUGH DIMENSIONS. ALL
2. ALL SUSPENDED CEILINGS INDICATED ARE SUBJECT TO MINOR HT. ADJ. IN CERTAIN SPACES. THIS WILL NOT APPLY FOR CORRIDORS
3. ALL SUSPENDED CEILG. WILL BE HUNG FROM METAL SUSPENSION SYSTEM W/ BUILDING CODE - C26-461.0
4. ALL DRYWALL PARTITIONS, PLASTER ↕ SUSPENDED PL ON LATH WORK SHALL OF 16'0.0. (AS PER C 26-400.0), EXCEPT WHERE NOTED

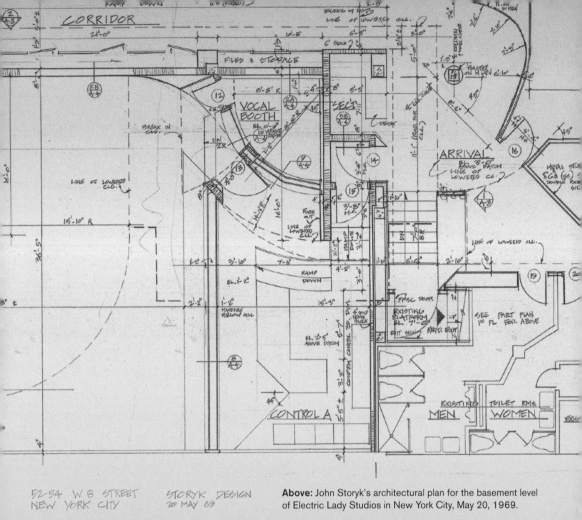

52-54 W. 8 STREET        STORYK DESIGN
NEW YORK CITY           20 MAY 69

**Above:** John Storyk's architectural plan for the basement level of Electric Lady Studios in New York City, May 20, 1969.

had been designed by Frederick Keisler in the 1920s. Keisler was and still is one of my favorite architects/sculptors. I was a fan of him throughout college.

"What's crazy about this, which was essentially a blues club, it had earlier been a polka club I used to go to a year or two earlier because I was in a blues band at Princeton and we had gigs in New York. So I knew all about this club. Hendrix had jammed there as well.

John Storyk, Electric Lady Studios architect and acoustician, c. 1970.

"And while I'm building Cerebrum, Jimi and Mike Jeffery decide to buy the Generation—not the building—the club, to buy the lease.

"Jimi says, 'Find the guy who did this downtown club that I like, because I want that designer to convert the club.'

"And I got a call from Michael Jeffery. I don't know how they got my phone number. I had a meeting with them to discuss redesigning the Generation Club, which of course I knew. I was age twenty-two, and had a meeting at the office on Park Avenue. And in the room was Michael Jeffery, Eddie Kramer, Jimi, and one other person, who had been hired to lead the project and basically manage the club, Jim Marron—he had been running Steve Paul's the Scene uptown, so he knew a lot about clubs—to supervise the transformation. 'I'd be honored,' I said.

"I leave and take a few weeks to design what would be my conversion of the club into what Jimi wanted, essentially similar things that he had seen at Cerebrum but with a lot of curves, even a curved stage. The ceiling had this curving shape. It was in the basement down the stairs. One of the ideas that Jimi and Eddie both had was that in the back of the club there would be a control room that would record everything that was happening in the club. Fifty years ago this was not that common.

"I put the room in the drawing. I'm now thinking we're gonna do the club. Then, one night late on a Sunday, I get a call from Jim Marron, who informs me that the club is being scrapped. And so my amazing client disappears as fast as it arrives. I was disappointed until the next sentence came out of his mouth: 'But they want you to stay on and do the recording studio.'

"What had happened is that Eddie convinced Jimi not to do a club but to do a full-on recording studio, because their recording studio bills were huge. Eddie and Mike also suggested a young producer, Phil Ramone, to help a bit on technicalities and layout. I had never been in a recording studio and went out and visited as many as I could.

"And then the project changed on a dime. Jim Marron would run the recording studio. Remember: there were few independent recording studios. 'You stay on and

Opposite: Music producer and engineer Eddie Kramer (seated center) and studio manager Jim Marron (standing) work with Hendrix on adjustments to the mixing board in the control room of Hendrix's Electric Lady Studio, June 17, 1970, two months before the studio opened.

we want you to do it.' So I quit my day job on the spot. You could do that in the six-ties. Money was easier. My wife at the time was working as a waitress. I created my own internship, to be honest. We hired a guy who knew a lot about isolation details for radio stations who we thought could help us with the isolation analysis for these rooms. I laid out the studios with Eddie.

"I did drafting for free for this person during the day in order to learn how to do this stuff. I did that for two months. I went back to Columbia University for six months, read everything I could read and did the design, and we just went right into construction. It took about a year to build it. I have a drawing from June '69, and by then Cerebrum was very well known. And the guy who was leading the Bucky Fuller Whole Earth course in New York approached me to be in the class. They selected twenty people. I was building Electric Lady on 8th Street, and in the afternoons I would walk down a block and a half in Greenwich Village to the New York Studio School on 8th Street and attend the class with Bucky.

"For the studio we got carpenters, mechanical engineers. I got a junior engineer from the electrical firm I was working with at my day job and another mechanical engineer who was a friend of a girlfriend who was a mechanical engineer from col-lege. And they became my lifetime design partners.

"Of course, the word got out before this was all done. My Princeton classmate Jon Taplin, road manager for the Band, introduced me to Albert Grossman, who man-aged them. I would eventually do his Bearsville recording studio and all his rooms.

"1969. An amazing summer. I went to the Woodstock festival in the car with Albert Grossman, who I really liked. He changed my life. I was backstage, but most of the time I was with Eddie Kramer in the recording truck. Eddie became a lifetime friend. He changed my life. My daughter's godfather.

"Jimi would come down to the construction site, usually late afternoons. That's the only time I would spend with Jimi. I didn't socialize with him. I went to his shows, Band of Gypsys at the Fillmore. I saw the quiet, respectful, almost shy Jimi. Jimi would point out certain things, but he would let Eddie and I do what we wanted to do. He was very happy. He had input. He didn't read architectural drawings very well, but he had ideas what he wanted.

**Opposite:** Interior view of Electric Lady Studios, 2014.

"There was one day where he did come down and made us replace the rectangular windows with round windows and also replace all the doors. Literally eight doors came off and found their way to these other studios in New York, which was hysterical. I guess I can tell the story now. [Laughs.]

"The studio design world really didn't really exist in 1969—a few people. I was making with Eddie a project studio, twenty years before the term was even invented. It was for Jimi and musicians. The control room had full ambient lighting, colored lights on the ceiling.

"Jimi did not want to work in the regular studios where basically the control rooms were small and dingy. They didn't have vibe. He wanted a studio that had vibe. Now, I had the advantage of simply not knowing any better. I just assumed that if you were making music, you're supposed to have vibe."

**Performances continued to ping-pong** between good, bad, and blah, depending on the vagaries of the road. The May 30 concert in Berkeley was filmed and recorded for commercial release. In June 1970, they performed at the San Bernardino Swing Auditorium, a surprisingly robust setting for rock bands in the rusty, dusty, climes of this blue-collar community. (Fun fact: the Rolling Stones' first-ever concert in North America was at this venue in June 1964.)

It was unclear whether any of the social unrest that was unfolding around them registered with Jimi. As far back as 1967, he had made a few comments interpreted as support for the Vietnam War. Most likely it was a fellow soldier showing solidarity with his "band of brothers." But now there were costs to being politically agnostic; fans wanted their musical heroes to carry the cudgel for moral righteousness . . . while playing their favorite songs.

### ELIZABETH DARROW JONES | fan and singer

"In June of 1970, I went to see Jimi Hendrix perform at the Swing Auditorium. We walked into the auditorium and it was early enough to wander around before the concert. I was dressed up in silk and velvet and ready for this concert to begin. We went looking for a restroom before the show. My friends opted to get something to drink, and I went looking for the ladies' room.

"In my search, I noticed someone with a guitar about a good twenty feet from me. I am thinking someone is tuning up guitars. I walk closer to see. He looks up and once again—it is Jimi. This time he smiles. I smile. I just turned nineteen years old, and my good sense told me to turn around and walk away. I left to go find my friends and watch him play.

"The first song? Debut of 'All Along the Watchtower.'"

### BRUCE D. HENDERSON | photographer

"The Swing Auditorium concert was the first of two back-to-back Jimi Hendrix concerts I'd snagged as freelance photo jobs from Bill Graham's Shady Productions promotion outfit in LA.

"I'd been to the Swing for a couple of other concerts, so I was familiar with the cavernous indoor arena, which was filling up when I got inside, and I had to push my way to get a seat a few rows back from stage center.

"I got a stage pass for the next day's concert at the Ventura County Fairgrounds. Just a side note: even though Jimi only performed for about 45 minutes the next night in Ventura, apparently because of the mist rolling in, it was so much better for

**Above and right:**
Photographer
Bruce Henderson's
pictures of Hendrix
performing at the
Swing Auditorium
in San Bernardino,
California, June 20,
1970.

me, as I was shooting from stage right and had mostly clear shots. The experience
was ethereal even with the occasional sound issues caused by dampness or poor
connections. Jimi got upset with his sound guy at one point, and I got to hear his
awesome 'talking guitar.' Without the echo of the auditorium, the sound was purer.

"The crowd, which the local paper reported numbered a record 7,300 people, was pretty pumped, and some people rushed the stage when Jimi came onstage. I remember being jostled a lot and having a hard time getting clear views for the camera, especially since I'm short. Jimi opened with 'All Along the Watchtower,' and his set included fan favorites like 'Foxy Lady,' 'Purple Haze,' and 'Machine Gun.' But I remembered especially liking 'Hear My Train a Comin',' which I hadn't heard before. Jimi performed for more than two and a half hours, but many in the audience were disappointed when he didn't go even longer. I remember being wowed by his onstage persona and incredible performance.

"I heard afterward that there had been a confrontation with police outside when an overflow of fans couldn't get inside, but I don't remember hearing the commotion from inside. Not surprising since the music was so loud and echoed throughout the auditorium."

### EDDIE KRAMER | recording engineer, producer

"Thank God Abe Jacob recorded so many great live Jimi shows during his career. And Jimi wanted to make sure the shit sounded good. I recorded Jimi at Woodstock and Miami Pop. And you had to be on your game. 'Cause you only had one shot.

"Berkeley 1970 is definitely up there as one of the finest. Abe Jacob actually did the basic recording. Of course, Abe and I go back many years, and we would always talk about stuff like how to record Jimi. I was very lucky to have him do some of those shows. I never had the opportunity to record Jimi live, but I always did all the mixing with him, starting with *Band of Gypsys*. I know what is needed to make it sound right. Certainly in today's market you want it to not only have the vintage feel but it's gotta punch, you know."

### ABE JACOB | sound engineer

"Bill Graham did the Berkeley 1970 show. He was a very dynamic individual. And he had a terrific personality. Sometimes it wasn't the personality you wanted to deal with. But his philosophy was always for the audience. He would do anything he did for the band and for the artist as long as they gave a performance to the audience. He told me, 'Bands have management and agents. Everybody else has somebody representing them. I'm here to represent the audience.'

"For Berkeley 1970, we got the Wally Heider truck. It was in the San Francisco area where I was from; it naturally worked out that I would be in the truck and Mike Neal would be doing the mix inside the theater.

"When we toured, the sound system for the Jimi Hendrix Experience was eight microphones. It was a little different for recording because we obviously had to mike the guitar and guitar to put it on tape, which you didn't in the live venue. Pretty much the drums, two vocal mikes, some audience mikes for ambience, and that was it.

"We had eight tracks available and everything went on a separate track, so it made it easy for Eddie Kramer to mix it later on. I just put a mike in front of what they played.

"The basic philosophy was that the sound that came off the stage was what you wanted to present to the live audience and that also was what you wanted to present when you recorded it.

"The one memory I have, and it has been reported, was that it was such a small room, people trying to get in, and we opened the back doors of the recording truck, and people gathered outside the theater to listen to our monitors in the truck. And it probably prevented a riot."

# Down South and Back Home Again

Jimi, Mitch, and Billy were the star attraction at the Atlanta International Pop Festival, held at the Atlanta International Raceway in Hampton Georgia, July 3–6, 1970. They headlined on the third. Jimi then had a fateful return to his hometown of Seattle on July 26, at Sick's Stadium.

**BILLY COX** | bassist, Gypsy Sun and Rainbows, and Band of Gypsys

"By this time we're getting used to these crowds. You know, it really didn't have anything to do with race. It was being linked together cosmically. He started off 'All Along the Watchtower' in the wrong key. I started off in the wrong key with him. Because wherever he went, I was right on him. Then Jimi got on the microphone and went to the original key and I was on him right then and there. When we got off the stage he said, 'You were right on me like white on rice.' 'No, I was right on you like a rat on cheese.' And we laughed at that.

"At Atlanta Pop, we did 'Freedom,' 'Straight Ahead,' 'Message of Love,' 'Room Full of Mirrors.' These are songs the audience never heard. And when we got off the stage Jimi said, 'You know, we must be pretty good, because they never heard [these songs] and they really went crazy. So we must be riding in the right direction.'

"We never had a set list. Jimi always starts the song off. So wherever he wanted to go, that's where we went. Normally it went from 'Foxy Lady' to 'Voodoo Child' to 'Freedom' and 'Straight Ahead.' So if Jimi wanted to extend it, he would look back, we knew what that cue was. Maybe he would raise his hands to the left or to the right. We knew the cue. He was the boss, and we knew where he wanted to go."

**JANIE HENDRIX** | Jimi's sister; CEO and President of Experience Hendrix

"I remember the last time Jimi was here and performed at the Sick's Stadium and Michael Jeffery came to the house to get him. And it was raining, thunder and lightning that day, and Jimi was not feeling well and he was still asleep. And they were driving down to Oregon. And Dad said, 'He's not going right now.' And Michael Jeffery said, 'But we have to perform tomorrow.' And Dad said, 'He'll take a plane tomorrow and he'll meet you there. He's not going right now.' And he fought with Michael. Michael was like, 'He needs to ride with us.'

"And Dad said, 'He is sick and he's going to rest. And if something happens to him, then what will happen? You won't have a group. So he's going to rest, and you are going to go down there and drive, and he will fly down tomorrow.' And that's the way it went.

"I know that my dad through life probably regretted, you know, not being able to be there, because my dad was a very sweet and wonderful person, but do know there was another side to my dad. There's a reason why Jimi and I have the work ethic that we do, and the reason why we got whuppings. [Laughs.] You do things and you say things, and if you're not walking the line you would be scolded. You would be punished. There was another side to my dad, and if you crossed that line, he was gonna stand strong. And he definitely did with Michael.

"I remember Jimi saying that—when he first came back to Seattle—he wanted us all to move to New York and manage him. And my dad was a landscape gardener. 'I don't know anything about the music industry.' But all Jimi was saying was 'I just wanted family around me so I can feel secure' and some sort of protection. Some sort of shield. Sometimes to help them realize: 'I'm not getting a good vibe from that person. I don't think they have your best interests at heart.'

"I think that's good and bad. Yes, we can learn both positive and the negative and turn it to positive from our own mistakes and from other people's mistakes, if we just pay attention. Nobody's perfect. You make mistakes. My dad used to say, 'Pull up your britches and bootstraps and keep going.' You can't sit and dwell about whatever just happened. People, managers, come along. Your choices are—at that time it was okay to say, 'I'll sign.' And maybe you didn't read the fine print. And then later it's like it haunts you for years. Do people learn from that? God, I hope so."

**Opposite:** Concertgoers watch the opening acts of Jimi Hendrix's Cry of Love Tour, Sick's Stadium, Seattle, July 26, 1970. **Above:** The audience at what would be Hendrix's last show in Seattle huddle in tents and under tarps against the rain.

### NILS LOFGREN | guitarist, songwriter

"In June 1970, my band Grin opened three Hendrix shows: Sacramento, San Bernardino, and Ventura. Art Linson was our manager. I don't know who was booking Jimi, but [it] may have well have been Frank Barsalona at Premier [Talent] Agency, who was booking us and everybody under the sun. Frank was a great guy and a fabulous friend. We played three nights opening for Hendrix. We were all out of our minds.

"One of the nights coincidently fell on my nineteenth birthday. The Ventura show was an outdoor festival. I was so blown away that we had an all-area pass to watch Jimi from the wings. I did not go out front. I saw him from out front in the audience many times.

"We watched from the wings and [were] very honored to see him. And on my birthday, June 21, 1970, just before our set, my producer, David Briggs, who was like my big brother and mentor, goaded me as a birthday gift to myself to go knock on Jimi's Winnebago dressing room door and say hello. I didn't think I could do that, but of course Briggs egged me on. So I knocked on Jimi's door.

"He answered it! I shook his hand and said I was his opening act, he was the reason I was a professional musician, 'Can't wait to see you play,' have seen him many times and wanted to thank him so much for his music.

"Jimi was sitting there with a shit-eating grin on his face. Looked a bit stoned, but he was happy. He was kind, sat there and listened to me and smiled. Before I got crazy and invited myself in for a guitar lesson I said, 'Just wanted to say, Jimi: thanks. I know you have a show to do. I'll be out watching. Have a great one.'"

# 13
# The Sky Is Crying

On August 27, 1970, Hendrix cut his last studio recording, an instrumental titled "Slow Blues." He then left with Billy Cox on an Air India flight for London to join Mitch Mitchell for their headlining spot at a huge music festival to be held on the Isle of Wight—the largest island in England, located several miles off the country's south coast.

**T**he festival market was exploding on both sides of the Atlantic. Organizers were of two minds; they were mostly as young as the artists and shared the same goals, an alluring altruism that would make attendees feel connected to a higher calling. But these were expensive enterprises to mount, and finding sponsorships with the burgeoning media industrial complex (for film, album and other ancillary rights) required some deft deal-making and compromises. It was a challenge to find that sweet spot between community and commerce, and not every festival succeeded at one or both.

# Isle of Wight Festival 1970

The Isle of Wight festival (August 26–31) dwarfed Woodstock in scale and scope. The audience of 600,000 was in a fiery and frenzied mood after turning the festival into a political arena, with fans trampling the fences and setting fire to structures and equipment. The consolation was in the range of artists who took that precarious stage, which included: the Who, Leonard Cohen, Joni Mitchell, the Doors, the Moody Blues, Jethro Tull, Free, Miles Davis (!), and numerous emerging (mostly British) bands that used music festivals to introduce themselves.

Jimi, again, came on late, and stammered through a piss-take of "God Save the Queen." There were technical cock-ups that frustrated him to the point of exasperation. There was no flow; the set drifted from some new songs to a bum's rush through the hits, to a gaggle of blues and more Mitch Mitchell drum solos than was good for anybody's well-being. Still, there were hints of greatness: a solo, a fiery exchange that portended the promise of this trio. Filmmaker Murray Lerner caught it all, and the resultant documentary captured Jimi in the final blush of his singular talents, leaving us to contemplate what might have been.

Murray Lerner was an Oscar-winning director who, in 1967, produced and directed *Festival!*, shot between 1963 and 1966 at the Newport Folk Festival, catching Dylan, Joan Baez, and Peter, Paul and Mary at their youthful zenith.

In 1995, Lerner's long-awaited *Message to Love: The Isle of Wight Festival* finally surfaced. The documentary captures the pervasive air of social breakdown, a kind of *Lord of the Flies* with the hippest soundtrack. Fans had mostly refused to pay for their admission and promoters were desperate to save their investment; they faced off in the loamy fields of an English isle, reaching only an unsatisfying draw. It is a thoughtful look at the darker side of the period's festival culture.

### MURRAY LERNER | director and filmmaker

"I had a loose outline between the idealism of the music and the commercialism of the music business. Leonard Cohen might have saved the festival at one point. There was a fire owing to some fireworks. And that place could have gotten out of hand. I really worried about it."

### BOB JOHNSTON | record producer

"I put a band together for Leonard Cohen in 1970 and did the Isle of Wight festival. All of these people had been sitting out there in the rain, and right after that they'd set fire to Hendrix's stage!"

### CARMINE APPICE | drummer, Vanilla Fudge

"Cactus played Friday night. Jimi loved [guitarist] Jim McCarty, who played with me in Cactus. They were good friends. He played with Jimi and worked with Buddy Miles. I had jammed with Jimi at Steve Paul's the Scene, and we'd go next door to the Record Plant and continue playing. Cactus recorded at Electric Lady and used to see Jimi there all the time and hang out. Matter of fact, the last show we saw Jimi was at the Isle of Wight in England. And it wasn't long after that that Jimi passed away."

### RICHARD WILLIAMS | music journalist

"By the time the Isle of Wight festival came around, I'd seen Jimi Hendrix at his razor-sharp best, in an early gig with the original Experience in front of 200 people, and at something close to his worst, barely capable of tuning up on a night when he was topping the bill of a package tour that also featured Pink Floyd and the Move. What he did in front of half a million people in the early morning of Monday, August 31, 1970, embraced both extremes. Delayed until long after midnight, the set began in a stoned haze that did the music no favors.

"His version of 'God Save the Queen' had none of the political impact of his tortured 'Star-Spangled Banner' at Woodstock the previous year. While Mitch

Mitchell and Billy Cox bravely strove to keep the set on track, Jimi took the best part of an hour to get himself together. But when he did, the result—for those who had stayed on, and stayed awake—was epic. Here, at last, was the Hendrix who had changed music as much as Charlie Parker had done a quarter of a century earlier.

"A couple of hours later, just as the sun was coming up, four of us made our way to a nearby airfield. We had to be back at work that morning, and we'd worked out that the best way of avoiding the huge queues for the ferries back to the mainland was to pay a local flying instructor £25—about $70 in those days—to take us across the water in a small plane. As we sat there in a hut by the grass runway, waiting for our pilot, a limousine came out of the morning mist. Out stepped Jimi, still swathed in his orange and red stage silks. He walked straight to a waiting helicopter, and a couple of minutes later he was disappearing into the sky, through the blue-grey mist. Eighteen days later, we learnt of his death."

Hendrix performing at the Isle of Wight festival, early August 31;
Mitch Mitchell was on drums and Billy Cox on bass.

**JUSTIN HAYWARD** | songwriter, lead singer, guitarist, the Moody Blues

"I'm often asked if I knew so-and-so in the sixties. I always say that I was acquainted with many people, but that that is not the same as 'knowing' someone.

"I expect many people will say they 'knew' Jimi, but I suspect very few really did—maybe only Mitch and Noel.

"I chose the people I wanted to know very carefully, because the music community in London in the 1960s was a wonderful, scatty, sometimes scary place and I was aware I should be careful.

"I met Jimi through Kathy Etchingham, who I always felt close to (before and after she was with Jimi), just because we were 1946 kids. She was kind, sexy, straight (unlike most of the rest of us who were pretty stoned) and could look after herself—she looked after him well too. I was acquainted with Jimi, and in his company two or three times, and played on the same bill maybe two or three times as well. I saw him one time at the Saville, and he, Noel, and Mitch were absolutely brilliant.

"I found him quiet, gentle, softly spoken, and very beautiful but a kind of stranger in a strange land. To be surrounded constantly by adoring white people but suffering the trials every black person faced, must sometimes have been terrifying.

"We talked of guitars, and about tuning them. (I had to tune to Ray Thomas's flute, and then turn and 'tune up' the other Moodies, which almost always meant we were rarely on 440 Hz.) Jimi tuned mostly a semitone down. It was the pitch where the guitar really 'sang' at super high volume. He took great care about string gauges too and after that I believe I changed gauges.

"It was an amusing good vibe conversation and a joint or two was shared. We were talking clothes (he had a superb 'eye' for gorgeous things to wear). He said, 'Oh, I just see them and pick them up—you know.' I remember thinking, 'If only it were that simple!'

"The last time I saw him on stage was at the notorious 1970 Isle of Wight festival. It had been a wonderful gig for us, coming only weeks after 'Question' was such a big hit.

"As we drove away that night Jimi was playing his set. The memory will always be with me of the lonely distress I believed he would have been in. Things just didn't sound or feel right. Some 'gremlin' in the equipment was disrupting the sound (he needed those amps to work properly for him) and the music was somehow confusing to the ear, and I was so sad.

"Maybe he was searching for music that he would have found—if only?

"I'm so lucky that I was 'acquainted' with the quiet, gentle, happy Jimi."

**Opposite:** Jimi Hendrix's last performance: onstage at the Love and Peace music festival on the island of Fehmarn in Germany on September 6, 1970.

**MURRAY LERNER**

"The Isle of Wight journey was worth it. That was the most exciting event I've ever been to. 'Cause it was so all-encompassing. And new, in terms of the possibility of the crowd killing us and always living on the edge of that precipice, and all the different personas that reacted to this thing."

# Love & Peace Festival, Isle of Fehmarn

Jimi's final performance was another festival, this time on the Isle of Fehmarn, in what was then West Germany. Held September 6, it was billed as the Love & Peace Festival, and it was anything but. The weather turned as nasty as a Nor'easter, blowing with gale force, leading to a litany of technical snafus. The crowds were turning ugly—too much drinking and the odious presence of skinheads itching for a fight brought the fraught proceedings to a near calamitous end.

Back at the hotel, Billy Cox was having his own private meltdown (it is believed someone had spiked one of his drinks with LSD a few days prior). Cox, never one for the shenanigans of rock stars—no drinking or drugs—was caught in the throes of a profound breakdown that alarmed the band. Nonetheless, the show must go on; it was adrenaline that dragged them all across the finish line, the music lost in the whirling winds.

**JAMES CUSHING** | poet, English professor, deejay

"On June 18, 1967, Jimi opened his Monterey International Pop Festival set with Howlin' Wolf's classic, 'Killing Floor.'

"There's a terrible poignancy to that, because the last concert he ever played [at the Isle of Fehmarn Festival, Germany, September 6, 1970], he also opened with 'Killing Floor.' The idea of death in the title conveys a tragic meaning that lingers like an awful scent."

# Coda

The band returned to England right after the concert, feeling like they'd gone twelve rounds with Joe Louis. Billy sought medical help to deal with his issues; Mitch retreated to Sussex, and Jimi lay low, expecting to return to New York in a few days. Sly Stone was heading to the Speakeasy Club, hoping to coax Jimi out for a jam. Mitch agreed to drive up and join them.

**ANYA WILSON** | music-business veteran

"On September 15, 1970, a Tuesday, I was working late and Laurence Myers and I were the only ones in the office when he asked if I would like to join him at Ronnie Scott's for dinner, as he had promised Eric Burdon that he would see the first night of the debut of [Eric's] new band, War.

"If you've ever been to Ronnie Scott's, you'll know it's an intimate space, and Eric had booked a table right at the front of the stage. The set was incredible, and partway through the set Eric looked out into the audience and said, 'Hi there Jim. . . . Climb on in,' and to my amazement Jimi Hendrix 'climbed on in' to join him and then delivered a stunning performance, giving the delighted crowd the treat of their lives! Jimi was literally three feet away from us.

"I think he joined Eric again the following night, and the day after that he died. As I look back now on the night I saw Jimi, he looked in fine form, not high or wasted, so his death came as a great shock to me."

**On Thursday, September 17, Jimi hadn't shown** for the Speakeasy jam. Mitch drove back, disappointed but unconcerned. He was awakened by a phone call from the band's long-time tour manager, Eric Barrett.

Hendrix had been admitted to St. Mary Abbot's Hospital in London on Friday the eighteenth at 11:45 a.m. after a girlfriend, Monika Dannemann, found him unresponsive at her flat in Notting Hill Gate. At 12:45 p.m. he was pronounced dead. The cause was aspiration of vomit precipitated by severe barbiturate intoxication.

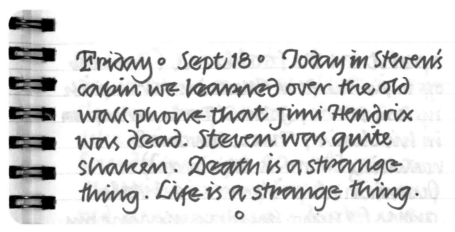

A sad entry in Henry Diltz's journal, written at Steven Stills's cabin, recounting how they learned of Jimi Hendrix's death on September 18, 1970.

### JAMES CUSHING

"On September 18, 1970, 'the absolute collided with the contingent,' as John Ashbery said about the death of Frank O'Hara.

"Jimi was working on *First Rays of the New Rising Sun*, the intended title for the double album Hendrix had been working on for many months in his New York studio, a sequel to *Electric Ladyland* that would consolidate its reach with the jazz directness of *Band of Gypsys*. The project was left forever incomplete.

"In fragmented form, it appeared in 1971 as a pair of single LPs, *The Cry of Love* and *Rainbow Bridge*, which was tied into a movie."

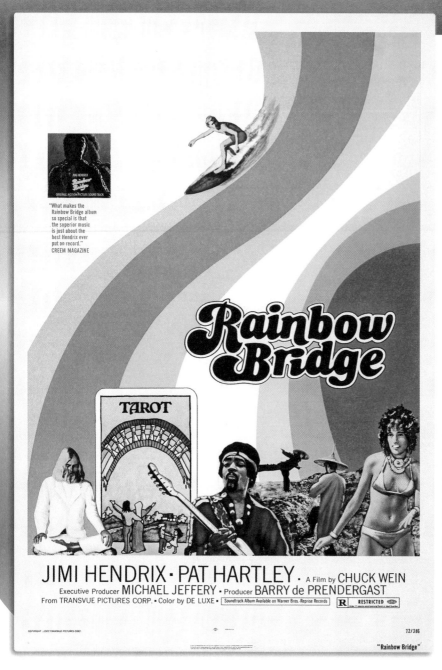

"What makes the Rainbow Bridge album so special is that the superior music is just about the best Hendrix ever put on record."
CREEM MAGAZINE

# Rainbow Bridge

TAROT

JIMI HENDRIX · PAT HARTLEY · A Film by CHUCK WEIN
Executive Producer MICHAEL JEFFERY · Producer BARRY de PRENDERGAST
From TRANSVUE PICTURES CORP. · Color by DE LUXE · Soundtrack Album Available on Warner Bros. Reprise Records · **R** RESTRICTED

COPYRIGHT ©1972 TRANSVUE PICTURES CORP.

72/386

"Rainbow Bridge"

The poster for the 1971 Chuck Wein film *Rainbow Bridge* about a model's experiences in Maui and which features seventeen minutes of a Hendrix concert filmed on the island on July 30, 1970. It also includes fragments of previously unreleased Hendrix songs.

### BOBBY WOMACK | guitarist and singer/songwriter

"Janis Joplin called me. She had just recorded my song 'Trust Me' at Sunset Sound with her producer Paul Rothchild.

"I remember her coming to the studio the next day and she was very upset because she was sayin' Jimi Hendrix passed. She was very upset. 'Oh baby, I know you feel bad.' So I shared my own experiences about meeting him.

"She then joked about 'Oh, I plan to kill my own self. Now with Jimi just leaving I ain't gonna get no publicity.' She was joking like that all the time.

"Then later in early October Paul Rothchild calls me and I hear about Janis. . . . That just broke my heart.

"Seeing somebody today and losing them tomorrow. Damn, I keep losing people. I love and didn't know I loved them this much until they aren't around.

"Maybe it's the thing where we become messengers for some people who aren't here. But boy, sometimes, I'm telling you, I need some help with these messages. Sometimes they go too fast."

## ROSEMARIE PATRONETTE | Newport '69 festival attendee

"I wish I could remember how Jimi came into my consciousness. I was age fifteen in '68, he just was . . . *there*. My brother Paul played guitar, so somehow we knew of and had heard Hendrix. We worshiped him completely.

"I do remember the day Jimi died very clearly, though. My dad had an intercom system installed in every room. In order to wake us up to get ready for school, he would yell into it, "Time to get up" and then blast the radio through it on radio stations KHJ or KRLA.

"But one day, my door at the end of the hallway quietly opened and my mom came in, sat on my bed, and told me that Jimi, our hero, had died. I could hear my brother wailing in his bedroom next door, and I immediately burst into sobs, too.

"We were allowed to stay home from school that day; we were absolutely devastated, as if we knew him personally, when we had merely seen him once in the San Fernando Valley at Devonshire Downs in 1969—and had our young minds permanently rearranged."

## NILS LOFGREN | guitarist, songwriter

"I still remember hearing about Jimi's death in September 1970 on the radio. I'm still not over it. It's still one of the worst deaths of my entire sixty-eight years. It wasn't the shock or feeling I had at age twelve when John F. Kennedy was killed. It had a worse vibe. JFK was on our black-and-white TV and it was the first time I saw my dad cry. But this was much worse for me. Music was like a sacred weapon for me that was saving my life daily—and still does. But as far as picking up your sword swinging, nobody had a bigger, more powerful healing sword than Jimi had. And there's nobody that the loss has cut deeper in my life. And we've lost so many greats. But that was the biggest one still."

"I TELL YOU WHEN I DIE I'M NOT GOING TO HAVE A FUNERAL. I'M GOING TO HAVE A JAM SESSION. . . . I SHALL HAVE THEM PLAYING EVERYTHING I DID MUSICALLY—EVERYTHING I ENJOYED DOING MOST. THE MUSIC WILL BE PLAYING LOUD AND IT WILL BE OUR MUSIC."

—Jimi Hendrix to journalist Bob Dawbarn in an interview published in *Melody Maker*, March 8, 1969.

# Jimi Hendrix and Australia— A Love Affair

DAVID N. PEPPERELL, WRITER AND MUSICIAN

"Jimi hit Australia like a comet! From the moment we first heard 'Hey Joe' in 1966 playing on the radio to when we saw a short video clip on TV of the Experience performing that same song in London, we were fans for life.

"His music was everywhere—every shop you walked into in Melbourne, Sydney, and Adelaide were playing his first album, *Are You Experienced?*, from track one to the end. Every radio station played practically every track on that amazing debut, which is always spoken of in the same breath as the greatest first albums, like *The Rolling Stones England's Newest Hit Makers*, *The Doors*, and *Court of the Crimson King*.

"Every band in the country played some or all of them, plus tracks from the album in their sets—if they didn't, they were practically booed off the stage! Every mod disco played Hendrix nonstop and featured a band playing Hendrix covers if they could find one good enough—it was Hendrixmania!

"We so looked forward to seeing Jimi play live after the *Monterey Pop* film where we finally saw what all the fuss was about regarding his live shows. Our jaws collectively dropped seeing someone not only play a guitar, but *become* a guitar and manifest as a total musical entity, both vocal and instrumental.

"But Jimi endlessly touring Europe and the USA . . . he never came here.

"But that was not to be.

"Jimi passed away in the back of an ambulance on September 18, 1970, so we never saw him play live in Australia. What a huge blow that was for all of us, mixing the sorrow at his passing with the terrible regret of missing out on actually seeing and hearing him.

"I remembered that black day so well. I was driving a delivery van, and I bought the daily newspaper to be greeted with the news he had died.

"Farewell Jimi—we never knew you, but you will remain in our hearts forever.

"It was unbelievable—one of the saddest days of my entire life. I wore a black armband at my job for the rest of the week and wrote a poem that was published on March 10, 1970, in *Go-Set*, the weekly Australian national pop paper":

## THE DAY HENDRIX DIED

the road remains hard
stretching out
lazy
in front of my tyres and window
endless white flashes
whilst the fences melt

to halt beneath a tree
on the corner of the world
to lower my eyes
to the printed sheet
below my arm
and wonder at the darkness there

for that sun
for those stars
I believed and died for
out of a feeling
I found impossible
out of a dream
I could not resolve

a stranger I met in the street
told me what I did not want to know
that jimi was gone

—David N. Pepperell, Melbourne,
Australia 18/09/1970

Miles Davis arrives at Hendrix's funeral on October 1, 1970, with his wife, singer Betty Mabry, left, and an unidentified woman.

**A private funeral for Jimi Hendrix** was held on October 1, 1970, in Seattle, at the Dunlop Baptist Church, where he was laid to rest at the Greenwood Cemetery in Renton.

Maybe two hundred or so fans gathered nearby, along with a small police consignment. The service was officiated by Reverend Harold Blackburn. Al Hendrix, and Jimi's stepmother, June, brother, Leon Hendrix, and his half-sister, Janie, and other relatives paid tribute. The pallbearers were Jimi's childhood friends and his valet/chauffeur from Hawaii, Herbert Price.

Seattle mayor Wes Uhlman was present, as well as concert promoter Tom Hulett, a confident of Jimi who had promoted his Seattle and West Coast concerts. Also in attendance were Michael Jeffery; Noel Redding; Mitch Mitchell; Eddie Kramer; writer Al Aronowitz, who came with Miles Davis; Eric Barrett and Gerry Stickells from the Hendrix road crew; Buddy Miles and his wife, singer Betty Mabry; Johnny Winter; John Hammond Jr.; soundman Abe Jacob; Steve Paul, owner of the Scene nightclub; and Chuck Wein, who directed *Rainbow Bridge.*

The coffin was opened briefly for those to cast a last look at the bright shining light that would lie, extinguished forever, in Greenwood Cemetery, near his beloved Lucille.

In his memoir, *Jimi Hendrix: Inside the Experience* (1990), Mitch Mitchell details that long day, as forlorn and sodden as the Seattle weather:

> Most of us were staying in the same hotel. Honestly, it felt like a gig. There was a knock at the door in the morning and Gerry Stickells stood there and said, "It's time to go now," and I'm sure I said, "What time's the gig?" I know it sounds sick, but maybe that was the only way I could deal with it.
>
> I think it started to hit me during the service, especially when we had to walk up the aisle and file past the open coffin. . . . Noel and I held hands—that's when it really hit me.

When Procol Harum's Robin Trower and band lyricist Keith Reid heard the news of Hendrix's death while touring in San Francisco, they wrote a tribute to him, "Song For a Dreamer," for 1971's *Broken Barricades.* Hendrix's influence on Trower is well-known; his solo career explodes with the early '70s release, *Bridge of Sighs*, a compendium of flangy, woozy, Stratocaster colorings that succeeded in honoring Jimi while foraging a fresh path forward for guitarists struggling to get out from under Hendrix's shadow. In many ways, this challenge mirrored the efforts of jazz saxophonists to free themselves from the tether of Charlie Parker, and later, John Coltrane.

And on November 29, 2019, the *Velvert Turner Group* album from 1972—Turner's only record, which had been out of print for decades—was re-released on vinyl for National Record Store Day. It closes with Hendrix's "Freedom."

**Opposite:** Detail of the Hendrix memorial at the Greenwood Memorial Park Cemetery in Renton, Washington, which was completed there in 2002.

# 14
# See You in the Next Life

At the time of his physical passing, Jimi Hendrix left no will and legal battles initially surrounded control of his estate.

Jimi resided in a world of his own design, an architect as audacious as Gaudí or Gehry. What matter were quotidian concerns when you're busy building castles made of particles and sound waves? When his brief, timeless transit came to its shattering full stop, there was, inevitably, a mad scramble to pick up the pieces.

**B**y 1995, Jimi's father, James "Al" Hendrix—sole heir to the lucrative empire—was able to establish the family company Experience Hendrix LLC, to administer the estate.

President and CEO Janie Hendrix, Experience Hendrix, and Authentic Hendrix oversee Jimi's legacy on a worldwide basis.

## EDDIE KRAMER | recording engineer, producer

"I was very fortunate to work with James Marshall Hendrix. I find when I do interviews I thank God I was able to work with a man like that, because he changed my life and many other people's lives. He was the greatest.

"I think it's the purity, the fact that there's this amazing dynamic all rolled up into one human being. There is the amazing presence. I can just say that whenever Jimi walked into a room, you had to turn your head. Because you felt you were in the presence of something quite unusual. And he had this way of commanding attention without commanding attention. His demeanor was so shy and self-effacing. He just sat there in a corner, but people were attracted to him. It's like magnetism. You have that aspect, which is the shy, wonderful, soft-spoken human being who at the turn of a switch as soon as he got on stage became this otherworldly being who could unleash gobs of power and lighting bolts at you. I think that's one aspect.

"Then you dive into all the other aspects, which, of course, is the music. This synergy or synthesis, if you will, of all of the bits and pieces of information that had flooded his brain. Whether it's blues, rock, pop, R&B, classical, and the sound of dropping out of an airplane when he did his parachuting.

"I think it's that auditory sponge-like brain that would take everything in with no filtering and probably would sit there for a day or two or three, or a month, or a year, whatever, and out of it would come in the form of a song. And it's a unique thing

"When you look back at how he first started to write songs, with Chas Chandler's encouragement, and he absorbed so much. And the surprising thing is that the music is so pure and so flamboyant and descriptive–it conjures up imagery which I feel very few rock artists have come close to, and the passion and the emotion and the bareness of it.

"Listen to 'Voodoo Child,' for God's sake!"

## BOB SAY | Freakbeat Records store

"People buy the first three albums and the greatest hits. The hardcore fans buy the weird reissues that come out. But the kids, the younger people and the continuing generations, always buy the classics. As far as popular Hendrix titles collectors seek, original vinyl mono *Axis: Bold as Love*. But for the average person, they don't know or go that deep. It was a legendary record, a different mix in mono. My favorite record of his is 'Crosstown Traffic.'"

Photographer Henry Diltz painting a mural of the *Axis: Bold as Love* album cover on a wall at the Aquarius Theatre in Hollywood, January 1968.

### JOHNNY ECHOLS | songwriter and guitarist, record producer, cofounder of Love

"The Jimi Hendrix Experience didn't have the hassles Love would have as a mixed-race band. I think had he not been black, I don't think Jimi would have resonated as much. But the showmanship, and the technique, and all of the pedals and things, all of this came together in one package. And it was different.

"Jimi was black during the time when we were in the fight for civil rights. All of this was converging and there he was, larger than life. And he put all of those things together. And I think that was what it was more than anything. White audiences weren't aware and so Jimi brought that to a whole new audience. And he just opened it up.

"And another thing: Jimi was out there by himself. He was the guy. In Love, we had three guys: Arthur, Bryan MacLean, and myself. We were vying for attention up on the stage and—where Jimi didn't have to do that. He was the man. People looked at him and they came to see him, and so that in itself was different than it was with other groups.

"Had Jimi come along at a different time, he wouldn't have had near the same impact that he had. It was just the right time, when kids were just flocking to Hollywood and flocking to gatherings. Jimi was able to tap into the teenage angst, anti-war and civil rights and all of that. And he was a symbol.

"That is another reason why Jimi is so popular. Jimi also popularized the Fender Stratocaster. Jimi's sound evolved, especially when he incorporated effects. And he was able to take all of those confluences and put them together and make a package. And that package was Jimi Hendrix, and he was larger than life. Jimi's emergence was a confluence of circumstances, and it all came together, and it was like all the stars just lined up in his favor."

### PATTI SMITH | singer-songwriter, musician, and author

"Radio used to be a cultural base. . . . A deejay would talk about how fucked up Vietnam was and then play Jimi Hendrix, the Rolling Stones, but then maybe play some Billie Holliday. You'd hear a Coltrane song, and then maybe a Rolling Stones song, then you'd hear Nirvana, My Bloody Valentine, you might hear Robert Johnson, all of our music. Not just one thing. And even the best pop. Songs that make you feel good. You could hear 'Good Vibrations,' 'Manic Depression,' and whatever. *Electric Ladyland* would always be on it. There's always going to be Coltrane on it. There's always going to be *Electric Ladyland* on it, without a doubt."

Patti Smith, in Long Beach, California, 1995.

**DANIEL WEIZMANN** | writer, music historian

"My brother Moshe gave me *Electric Ladyland* on wax for my fifteenth birthday, during the height of LA's Paisley Underground, when I was stuck on the Byrds, Love, and the Seeds. He said, 'You need this, Danny, since I know you'll never buy anything this cool for yourself.' Of course, he was right.

"The best Hendrix illustration I can think of is his treatment of 'Hey Joe.' Nobody's 100 percent sure who wrote the song—some say it's a traditional—but it was registered in '62 by Billy Roberts, a folksinger on the Cali coffeehouse circuit. But it quickly became a staple of every third band on the Sunset Strip, with versions recorded by the Leaves, the Standells, the Surfaris, Love, the Music Machine, and the Byrds, all inside the heady twenty-four months of '65–'66. Listened to back-to-back, they range from poppy to punky to herky-jerky to countrified . . . but they are more similar than not, and they never overheat.

"Now here comes Jimi, stepping into the studio on October 23, 1966, at De Lane Lea in London to tackle the beast. I don't have to tell you the rest, 'cause you already know it. His 'Joe' swaggers, burrows into the groove, and builds to a frenzy that's erotic, passionate, anguished, and at once heavier and yet lighter on its feet than all the other versions. Incredibly, he somehow manages to 'return' the blues to a John Lee Hooker Delta deepness, and yet shoot it into outer space at the same time. That's the Hendrix magic.

"I think Jimi's voice is a cornerstone of his art, a savvy and unusual approach. He brings an attitude, a cadence, and a tone that helps frame and even beautify the greatest electric guitar playing ever recorded.

"To understand the vocal choices Jimi made, you first have to dig what he chose not to do. Jimi rarely wailed, growled, or went for 'long yardage' and high emotion like so many bluesmen of the day, black or white. In the rock world, where he was frequently the sole African American onstage, he never did traditional 'Soul with a capital S' and he didn't even 'rock' vocally the way, say, a Robert Plant might be known to rock—to throw his guts into the notes.

"On the best jams—especially live stuff like 'Foxy Lady' at Miami Pop, 'Hear My Train a Comin'' at Fillmore East—there's an almost rabbinic incantation to his voice, simple but mesmerizing. He simply refuses to gild the melody's lily—no mean feat for a guy who knows from musical elaboration."

**CELESTE GOYER** | poet

"Beethoven and the others of the European Romantic movement in the late nineteenth and early twentieth centuries believed in the transformative power of art to unite people and lift them up, in contrast to what they saw as the alienating effects of increasing materialism and the advances of mechanistic science. And here's William Blake: 'The Imagination is not a State: it is the Human Existence Itself.'

"This thread leads from Wagner and Goethe to Karlheinz Stockhausen, whose invention of intuitive music was designed to create holes in consciousness through which divine inspiration could enter.

"*Amazing Grace*, the Aretha Franklin documentary, wonderfully demonstrates the transformative function of music to bring love and community to vivid life in a place where it would be easy to despair. Think of Jimi Hendrix, part Cherokee, part black American. Does a past get any more rubbed out than that? He didn't just imagine or pray for a better future—he actively sought to bring it about with his music."

## JAMES CUSHING | poet, English professor, deejay

"I think it was [cultural critic] Pauline Kael who said somewhere in an essay [that] the only thing we ask of any artist in any genre, painting, theater, is that the artist astonish us. And Jimi Hendrix is never less than astonishing. And he still inspires us, for the same reason I want to hear every Charlie Parker, John Coltrane, Captain Beefheart, Cecil Taylor, and Miles Davis album—because these people were geniuses. And the level of genius that they have is such that everything they did was somewhat touched by it. And we learn from it. His death is tawdry and tragic. And it happened way too soon and should never have happened. But his life is well worth celebrating."

## MICHAEL DES BARRES | actor, musician

"Jimi was rare. Like a white buffalo or a blue diamond. It's because they are unique. There's nobody like them. There are many pretenders, which is perfectly reasonable. I applaud anybody who tries. I would never critique anybody for having a go. But the importance of Jimi Hendrix is like Lenny Bruce. People who came with something new, different and beautiful.

"Also, secondly, there's a premature death. Premature death is romantic, no matter in what culture you are or what age. Die young. Leaving a beautiful corpse and great solos is immortality.

"The sound that he created, he hated. Because the more he had to be Jimi Hendrix, the less he enjoyed being Jimi Hendrix."

## DEL BRECKENFELD | former director, entertainment marketing, Fender

"It's very deep for me, meeting Mitch and Noel, working with them in promotional capacities. Around 1996, Bob Hendrix and I presented Buddy Miles onstage at the

House of Blues in LA with a white Strat. We gave him the gold record of *Band of Gypsys* when it finally went gold. Buddy started crying.

"Whenever I hear Jimi, it takes me back to the moment seeing him and how unique and special it was in my world. And it also makes me really proud that he is not forgotten.

"And I feel like I know him. I met the other members and Eddie Kramer, a longtime associate, with my work with Fender and working with Janie on many projects. And I give Janie Hendrix a lot of credit for protecting his legacy."

Rich Siegle, Director of Branding at Fender Academy, explains the ad seen here: "When Jimi flipped his right-handed Stratocaster and restrung it to accommodate his left-handed style, the dynamics of the guitar changed: the individual string lengths changed with the reversed headstock, and the slanted bridge pickup put more emphasis on the low E and A strings. This Jimi Hendrix model from 2015 re-created those dynamics for the right-handed player, and Jimi's song title was the perfect analogy for the concept. The photograph used in the ad is by Gered Mankowitz."

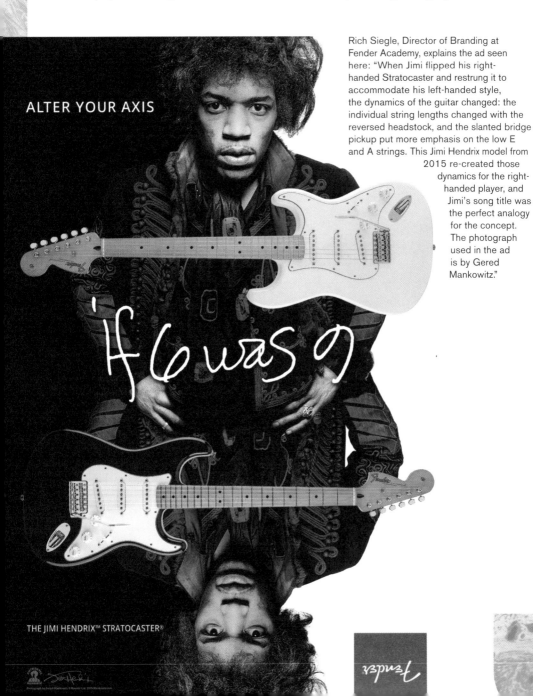

ALTER YOUR AXIS

'If 6 was 9'

THE JIMI HENDRIX™ STRATOCASTER®

Fender

Photography by Gered Mankowitz © Bowstir Ltd. 2015 Mankowitz.com

## PRESCOTT NILES | bassist, the Knack

"When Jimi died, I called Velvert Turner. We mourned the loss. Velvert was distraught. Jimi seemed so vibrant and not just a guy in a group.

"In late 1970, people in the music business started calling Velvert all of a sudden. And he asked me to fly back to New York and do music.

"People knew that Jimi had been interested in Velvert. Jimi gave Velvert a guitar, a white Strat. We cut a demo at the Record Plant. Michael Lang had Sunshine Records, a subsidiary of Paramount/Gulf and Western. It was a version of 'Freedom,' very different from Jimi's. We actually had an organ player overdub.

"We got a record deal and moved to LA. There were no copycats back then. Velvert had cred. The vibes were connecting. Then Artie Ripp came on the scene later. His Family Productions bought Sunshine Records.

"I eventually settled in Los Angeles during 1975 and went to Los Angeles City College to study electronics and doing deejay stuff. In my class was Fayne Pridgon, Jimi's true love. She knew me as Scotty.

Lithofayne "Fayne" Pridgon, on the campus of Los Angeles City College, mid-1970s.

"I had met her earlier in New York with Velvert when she was dating Jimi. She was at *Electric Ladyland* sessions. Her name and LA number is still in one of my phone books. Her nickname was Peaches."

## BILLY COX | bassist, Gypsy Sun and Rainbows, and Band of Gypsys

"Jimi knew he had something to offer to this world. He was a cosmic messenger, and his music today is just timeless, because right now I see all these young kids picking up guitars. If a periodical wants to see more copies than the previous month, they put his picture on the front cover. So his music right now reaches down through generations. It transcends cultural boundaries! Anywhere you go around the world, there are young kids with guitars and playing them. Like Beethoven, Mozart, and Handel, Jimi left one hell of a legacy.

"Jimi was bombarded a lot of time with bull crap by attorneys and management that was unnecessary for a man who was supposed to be about the music. Why does a creative individual have to go through all that bull crap? A lot of times you could see it on his face. 'What's wrong with him? Well he's worried about . . . this is goin' through his mind . . .'

"However, all in all, there were moments when he was the same guy. But Jimi became more and more a spiritual person. He knew that spiritual multiplies. It never divides. So his music just brings people together.

"Jimi and I covered a lot of ground together and had traveled many miles together. He was like a brother. And it was sad to lose one of my brothers."

Janie Hendrix, 1999.

## JANIE HENDRIX

"My dad was a man of few words, but what he said was profound when he spoke. . . and I always find myself hearing his voice. Not weirdly. The different sayings that he would say and Jimi embraced that. And he was quite shy, and when he was a kid he stuttered, so he didn't speak a whole lot. And I think that also enabled him to choose his words wisely when he did speak.

"I think that you get a very innocent and sweet, down-to-earth—almost childlike is what you see, because he always held on to that. He was fun to be around and he loved to laugh. A lot of the pictures are showing him happy. He always found that silver lining and always had fun even in the midst of even serious moments.

"I saw five concerts. And for me, I get to know Jimi more and more, better and better, as if I was there or he's still here, every day that I work with his music. Reflecting on some of things I would see when Jimi came home. Like the funny talks at the dinner table. Jimi loved my mother's chicken teriyaki. . . .

"I think technology has caught up to what Jimi visualized. I think when Jimi was creating the music he was so far ahead of the time he was already hearing that in the way we hear it now. . . .

"I just feel somebody whispered in his ear, 'You have until you're 27. Go!' He always felt like he wasn't going to live past 27. And he stated that a few times. Did an angel come by and whisper in his ear and say, 'Time's ticking. You got until you're 27 to let the world hear your music and tell your message'?

"Carlos Santana met Jimi in an elevator with Devon Wilson at Electric Lady Studios. He wanted to give Jimi a medallion to protect him when he saw that Jimi already had a mess of bling around his neck. And he thought, 'He's protected. He has enough. I'm not gonna give it to him.' And of course Jimi goes on tour and doesn't come back.

"And Carlos always felt like, 'Well, if I would have given that to him, what would have happened? Would it have protected him? Would he have come back?' And so, consequently, you know, Carlos has always been kind of a big brother in my life. He'll call me up sometimes out of the blue: 'I'm watching out for you, being that Jimi is not here.'"

**CARLOS SANTANA** | Santana

"To me, the real practicality is that some people are chosen instruments to carve a certain message, a certain mood, whatever. Not frozen but forever encapsulated and to anything that will be eternally relevant with the youngsters.

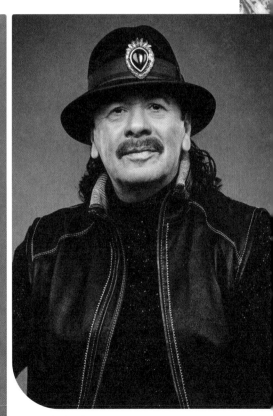

"How do you describe 'Here it comes' in one note? The doors are connected forever. You take a solo, play a few bars, and give it to somebody else. You have that awareness. When you are a musician of this caliber, you will always remain."

—Carlos Santana

Carlos Santana, 2016.

# Epilogue

Of all the creative artists whose works demand to be remembered, few communicated with more urgency than Jimi Hendrix. He landed in our midst like a subversive extraterrestrial, a nomad who tapped into a sonic fiction that took pop music many steps beyond its teenyboppish domain into the realm of the uncanny. He was a savant of the guitar, a style icon, a sociocultural touchstone who, like a refracted image in a fun-house mirror, could be seen in any guise that suited the listener. He was born to a wounded community, financially/opportunistically impoverished, and yet his success speaks to that uniquely American dream of self-actualization finding its providential reward. That he had to cross the Atlantic ("Head east, young brother") to fusty ole England to find his way back home, only italicizes the Odyssean scale of his travails.

Again and again, correspondents who spent time in his company noted his humility, his gentle manner—a bashful effacement that, with a snap of those prodigious fingers, could reanimate into an elemental force of nature. He was not alone in this weirdly disjunctive polarity; Michael Jackson, another preternatural talent, was even more extreme in his ability to transform from a silhouette into a human dynamo. As fans who obsess and crave a kind of privileged access, we nevertheless accept that this capacity to tap into a parallel life force remains forever outside our bewildered comprehension.

As much as Jimi resisted any sort of categorization, there is no gainsaying how neatly his music found common ground with "Afrofuturism," a term coined by Mark Dery in his essay "Black to the Future" (*South Atlantic Quarterly*, 1995). This is the sound of John Coltrane's *Interstellar Space*, of Sun Ra's celestial Arkestra, of George Clinton helming the P-Funk Mothership, of Miles Davis's mid-seventies metallic grooves that percolated like an alternative score to *Starship Troopers*. Jimi was right there with them, hurtling through space and time, marveling at his own impetuosity.

It is hard to resist drowning Jimi in superlatives. Greg Tate, in his book *Midnight Lightning: Jimi Hendrix and the Black Experience* (2003), describes him as "the electric guitar's Einstein if not its Edison." Another vivid analogy would be to compare him to Schrödinger's beguiling cat, a whimsical allusion to a force in the universe that conjures the sublime.

The brilliant classical pianist Stephen Hough often lends his lapidary touch to words. In *Rough Ideas: Reflections on Music and More* (2019), he writes:

> For me, great music should be able to be "heard" after it's stopped sounding. The vibrations that were created in the air of the concert hall or on the recording must be "cherishable." When we listen to music we want some element of the piece to become part of us. . . . Ultimately if we cannot take away an aura from music, however complex the piece or indefinable the emanation, I don't think the music is really worth anything.

If nothing else, this book is intended (ideally) to convey these very qualities—resonance, vibrations, aura—in the words and images of enthusiasts (from the Greek *enthousiaste*—a person inspired by god) who, decades on, continue to burn the midnight lamp in honor of James Marshall Hendrix.

**"Everyone's hourglass was running down. Everyone's but Beethoven's. As soon as you are born the sand starts falling and only by demanding to be remembered do you stand a chance of it being upturned again and again."**

—Lisa Halliday, *Asymmetry* (2018)

# Appendix I

# Jimi and Jazz—A Marriage Never Consummated

**B**ill Graham, the legendary rock music promoter, had a temperament that roiled like the currents surging under the Golden Gate Bridge, in his home port of San Francisco. He could bark louder than the stacks of Marshall amps mounted on his stage, putting the fear of his iron will into a subordinate or rival promoter, while treating his acts and audience like beloved family members at a Passover Seder. His respect for the music was most evident in his innovative booking policies, which routinely brought disparate genres together before an audience willing to grow along with the artists themselves.

As early as January 1967, just months after opening the Fillmore Auditorium in San Francisco, he booked saxophonist Charles Lloyd to perform for a crowd used to the acidic backbeats of the Airplane, the Dead, Quicksilver, and Big Brother. Lloyd's acoustic quartet, which featured the prodigiously gifted young pianist Keith Jarrett*, created a sensation; their blend of bebop, funky four-to-the-floor grooves, and voguish fashion attire—Nehru jackets and love beads supplanting the traditional jazz attire of suits and ties—caught the fancy of a mostly white,

---

*Talking to writer Edward Strickland for *Fanfare Magazine* [May/June, 1987], Jarrett recalled that "It's as though I've seen the whole spectrum of music. In the Charles Lloyd band at the Fillmore I talked to Jimi Hendrix and Janis Joplin. I was going to write some ragtime pieces for Janis and collaborate with Jimi. Then they both died."

college-aged assembly who were unlikely to have heard much serious improvisational music, let alone from a group opening for a Chicago bluesman or a trippy Bay Area jam band.

In fact, jazz, like all the liveliest arts, was going through its own revolution; the once parlous flights of Charlie "Bird" Parker and Dizzy Gillespie, of Charles Mingus and Thelonious Monk, were being superseded by a more contentious sound that echoed the post-Modernist conjuring of composers like György Ligeti, Pierre Boulez, and Karlheinz Stockhausen.

Michael Chanan articulates this shift in sound and sensibility in his book *From Handel to Hendrix: The Composer in the Public Sphere* (1999). He writes: "By the 1960s the jazz avant-garde had [created] a radical idiom every bit as abrasive—harmonically, melodically, rhythmically—as their classical counterparts. . . . Jazz players like Ornette Coleman, John Coltrane, or Archie Shepp were no less uncompromising in the demands they made on their listeners to enter new musical territory."

Jimi Hendrix was not a jazz guitarist, not in the way that Wes Montgomery or Kenny Burrell or Jim Hall were so clearly identified. He did, however, embrace their investment in improvisation that subordinated empty technical displays to an intimate emotional release. In that regard, Jimi's wailing is of a piece with Sonny Rollins blowing on the Williamsburg Bridge or a Coltrane cloudburst on any night at the Village Vanguard. Further, Jimi arrived at the exact moment when the different creative disciplines found a robust common cause: to share their talents and strategies before a community eager to soak up the spillover. Warhol designed album covers for Monk and others; Jack Kerouac riffed over edgy, major-minor modes; Jackson Pollock and the Abstract Expressionists met their match in the rhythmic splatter of Cecil Taylor's pianistic assaults.

And then there was Miles Davis, his eyes and ears locked and loaded, alert to the next new thing to arrive. He once answered a fan who complained that his music was moving too fast for his taste: "Should I wait for you, motherfucker?" Miles' girlfriend was "Mademoiselle Mabry," Betty Mabry, a sultry young singer whose blend of funk and R&B put the *x* in *foxy*. She was hip to James Brown and Sly Stone, and to Jimi Hendrix, who shared her love of flamboyant clothes, hair, and attitude. If Miles was mapping new directions in music, it was Mabry who served as his chief surveyor.

Miles was going electric, not only to stay au courant, but to reach a wider audience. Tired of working the jazz club circuit, he was keen to reach the exploding white rock audience, accepting engagements at the Fillmore, opening for crossover acts like Blood, Sweat, and Tears at Madison Square Garden. His backing musicians, a mix of blacks and whites who'd come of age under the influence of the Beatles as much as of their jazz heroes, were equally excited about Jimi Hendrix.

Drummer Tony Williams told Pat Cox of *Downbeat Magazine* (May 28, 1970) about his desire to expand his musical horizons:

> I had played with everybody I had wanted to play with . . . Then I started feeling, well, there's got to be something else, because John Coltrane left such an impression—on not only the jazz scene, but the whole music scene with what his band produced . . . At this time, something started filtering in. I started hearing a lot of electricity. The first thing I can remember . . . was Jimi Hendrix's first record, and the sound of it . . . the amplified electricity, the sound of the guitars, and that started to excite me and I wanted to hear more of that.

Miles was listening closely as well; he told *Rolling Stone* in December 1969, "White groups don't reach me. I can tell a white group just from the sound, don't have to see them. . . . All the white groups have got a lot of hair and funny clothes . . . they got to have on that shit to get it across. Some of the white groups are nice . . . [but] Jimi Hendrix can take two white guys and make them play their asses off."

It wasn't only Jimi's persona that captured Davis's attention—it was his sound. In his 1989 autobiography, Davis wrote:

> I was getting away from using a lot of solos in my group sound, moving more toward an ensemble thing, like the funk and rock bands. . . . By now I was using wah-wah on my trumpet all the time so I could get closer to the voice Jimi had when he used a wah-wah on his guitar. I had always played trumpet like a guitar and the wah-wah just made the sound closer.

Other members of Miles's group were connecting with Jimi too. Guitarist John McLaughlin had been a top session musician in London before relocating to the

States. He'd been aware of Jimi's impact at home and would later, in New York, finally connect with him. The results of their brief encounter—just a jam—have tantalized fans for years. But nothing of real value ever surfaced; a missed opportunity perhaps, or a prelude to something grander, if only . . .

The fans, the players, and even the music industry were buzzing at the prospect of a Miles/Hendrix collaboration. It seemed inevitable, these two icons charging into each other's proximity like twin star systems. The July 1970 Randall's Island Pop Festival featured Jimi, and promised a guest appearance by Miles with Tony Williams' group with jazz guitarist John McLaughlin, Lifetime. Miles, true to form, canceled. Two months later, the curtain closed for good.

Author Colin Harper, in his book *Bathed in Lightning: John McLaughlin, the '60s and the Emerald Beyond* (2014), examines the torturous history that scuttled the prospect of a Jimi and Miles musical summit:

> There was at one point an arrangement between Jimi Hendrix's people and Miles Davis (with Tony Williams also scheduled) for a joint recording. Miles, on the day of the session, phoned, requiring $50,000 up front. Hendrix producer Alan Douglas has said that Tony Williams, when he heard that Miles had asked for this, phoned to demand the same sum. Obviously, the session was canceled. Nevertheless, a session involving Hendrix and Miles' favored arranger, Gil Evans—with Miles likely to be involved—was due to take place shortly after Jimi died, in September 1970.

In Harper's *Bathed in Lightning*, John McLaughlin discusses Coltrane, Jimi, and Miles:

> We were all looking for new tones on the guitar. I was bored with this kind of jazz guitar tone, you know. I was listening to Coltrane, and he was breaking the barriers of sound. And Jimi came, and he too started to break the barriers of sound. Jimi had an influence on me like he had on everybody else.
>
> I remember taking Miles to see Jimi on the *Monterey Pop* film. Miles had never seen him [playing] before and couldn't believe it.

Jazz guitarist and composer John McLaughlin playing electric guitar at the 50th anniversary Monterey Jazz Festival, Monterey, California September 21, 2007.

**Gil Evans (jazz pianist, arranger, composer):** "We were talking about doing a guitar album . . . all new material. I was supposed to meet him on Monday, but he died on Friday. It was the big shock of my life."

Evans would go on to record several albums featuring Jimi's compositions, including some richly evocative arrangements for Sting's Hendrix tribute.

**James Newton (composer, flutist, professor of jazz studies):** "In 2017, I taught a class on Hendrix at UCLA ETHNMUS C 165 – *Selected Topics on Composition: Jimi Hendrix* and the students were profoundly invested in the music. There was a level of excitement that left me incredulous, like I'm getting paid to teach this! We had ethnomusicologists breaking down Jimi's historical context. We had composition majors write original music based on their interpretations of Jimi's work. In essence, we built a class around Jimi's own approach to the creative process. We delved deeply into each album, each grouping, country and urban blues.

"Let's consider Jimi's rhythm section: Mitch Mitchell was a jazz drummer and had his own unique connection to a 'black' sound. He loved Elvin Jones. He was, like so many of his fellow English musicians, steeped in American blues and was deeply respectful of any opportunity to play authentic black music. Let's break down a particular tune: 'House Burning Down.' The bass and guitar accompaniment melds with the rhythmic groove and you end up with a tango—who was doing that in rock at that time?! And check out the 'floating quality' in '(Have You Ever Been to) Electric Ladyland.' When Hendrix hits the guitar three times to establish the tempo I'm thinking, 'Okay, it's in 3 but it's not really—most people hear it in 4/4.' Again, a polyrhythm is established, which is not something you hear in pop music, then or now. It's Mitch channeling Elvin. 'If 6 Was 9' has sections where Mitch is playing straight time but other moments when it feels free.

"Let's take it in a different direction. Hendrix saw the blues as a spaceship; he was a master of country blues, not just urban blues. 'Machine Gun' is a perfect example of moving the blues into the future. John Coltrane was moving back and forth between spirituals and the blues. Jimi follows in that tradition. And it's the biggest reason for explaining his enormous influence on Miles Davis, an influence eclipsed only by [that of] Charlie Parker.

"There was a vital connection between them. Consider 'Mademoiselle Mabry' [from *Filles de Kilimanjaro*] and 'The Wind Cries Mary.' There's a chromatic lick at the beginning they both share. And they also share a link with Ms. Mabry herself. Betty Mabry was a young funk goddess who never got the credit for turning Miles on to Jimi, Sly, James Brown, and moving his sound in that electric direction. There was a lot of fluidity in this scene. And by 1970, there was a huge

James Newton, composer, flutist, and distinguished professor, composition jazz studies at UCLA's Herb Alpert School of Music, 2018.

shift in the language of jazz, going electric. It's not unlike the time two decades earlier when Parker and Dizzy and Max Roach and Bud Powell introduced their lexicon into jazz. Jimi brings a blues foundation and sonic vocabulary, which was a perfect analog for the time. Miles had to embrace those changes because he wanted to remain on the cutting edge.

"Think of the company he kept during that time: artists, politicians, athletes. Miles was always at the center of whatever was happening, and now he's turning to Jimi. He's playing the Fillmore, opening for major rock bands, appearing on the cover of *Rolling Stone*.

"No other jazz musician has the temerity to command this kind of attention. This was a man from an upper-middle-class black family, comfortable in a sharp Brooks Brothers suit, looking to Jimi for fashion statements. It's what great artists do; they look around the contemporary environment, take what they need, and make their mark.

"Let's focus on why jazz musicians listen to Hendrix. Take the cut '(Have You Ever Been to) Electric Ladyland'—it is so sophisticated. Hendrix is borrowing Curtis Mayfield's falsetto to carry the melodic material; Mitch Mitchell is in lockstep with Jimi's bass line; the timbre is unlike anything else happening in pop, R&B, blues, even serious composition.

"A jazz player is going to listen to that cut and be breathless. Jimi found a perfect balance between complexity and approachability."

# Appendix II
# Room Full of Gear

Leo Fender's ambitions were modest when he introduced his first electric guitar in 1949. He was trying to eliminate the nuisance of feedback that was characteristic of the then popular hollow-bodied guitars. His initial attempt morphed into what would become the Telecaster, a caduceus with six wings and a design as all-American as the Louisville Slugger and the Coca-Cola bottle, form and function melding in perfect harmony.

But it was Fender's next iteration that would set the guitar world on fire. Leo was preoccupied with the process of getting it right; there was always more tweaking, refining, fine-tuning. And so, after the launch of the Telecaster, he began anew, with an artisan's eye for symmetry, to sculpt a piece of wood into a life-force whose balance and aesthetic flair would rival an Olympic gymnast's effortless mastery. Debuting in 1954, the "Stratocaster" was, according to Fender's accompanying press release, "comfort contoured," an "electric Spanish guitar—with or without built in tremolo." In almost giddy tones, it highlights a body design that "is shaped in such a way that, in reality, it would become part of the player and is the most comfortable instrument to play ever to be made." It was as if Fender had built it with one person in mind—another obsessive whose search for the right instrument to realize the music of his mind would make his name synonymous with the Stratocaster itself.

Just thinking about Jimi Hendrix's gear—the legion of Strats, battered and bruised like infantry in full retreat; the mountains of Marshalls, as hulking and indomitable as Russian tanks on the plains of Kursk; the slinky effect devices that could change the course of the music with a single stomp— induces vertigo. Make no mistake: outfitting Jimi onstage was like going to war. He treated all his equipment with ruthless dispatch. According to his equipment manager, Eric Barrett, he carried as many as thirteen Strats on tour, "between a dozen and eighteen [Marshall amp] tops, and box upon box of speakers, which had to be changed daily after Jimi tore through them with his guitar. The grill cloth, however, was left hanging." And don't forget the two dozen Fuzz Faces, at least a dozen Univibes, and two dozen wah-wah pedals.

Manufacturers were desperate to align with him, and he, in turn, was open to any and all overtures. Sunn Amplifiers worked tirelessly to obtain his endorsement; Noel Redding quite liked their product, but Jimi demurred. He ultimately returned to the Marshall fold, confident in their amps' power and durability. This pairing with the Strat, like Thor with his hammer, came to epitomize the rock guitarist as a totemic god. Ironically, although Leo Fender's quest was to limit feedback, that bane of most early electric guitarists, feedback would become Jimi's most enduring sonic signature.

**Del Breckenfeld (former director, entertainment marketing, Fender):** "I knew Leo Fender, and his wife Phyllis said that 'Leo thought of the guitars as his children. When they went out they were his children.' There's a quote she has about Leo admiring Jimi Hendrix's technical skills, that he was innovative with how he used his guitars left-handed. Privately Leo was not happy about Jimi smashing Stratocasters or setting fire on them. Those guitars were his babies. Leo spent all his time making high-quality musical instruments, and he always treated the guitars with tender care and respect.

"Jimi had a Jazzmaster guitar when he played with King Curtis. When he played live, the Strat was it. There's a tape where he is talking to an engineer or a tech: 'Hey, you get me a guitar? Get me a Fender Strat 'cause that's the only thing I ever play.' Jimi still used the Showman amps on some of his great recordings done at Electric Lady.

"George Fullerton was a longtime associate of Leo at Fender [Leo founded Fender in Fullerton, California, in 1946]. They had G&L Musical Instruments along with Dale Hyatt going back to the late forties. George was very involved with designing the solid-body Telecaster electric guitar. . . .

"I asked George, 'What did you tell artists back in the day, the early sixties?' 'We just listened.'"

**Richard Bosworth (record producer, engineer):** "Hendrix's awareness of and interaction with Dick Dale also influenced his choosing the Stratocaster. He picked up a lot of stuff from Dick Dale's playing style. The powerful sound, the double picking and the wild sound effects that Dale got, and the fact that they were both left-handed. Dick told me about hanging out with Hendrix and showing him some technique and sound stuff.

"I'm sure Jimi was aware of the amp Dick used, the original blonde Fender Showman JBL D130 15" single speaker with the very special 'tone ring' cabinet that Leo Fender designed at Dick's request. Keyboardist Mike Finnegan confirms that was the exact amp and cabinet Jimi used on 'Rainy Day, Dream Away.'"

**Michael Bloomfield (guitarist):** "Somehow by tapping the back of his guitar neck (which he constantly did) and by using the [tremolo] bar, Jimi could control feedback. You would hear a rumbling start—he knew which note would feed back and what harmonic he was shooting for, and then he controlled it. Somehow, when he

An ad for V. C. Squier's Esquier guitar strings—used by Fender—featuring Jimi Hendrix, from a 1968 *Fender Album of Stars* promotional magazine.

had all the notes open, he would raise the pitch level by using the bar and he'd get a higher note to feed back, or he would make the bass note feed back harmonically.

He was listening for such things, and I believe he heard them on the English records, particularly by the Yardbirds and Jeff Beck. He was very modest. . . . He said, 'I fool with it, and what I'm doing now is the fruits of my fooling around.'"

**Frank Orlando (guitarist and music teacher):** "I saw the Jimi Hendrix Experience in San Diego at Balboa Stadium [in] 1968. Jimi's relationship to Fender guitars and why he used it over a lot of the other choices was based on some of the unique characteristics of the Strat. Strap it around your neck and play for an hour or more. There's an ease with that instrument that eclipses a Gibson Les Paul, which is a lot heavier. The Stratocaster also lent itself a bit more to the theatrics he employed because it was lighter.

"In addition, his playing style would not have been accommodated by a guitar other than the Strat. It had a longer scale. The string length between bridge and the nut was slightly longer, at twenty-five inches, than [that of] many of the other brands and Fender models. Because they're longer, there's more tension and less problems with string buzz.

"Hendrix did not use the normal string gauge that other guitar players generally used. He pitched the guitar a half step lower, meaning that if the guitar low string is an E, he would tune it down to E flat. So it's lower and heavier. Also, he would also use smaller gauge strings on the three lower strings. With the extra length, things were not getting quite as muddy. The Stratocaster before Jimi started playing it wasn't a top-of-the-line Fender. Hendrix popularized the model.

"Jimi was playing it left-handed. His playing style allowed him to use his thumb to play bass notes and his fingers to play things that legitimately could give you the impression that there were two guys playing at the same time. Some of it had to do with the size of his hands. A lot of it had to do with the fact that the fingerboard of the Stratocaster is curved. The Les Paul is a little more flat."

Randy Holden was a noted guitarist around LA in the late sixties when he was offered the gig to replace Leigh Stephens in the wicked-loud power trio Blue Cheer. He'd tasted some success, having recorded singles for Imperial Records, performed with popular Sunset Strip regulars the Sons of Adam, and cut an album with the Other Half, who worked the ballroom circuit in San Francisco. Joining Blue Cheer looked great on paper: a chance to tour, to record, to get a bump up to the big time.

He did, however, earn distinction for routinely detonating a Hadrian's Wall of Sunn amplifiers whenever he hit the stage, which was no small accomplishment.

On April 30, 1970, Randy met Hendrix backstage at the Forum, while Jimi was on tour with Mitch Mitchell and Billy Cox. Through a mutual friend, Holden was given the rare opportunity to examine one of Jimi's Strats up close.

In the summer 2019 issue 51 of *Ugly Things* magazine, Randy shared his observations in an article written by Mike Stax and Eliot Kissileff:

> It was his sound. Listening to me play a couple of his songs on it, you wouldn't have been able to tell it was me playing if you were in another room. I was pretty freaked out about it, wanting to know what on Earth had been done with it to make it sound like that. A friend told me that Jimi's guitar tech did a little wiring trick where he soldered in line a capacitor, or a resistor, between the pickup and the output jack. The effect was to reduce the output of the guitar, which allowed more of the natural sound of the wood of the unplugged guitar to pass through to the amp. Stratocasters have a kind of natural bell-like tone when playing unplugged, and you heard that through the amp. Instantly I realized what he was doing. It quieted the electrical power of the guitar, and let him push up the volume of the amp, allowing it to sustain more.
>
> Years later I learned an old school guitarist, Roy Buchanan, was the guy who came up with the idea," added Holden in *Ugly Things*.
>
> Jimi asked him how he got the sound he had, and he showed Jimi how he did it and what he did, and Jimi used that from then on. Roy used to use reverb to get sustain, but he wanted to push the amp harder to get it, and you needed volume from the amp to do that, but there was too much volume coming from the guitar, so he cut the guitar volume of the guitar by putting a resistor in line between pickup and output. That kind of blew me away to learn it was Roy's idea. It was a damn brilliant idea, and super

smart by Jimi to use it. When going through the new Marshall Amps, that only Cream and Hendrix had at the time, with those amps and that wiring trick, the sound was like nothing ever done, or heard before.

Guitarist, producer, and engineer Glen Laughlin, 2014.

**Glen Laughlin (guitarist, producer, engineer):** "In the early days, Hendrix played through Sound City amplifiers. Designed by Dave Reeves, they were the precursors to Hiwatt Amplifiers. The Who was also a famous patron of both marques. Both Hiwatt and the original Sound City amps were notable for blistering volume, but were extremely efficient or 'clean' amps, meaning that even at high volumes the amps operated with little overt distortion. I think most informed technicians would agree that these amps were extremely well designed. Listening to Hendrix's version of 'Hey Joe,' you will note that he does not rely on effects, feedback, or distortion. The guitar sound is notable for the exquisite responsive and evocative tone, clean and unaffected. When employing fuzz, Octavia, wah-wah, Univibe (electronic simulation of a rotating Leslie organ speaker), or other effects Hendrix regularly employed, it seems unnecessary to overdrive the amplifier. Doing so, in my experience, actually diminishes or obscures the effects.

"Hendrix moved on from Sound City and Hiwatt to Marshalls. These early examples were crudely made and did not have safeguards that later models did. The impedance selectors were inferior, and the internal components were not made of spring steel. With use over time, the poor contacts would cause the output transformer to fail. It also seems likely that additional cabinets were added to the famed 'Marshall stacks,' which changed the impedance and made the rig even more unstable, especially if the impedance selector was not positioned correctly. The early Marshalls were also prone to radio interference and audiences were sometimes treated to impromptu hits of the day. The Fender amps that Hendrix also used were more stable, but under the conditions on the road were hardly impervious to some of the same issues. I can only imagine that fuzz boxes and the like, notorious for radio interference, added to the problem."

Michel Delville, Belgian musician and professor of literature at the University of Liège, 2014; one of his bands is Machine Mass.

**Michel Delville (guitarist, professor of literature at the University of Liège):** "What I find fascinating is Jimi's use of effects and the influence it had on the development of the band's aesthetics. *Are You Experienced?* appeared in 1967, at a time when the Octavia and the Fuzz Face were only beginning to be used by a

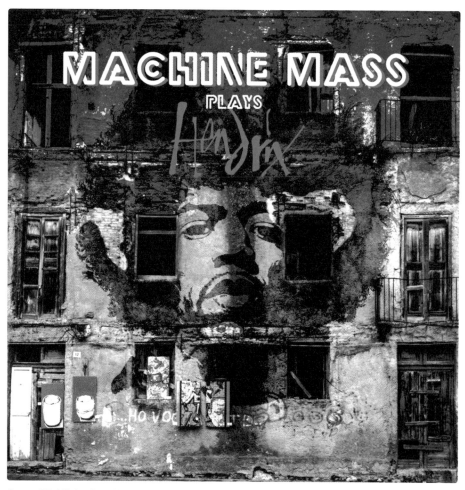

Cover of Delville's album *Machine Mass Plays Hendrix* (2017).

handful of musicians. The sheer feeling of discovering the gear must have been so exciting—not being influenced by a tradition or preexisting models, but taking risks, relishing in discovering the unschooled pleasures and possibilities of making the guitar sound like a machine gun or a hurricane, or a wind instrument, or the human voice. And, of course, his use of the wah-wah—whose first prototypes were built a year or so before the release of *Are You Experienced?* was hugely influential on me—his solos invariably tell a good, gripping story but always tell it at a slant, through artful patterns and seamless transitions. His use of feedback also remains a huge influence to the extent that he never used feedback as an end in itself but with a view to creating interesting and hitherto unheard harmonics on the electric guitar.

"Jimi's style is mercurial, and not just in a metaphorical sense: if you try to emulate it, it'll slip through your fingers. I mean Stevie Ray Vaughan sounded great and so do many later Hendrix impersonators, but to bring something new to his repertoire, to approach it from a different angle, is an altogether different affair. I think it's because it's intimidating, which is probably why I did not attempt a Hendrix 'tribute' until I was in my late forties. Jimi's music is sacred to many musicians, but that shouldn't be an obstacle to re-readings and revisitations of his works.

"What we attempted with *Machine Mass Plays Hendrix* was to rethink the power trio format (using a keyboard player rather than a bass player), deconstructing the structures of the original songs, and using the familiar themes and riffs as building blocks for groovy improvs. It's like the Doors or maybe the early Soft Machine playing Hendrix while listening to Coltrane! Again, it'd be pointless to try and reproduce the sonic textures of the original recordings—what one can do instead is to emulate the spirit of adventure, the experimental attitude which characterized the Experience by using contemporary effects and instruments."

**Hugh Banton (organist, Van der Graaf Generator):** "Sonic explorations—frankly, everybody was at it by the late sixties, great fun to be had! 'Fuzz' had started turning up on just a handful of records—i.e. "Keep on Running," "Satisfaction," fuzz-bass on the Beatles' 'Think for Yourself'—and at the time most such effects were studio generated. Enterprising engineers at Abbey Road with soldering irons and time on their hands, no doubt. Tape phasing and backwards recording were also very much in fashion; I found it all completely fascinating.

"Compact battery-powered effects were a new thing in the late sixties; before that I can only recall various echo machines, mostly tape based. It was only around this time that there was the beginning of a shift from tube-based equipment to transistors, although guitarists have understandably continued to favor the former to this day. From '66 onwards fuzz boxes began to appear in shops, swiftly followed by the wah pedal, then octave dividers, phasers, chorus, etc. etc. Applying my engineering background (my other hobby), I was able to totally customize my VdGG organ by using all this stuff, often building circuits myself.

"Many talk endlessly about Jimi's 'sound,' the distortion and the effects, but to me it's more what you find in, say, 'Little Wing'—that amazing detail in his expression and phrasing. Where most would simply play straight chords, he constantly reels off cascades of licks and passing notes, musical manna from heaven. His extraordinary fluidity was immediately evident in that very first live performance of 'Hey Joe' on TV. As on the record, the guitar sound is pretty clean (except where he turns it up to 11 for the behind-the-head solo) and again, in every bar of the song the guitar part is full of detail and added phrases. It's a mystery how he could produce this amount of complexity and sing at the same time—a phenomenal ability.

"The 8-string Hagstrom basses that Jimi and Noel played on *Axis* also became a fascination to me when the album was released. I think they're only on a couple of tracks—'You've Got Me Floating' and 'Spanish Castle Magic,' if memory serves. I bought myself a 10-string (yer 5-string bassist's equivalent) a few years back; it's a bit unwieldy to play but makes that same sound. I remain a frustrated guitarist!"

**John Etheridge (guitarist, Soft Machine):** "When I first saw Hendrix he would have used the Stratocaster, Marshall 100-watt amp with two 4×12 cabinets (the Pete Townshend setup). Marshalls were completely unavailable in the USA—so this would have completely liberated his sound (check out the Isley Brothers with JH video, where he has a very jangly American sound).

"He also had the Fuzz Face and the wah. By the time I saw him in Sweden, he would have had the Univibe (maybe!), which was an essential ingredient of his mature sound. The other thing which was very novel was the use of what was called at the time the "tremolo arm" (whammy bar). This had been used extensively by Hank Marvin of the Shadows as a substitute for finger vibrato, but since then had dropped off most guitars at the time (Eric [Clapton], Jeff Beck, Pete Townshend would have eschewed it). Hendrix obviously used it in a completely expressionistic way, and this may have ended up as one of his major legacies.

"As far as copping licks, etc. . . . Well, I had made up my mind when seeing Eric that I wasn't going to copy that (as devastating as it was), which is why I was so aggravated by the blatant imitation that went on—only Steve Howe, Albert Lee, Robert Fripp, [and] Pete Banks seemed to be able to keep on their paths.

"But the inspiration is always with me—probably more so than ever. With the Soft Machine I've become very interested in sonic exploration, pedals, etc. So over the last few years I'd say the influence has been greater.

"Hendrix was a great sitter-in and I know a lot of guys who had jam session brushes with him and speak of his generosity and open-mindedness.

"The last time I saw Jimi live was in summer '67 at Gröna Lund in Stockholm. He was already beginning to drop the exuberant antics, but the guitar sound and playing was really deep and penetrating—this was the mature Hendrix."

**Nels Cline (guitarist, Wilco):** "When *Are You Experienced?* was released, my twin brother (and drummer already) Alex and I were already fully obsessed with music, with rock 'n' roll, and particularly with all things 'psychedelic.' We spent every cent of our allowance on records, starting with 7" 45s, then stepping up to LPs. This was before so-called 'underground FM' radio (which ultimately meant KPPC in Los Angeles where we grew up), so the only way we heard records then was on 'top 30' radio or by just rolling the dice and risking getting a really cool-looking record that often had only a couple of decent tracks on it.

Wilco guitarist Nels Cline performing at the Chicago Theatre, February 23, 2017.

"Since we had been burned a couple of times in such a manner, we were cautious when first seeing *Are You Experienced?* in record and department stores, even though we agreed that it looked like it might be one of the coolest records of all time. That fish-eye band photo! That eyeball jacket! That hair! A black guy! . . . The only other record cover offering as much radical visual coolness/wildness at the time was *Freak Out!* by the Mothers of Invention, and as a double album priced at $5.49, it was too expensive. We spent two weeks' allowance on a record every two weeks, and I guess three weeks was just an impossibly agonizing wait.

"Anyway, one Saturday afternoon while Alex and I were sitting around the Garrard hi-fi listening to 93 KHJ (AM), 'Manic Depression' came on. We looked at each other a few seconds into it and actually started jumping up and down and shouting, 'This is that Jimi Hendrix record!' We could tell it was a black guy singing and, crucially, that it was a trio offering up absolutely the most exciting music/guitar playing/drumming we had ever heard! When the legendary ascending melody that Jimi sings wordlessly along with his guitar happened and catapulted me into that ripping guitar solo, my whole body felt like it was being zapped by powerful-yet-benign electricity and—no lie—I decided then and there to play guitar and participate in the creation of music for the rest of my life.

"The legacy of Jimi Hendrix lives on. Guitar magazines seem to stay solvent just by putting him on their cover once or twice a year, even now. His career was tragically brief, his impact massively huge. Plenty of words have been uttered, perhaps most often about his virtuosic and charismatic performances, his 'shredding.' I would just like to mention that yes, Jimi Hendrix remains one [of] the most exciting and visionary guitarists in history but, additionally, he was a sonic visionary, an innovator, and a marvelous songwriter. From the psychedelic overwhelm of 'Third Stone from the Sun' and 'Are You Experienced' (the song), Jimi expanded his writing and sonic innovations on *Axis: Bold as Love* and into what I may call his masterwork, *Electric Ladyland*.

"It is this sonic artistry coupled with exciting playing that catapulted me into the magic of sound, to the guitar, to my own artistic aspirations. I never tried to play like Jimi Hendrix. Well, decades after absorbing Jimi's many recordings and bootlegs, some of his sound and approach started to sort of leak out occasionally! But back then? No way. He seemed like a magician, a shaman, an ascended master.

"If one reads a book called *Starting at Zero,* which compiles Jimi's letters and diary entries chronologically until his death, one gets a real picture of a young man being sucked dry, drained by constant touring, by adulation, by the business side of things. He also felt that a voodoo priestess had cursed him. The sense of pure fatigue and creative stagnation is palpable, and I personally have always felt it in the posthumously released recordings, though of course they do offer up some wonders—mostly wistful ones like 'Angel,' 'Drifting,' 'Belly Button Window.' I have often felt a deep ache, a sadness, when listening to some of these recordings, to bootlegs wherein Jimi's vocals sound tired and/or half-hearted while he is just trying to keep his guitar in tune as he pushes it to the limits of its capabilities. In these moments I return to his first three albums and feel that energy and creative vision and I am at peace—at peace while also stimulated, excited, and inspired, much as I was upon hearing 'Manic Depression' on the radio fifty years ago. I have never been the same since that afternoon."

**Del Breckenfeld:** "My daughter Holly Quirk runs the biggest School of Rock in the world in Chicago. Jimi Hendrix is the number one artist that kids fourteen to eighteen emulate. And it's not just his playing. It's the whole package. He was an innovator. They know about him from YouTube and are not nostalgic on vinyl, because they don't remember it. They love analog. They are a digital world. They want soul. They want to listen to the records in the order they came out, so that they can see or hear the evolution. He was still innovating at his death.

"My daughter told me that Jimi Hendrix is by far the number one artist at the School of Rock—and 40 percent of the students are young girls, by the way, we're not talking about guys. And her word is that they are going to emulate him. That makes me proud."

# Acknowledgments

Harvey Kubernik and Kenneth Kubernik would like to give special thanks to the team at Sterling Publishing, especially executive editor Barbara Berger, who had the courage to initiate the expedition; we are also grateful as well for her ongoing support and guidance. Photo editor Linda Liang was particularly sensitive to the images and artifacts that informed the undertaking. We also thank cover designer Igor Satanovsky and interior designer Gavin Montnyk for the stunning psychedelic designs. Kubernik kudos to other associates at Sterling: production editors Scott Amerman and Michael Cea; production manager Ellen Hudson; and line editor Joanie Eppinga.

Harvey is extremely grateful to the Lou Brockian–like efforts and technical contributions of my archivist and photo librarian Gary Strobl, who hit for the cycle; his Gemini brother Greg; and musician/photographer Henry Diltz for the groovy environment at his studio.

The mission continues.

Our destination point was further aided and enriched by Jimi, Mitch, and Noel. Also by Travis and Judy Pike at Otherworld Cottage Industries, Chris Darrow, Andrew Loog Oldham, Daniel Weizmann, Rodney Bingenheimer, Gary Pig Gold, Andrew Solt and SOFA Entertainment, Dr. David B. Wolfe, Jim Kaplan at *Record Collector News* magazine, Andy Morten at *Shindig!* magazine, Mike Stax at *Ugly Things* magazine, Micky Dolenz, Ed Caraeff, Peter Piper, Arthur Lee, Johnny Echols, Ron Lando, Elliot Kendall and Crystal Ann Lea, Del Breckenfeld, Cindy Kona, David A. Barmack, Gary Schneider, David Carr, Gary Stewart, Nancy Rose Retchin, Ram Dass, Harry E. Northup and Holly Prado, Dr. James Cushing and Celeste Goyer, Jim and Brandon Salzer, David Leaf, Russ Regan, Joe Smith, Bob Merlis at M.f.h., Janie Hendrix, Eddie Kramer, Billy Cox, Paul Tarnopol, John Van Hamersveld and Alina Post, Dennis Loren, Laura Grimshaw, Ken Voss and the Voodoo Child website at the Jimi Hendrix Information Management Institute, Hal Blaine, Richard Williams, D. A. Pennebaker, Michael Hacker, Jeff Gold at Record Mecca, Ken Resser, Steven Gaydos, Richard Bosworth, Alex Del Zoppo, Steve Bailey at Hummingbird Media, Elizabeth Darrow Jones, Joel Selvin, Marko Budgyk, Frazer Pennebaker, Jim and Cynthia Keltner, Stephen J. Kalinich, Nik Venet, Dan Bourgoise, Brian Young, Mark Bentley, Todd Thompson, Martin Lewis, Bob "Deacon" Kushner, Jan Alan Henderson, Keith, Michael Macdonald, David N. Pepperell, Larry LeBlanc, Leslie Ann-Coles, Danny Eccleston at *MOJO* magazine, Michael Jensen at Jensen Communications, Paramahansa Yogananda, Krishnamurti Foundation of America, Cantor Nathan Lam, Rabbi Yoshi Zweiback, Joseph McCombs, Shari Foos, Tom Cording, Randy Haecker, Maria Malta at Sony Music, Leonard Cohen, Sarah Kramer, George Harrison, Ravi Shankar, Howard Kaylan, Rebecca Baltutis, Drew Steele, Dennis Dragon, Bruce Gary, Buddy Miles, Velvert Turner, Rosemarie Patronette and Scott Stoddard, Greg

Franco, Rob Hill, Steven Van Zandt, Carol Schofield and MsMusic Productions, Lou Adler, Howard Frank, Kirk Silsbee, David Kessel at CaveHollywood.com, Roger and Mary Steffens, Gary Calamar, Jeff Brough, Clint Weiler, Mark Pucci, Michael Simmons, Jeff Goldman and Santa Monica Press, Erin Ediken, Gene Aguilera, Dan Kessel, Robert Sherman, Brian Skyra, Bill Walton, Barney Hoskyns, Ray Coleman, Roy Trakin, Jeff Gelb, Open Mynd Collectibles, Humble Harv, Real Don Steele, Jimmy Rabbitt, Jim Ladd, B. Mitchel Reed, Tom Reed, KHJ-AM, KRLA-AM, KFWB-AM, KBLA-AM, KGFJ-FM, KPPC-FM, KLOS-FM, KMET-FM, Dwight Russ, WLAC-AM, Mike Johnson, Ben McLane, Ray Manzarek, James Douglas Morrison, Ray Davies, Pat Baker, Christopher M. Allport, Lori Lousararian at Rogers & Cowan, David Berger, Art Fleischer, Jim Roup, Miss Pamela, Eric Burdon, Carlos Santana, Chris Hillman, Eva Leaf, Jam, Inc., Robby Krieger, Lonn Friend, Jeanne Mar, Next Level CBD, Brian Jones, Guy Webster, Merry Webster, Drew Evans, Lisa Gizara, The Dark Bob, Laurette Hayden, Scott Aitkin, Bob Say at Freakbeat Records, Bob Say and Tom Gracyk at Freakbeat Records, Wallichs Music City, Rich Siegle at Fender, Prescott Niles, Laura Bialobos, Greg Basser and David Anton of Century City Entertainment, Mark Nardone, Janis Joplin, Sandy Robertson, Fran, Leslie, Bobby Womack, Gail, *Disc* magazine, Tim Doherty, Jim Delehant, *Hit Parader,* Keith Altham, Dolphin's of Hollywood, Flash Records, *Sports Stories with Denny Lennon,* Jeff Tamarkin, Curtis Mayfield, Kent Kotal, Jan Henderson, Edith Wolfe, Bob Dylan, Pat Prince at *Goldmine* magazine, Bob Marley, Eric Kulberg, The Frigate, Lewin Record Paradise, Elmer Valentine and Mario Maglieri, Denny Rosencrantz, Grelun Landon, Justin Pierce, Marina, Spock, Dave Kephart, Lenny Dawson, Lance Alworth, Elgin and Jerry, John R. Wooden, Dan Patrick, Colin Cowherd, Denny Bruce, Dennis Pernu at Voyageur Press, Hal Lifson, Kevin Gershan, Buddy Colette, Kim Fowley, Gold Star Recording Studio, Jack Nitzsche, Brad Ross, Jonathan Rosenberg, Barry Gordon, Tracey Jordan, Frank Orlando, ForgottenHits.com, Heather Harris and Mr. Twister, Jeremy Gilien, Mark London, Paul Body, Robert Marchese, Ola Hudson, Pooch, Tom Johnson, Cake, Dean Dean the Taping Machine, Slash, Benjamin Piekut—author of *Henry Cow: The World Is a Problem,* for putting a fresh spin on uncertainty—and Marshall and Hilda Kubernik.

Kenneth would like to thank Leonardo "Nardini" Pavkovic, for opening doors; John Etheridge and Hugh Banton, for being there then; Nels Cline, for finding the time; James Newton ("Yes, let's talk about James Jamerson"); Michel Delville; the Bruin boys, Daniel "Wicker Man" Rucker and Umberto Belfiore; the Harrison clan—Thomas, Robert, and Sandra—for bearing witness; Roberto Crema, *grazie mille*; my brothers in bop, Carl Bromley and Adam Shatz; MD Tiberi (natch); Fiona Adams, who almost made it; Peter Alan Roberts, again; Brian Auger, survivor extraordinaire; Teo Ruiz, for being so neighborly; Deborah and Glen, for fighting against the currents; Christine Hopper, for graciously allowing us to keep Hugh's voice alive; and Hilda K., who, like the Dude, abides.

# Sources

## QUOTE CITATIONS

v  "We play our music": Charles R. Cross, *Room Full of Mirrors: A Biography of Jimi Hendrix* (New York: Hyperion, 2005).

viii  "A girlfriend rang up": https://www.youtube.com/watch?v=EVBf-N4smZ4.

5  "The substantive issue": Paul Gilroy, *Darker than Blue: On the Moral Economies of Black Atlantic Culture* (The W. E. B. Du Bois Lectures) (Cambridge, MA: Belknap, Harvard Univ. Press, 2011).

6  "He was so special": Stuart Millar, "An English Heritage Plaque Is Unveiled to the Legendary Guitarist Jimi Hendrix in London," *The Guardian*, September 15, 1997.

6  "radical incompleteness": Gilroy, *Darker than Blue*.

8  "It's groovy, man": *A Film About Jimi Hendrix*, 1973, directed by Joe Boyd, John Head, and Gary Weis.

8  "Many of Hendrix's immortal articulations": Gilroy, *Darker than Blue*.

14  "You get rid of that shirt, boy!": Sharon Lawrence, *Jimi Hendrix: The Man, the Magic, the Truth* (New York: HarperCollins, 2005).

21  "The United States and Canadian rights": "Warners Obtains Hendrix Rights in U.S. & Canada in Chalpin Settlement," *Cashbox*, July 27, 1968.

43  "Beyond any shadow of a doubt": Bill Harry, *Record Mirror*, January 21, 1967.

151  "casually voracious 'nowness'": Ian MacDonald, *Revolution in the Head: The Beatles' Records and the Sixties* (Chicago: Chicago Review Press, 2007).

153  "I watched him work": Larry Coryell, *Guitar Player*, September 1975.

238  "I tell you": Jimi Hendrix to Bob Dawbarn, interview in *Melody Maker*, March 8, 1969.

240  "The Day Hendrix Died," poem by David N. Pepperell, published in *Go-Set*, March 10, 1970; supplied by Pepperell to Harvey Kubernik.

242  "Most of us were staying": Mitch Mitchell with John Platt, *Jimi Hendrix: Inside the Experience* (New York: Harmony, 1990).

255  "electric guitar's Einstein": Greg Tate, *Midnight Lightning: Jimi Hendrix and the Black Experience* (Chicago: Chicago Review Press, 2003).

255  "For me, great music": Stephen Hough, *Rough Ideas: Reflections on Music and More* (New York: Farrar, Straus and Giroux, 2020).

255  "Everyone's hourglass was running down": Lisa Halliday, *Asymmetry* (New York: Simon & Schuster, 2018).

256  "It's as though I've seen": Edward Strickland, *Fanfare*, May/June 1987.

257  "By the 1960s": Michael Chanan, *From Handel to Hendrix: The Composer in the Public Sphere* (New York: Verso, 1999).

257  "Should I wait for you, motherfucker?": Miles Davis, in George Cole, *The Last Miles: The Music of Miles Davis, 1980–1991* (London: Equinox, 2005).

258  "I had played with everybody": Tony William to Pat Cox, interview in *Downbeat*, May 28, 1970.

258  "White groups don't reach me": Miles Davis interview in *Rolling Stone*, December 1969.

258  "I was getting away": Miles Davis, *Miles: The Autobiography* (New York: Simon & Schuster, 1989).

259  "There was at one point": Colin Harper, *Bathed in Lightning: John McLaughlin, the 60s and the Emerald Beyond* (London: Jawbone Press, 2014).

259:  "We were all looking": John McLaughlin in Harper, *Bathed in Lightning*.

267:  "It was his sound": Randy Holden, in Mike Stax and Eliot Kissileff, *Ugly Things*, summer 2019.

## INTERVIEW CITATIONS

Harvey Kubernik newly conducted interviews for this book and previous Kubernik written and published magazine/periodicals/online and non-published sources. All incorporated Harvey Kubernik–penned magazine articles and excerpts from digital endeavors were utilized from the Harvey Kubernik archives along with newly conducted Kenneth Kubernik interviews (identified as by Kenneth Kubernik) except where noted.

Citations for repeated interviews within a chapter are only listed at first occurrence of interview in a chapter.

### 1: The Meaning of the Blues
Mike Stoller: Interview, 1993, for *HITS*, 1993; excerpted in *Goldmine*, 1995.
Janie Hendrix: Interview, 2011, for *Record Collector News*, 2011.
Jerry Miller: Interview, 2007, for *Goldmine*, 2007.
Don Wilson: Interview, 2008, for *Discoveries*, 2008.
Bobby Womack: Interview, 2009.
Steve Cropper: Interview, 2007; excerpted in *MOJO*, 2007.
Johnny Echols: Interview, 2019.
Chris Hillman: Interview, 2007, for *MOJO*, 2007; excerpted in *Goldmine*, 2012; excerpted in Harvey
     Kubernik and Kenneth Kubernik, *A Perfect Haze: The Illustrated History of the Monterey Pop
     Festival* (Solana Beach, CA: Santa Monica Press, 2011).

### 2: New York, New York, a Helluva Town
Ernie Isley: Interview, A. Scott Galloway, *Wax Poetics*, no. 30, 2008.
James Cushing: Interview, 2019.
Jerry Schatzberg: Interview, 2015, for *Record Collector News*, 2015.
Carmine Appice: Interview, 2019.
Carl Hauser: Telephone interview by Mike Stax, 1990; supplied to Harvey Kubernik.
John Ridley: Interview, 2014, for *Record Collector News*, 2014.
Ronnie Schneider: Interview by Kenneth Kubernik, 2019.
Barry Goldberg: Interview, 2007, for *Goldmine*, 2012; excerpted in Kubernik and Kubernik,
     *Perfect Haze*.
Al Kooper: Interview, 2007, for *Goldmine*, 2012; excerpted in Kubernik and Kubernik, *Perfect Haze*.
James Newton: Interview by Kenneth Kubernik, 2019.

### 3: Ready Steady . . . Go!
Michael Des Barres: Interview, 2019.
Kim Fowley: Interview, 2007.
John Mayall: Interview, 2019, for CaveHollywood.com, 2019.
Eddie Kramer: Interview for *Record Collector News*, 2019.
Dave Mason: Interview, 2019.
Brian Auger: Interview by Kenneth Kubernik, 2019.
John Etheridge: E-mail interview by Kenneth Kubernik, 2019.
Michael Lindsay-Hogg: Interview, 2019, for *Record Collector News*, 2019.
Hugh Banton: Interview by Kenneth Kubernik, 2019.
Barrie Wentzell: Interview, 2019.

Kim Simmonds: Interview, 2019.

David Kessel: Interview, 2019.

Dan Kessel: Interview, 2019.

Marijke Koger-Dunham: Interview, 2019.

Anya Wilson: Interview, 2019.

## 4: Are You Experienced? We Are Now

Eddie Kramer: Interview, 2019, for *Record Collector News*, 2019.

Richard Bosworth: Interview, 2019.

James Cushing: Interview, 2019.

Brian Auger: Interview by Kenneth Kubernik, 2019.

Kim Fowley: Interview, 2007; excerpted in CaveHollywood.com, 2007.

Russ Regan: Interview, 2012 and 2017.

Denny Bruce: Interview, 2019.

Joe Smith: Interview, 2007; excerpted in *MOJO*, 2007.

Gene Cornish:  Interview, 2013.

## 5: Pop Goes the Festival

Eric Burden: Interview, 2007; excerpted in *Goldmine*, 2012; excerpted in Kubernik and Kubernik, *Perfect Haze*.

Andrew Loog Oldham: Interview, 2007 and 2019; excerpted in *MOJO*, 2007.

Jim Salzer: Interview, 2019.

Jenni Dean Harte: Interview, 2007; excerpted in Kubernik and Kubernik, *Perfect Haze*.

Al Kooper: Interview, 2007; excerpted in *Goldmine, 2012;* excerpted in Kubernik and Kubernik, *Perfect Haze*.

Pete Townshend: Interview, 2007, for *MOJO*, 2007; excerpted in *Goldmine*, 2012; excerpted in Kubernik and Kubernik, *Perfect Haze*.

Al Kooper: Interview, 2007; excerpted in *Goldmine*, 2012; excerpted in Kubernik and Kubernik, *Perfect Haze*.

Roger Daltrey: Interview, 2007; excerpted in *Goldmine*, 2012; excerpted in Kubernik and Kubernik, *Perfect Haze*.

Jerry Wexler: Interview, 2007; excerpted in *Goldmine*, 2012; excerpted in Kubernik and Kubernik, *Perfect Haze*.

Larry Taylor: Interview, 2007; excerpted in *Goldmine*, 2012; excerpted in Kubernik and Kubernik, *Perfect Haze*.

Chris Hillman: Interview, 2007; excerpted in *Goldmine*, 2012; excerpted in Kubernik and Kubernik, *Perfect Haze*.

Paul Body: Interview, 2007; excerpted in *Goldmine*, 2012; excerpted in Kubernik and Kubernik, *Perfect Haze*.

Robert Marchese: Interview, 2007; excerpted in *Goldmine*, 2012; excerpted in Kubernik and Kubernik, *Perfect Haze*.

Michelle Phillips: Interview, 2007; excerpted in *Goldmine*, 2012; excerpted in Kubernik and Kubernik, *Perfect Haze*.

Peter Lewis: Interview, 2019.

Djinn Ruffner: Interview, 2019.

Paul Kantner: Interview, 2007 and 2011; excerpted in Kubernik and Kubernik, *Perfect Haze*.

Jerry Miller: Interview, 2007; excerpted in *Goldmine*, 2012; excerpted in Kubernik and Kubernik, *Perfect Haze*.

Barry Goldberg: Interview, 2007; excerpted in *Goldmine*, 2012; excerpted in Kubernik and Kubernik, *Perfect Haze*.

Alex Del Zoppo: Interview, 2019.

Micky Dolenz: Interview, 2007; excerpted in *Goldmine*, 2012; excerpted in Kubernik and Kubernik, *Perfect Haze*.

Abe Jacob: Interview, 2013; excerpted in *Goldmine*, 2015.

Lou Adler: Interview, 2007; excerpted in *Goldmine*, 2012; *Goldmine*, 2007.

Jann Wenner: Interview, 2011; excerpted in Kubernik and Kubernik, *Perfect Haze*.

Jim Salzer: Interview, 2019.

Keith Altham: Interview, 2015.

Jerry Heller: Interview, 2007; excerpted in Kubernik and Kubernik, *Perfect Haze*.

Henry Diltz: Interview, 2007; excerpted in *Goldmine*, 2012; excerpted in Kubernik and Kubernik, *Perfect Haze*.

Clive Davis: Interview, 2007, for *MOJO*, 2007; excerpted in *Goldmine*, 2012; excerpted in Kubernik and Kubernik, *Perfect Haze*.

## 6: On the Road Again

Marty Balin: Interview, 2015, for *Record Collector News*, 2015.

Dennis Loren: Interview, 2019.

Jim Salzer: Interview, 2019.

Johnny Echols: Interview, 2019.

Robby Krieger: Interview, 2019.

John Densmore: Interview, 2007, for *MOJO*, 2007.

Seymour Cassel: Interview, 2010, for *THC Exposé*, 2010.

Don Wilson: Interview, 2008, for *Discoveries*, 2008.

Stephen Stills: Interview by Gary Strobl, 1988; supplied to Harvey Kubernik.

David Price: Interview by Gary Strobl, 2016; supplied to Harvey Kubernik.

Dick Clark: Interview, 2004, for *HITS*, 2004.

Andrew Loog Oldham: Interview, 2007; excerpted in *MOJO*, 2007.

Bobby Rogers: Interview, 1975, for *Melody Maker*, 1975.

David Ruffin: Interview, 1975, for *Melody Maker*, 1975.

Ernie Isley: Interview, 1975, for *Melody Maker*, 1975.

Keith Altham: Interview, 2015.

Abe Jacob: Interview, 2013.

Nils Lofgren: Interview, 2019.

Jan Alan Henderson: Interview, 2019.

Robert Marchese: Interview, 2007.

Guy Webster: Interview, 2010, for *THC Exposé*, 2010.

John York: Interview, 2019.

Jon Povey: E-mail interview by Mike Stax, 2019; supplied to Harvey Kubernik.

Howard Kaylan: Interview, 2013, for *Record Collector News*, 2013.

Marshall Chess: Interviews, 2006 and 2009; excerpted in *Goldmine*, 2006.

## 7: Tilting the World Off Its Axis

James Cushing: Interview, 2019.

Eddie Kramer: Interview, 2019, for *Record Collector News*, 2019.

John Mayall: Interview, 2019.

Tom Gundelfinger O'Neal: Interview, 2014; excerpted in *Treats!*, 2014.

Dennis Loren: Interview, 2019.

Joel Selvin: Interview, 2019.

Carol Schofield: Interview, 2019.

Robert Knight: Interview, 2019.

John Van Hamersveld: Interview, 2014; excepted in *Treats!*, 2014,
     and *Record Collector News*, 2015.

Marina Muhlfriedel: Interview, 2019.

Dave Pearson: Adapted from "In the Thrall of Michael Bloomfield," by Dave Pearson, 2008,
     published on David Dann's www.mikebloomfieldamericanmusic.com, supplied by David Dann
     to Harvey Kubernik.

Denny Bruce: Interview, 2019.

Ed Caraeff: Interview, 2019.

Mark Roman: Interview, 2019.

Andrew Solt: Interview, 2019.

Jeff Gelb: Interview, 2019.

## 8: Studio Daze, Those Hollywood Nights

Eddie Kramer: Interview, 2019.

Allan Arkush: Interview, 2019.

Prescott Niles: Interview, 2019.

Anya Wilson: Interview, 2019.

Thomas Harrison: Interview by Kenneth Kubernik, 2019.

Robert Pogue Harrison: Interview by Kenneth Kubernik, 2019.

Filippo La Porta: Interview by Thomas Harrison, 2019; supplied to Kenneth Kubernik.

Sandra Harrison: Interview by Kenneth Kubernik, 2019.

Marco Persichetti: Interview by Thomas Harrison, 2019; supplied to Kenneth Kubernik.

Richard Bosworth: Interview, 2019.

Carmine Appice: Interview, 2019.

Alex Del Zoppo: Interview, 2019.

Carmine Appice: Interview, 2019.

Ed Caraeff: Interview, 2019.

Nancy Rose: Interview, 2019.

Lanny Waggoner: Interview, 2019.

Jim Keltner: Interview, 2019.

Peter Piper: Interview 2017; excepted in *Record Collector News*, 2018, and CaveHollywood.com, 2018.

Bill Halverson: Interview, 2014; excerpted in CaveHollywood.com, 2019.

Rodney Bingenheimer: Interview, 2019.

Marshall Chess: Interviews, 2006 and 2009; excerpted in *Goldmine*, 2006.

Kim Fowley: Interview, 2013.

Richard Bosworth: Interview, 2019.

Dennis Loren: Interview, 2019.

Hugh Hopper: From the personal archive of Hugh Hopper, supplied to Kenneth Kubernik, 2004.

## 9: *Electric Ladyland*

James Cushing: Interview, 2019.

Teofilo F. Ruiz: Interview by Kenneth Kubernik, 2019.

Dave Mason: Interview, 2019.

Jim Keltner: Interview, 2019

Michael Hacker: Interview, 2019.

Steven Van Zandt: Interview, 2007; excerpted in *Record Collector News*, 2007.

Daniel Weizmann: Interview, 2019.

Janie Hendrix: Interview, 2011, for *Record Collector News*, 2011.

Roger Steffens: Interview, 2019.

D. A. Pennebaker: Interviews 2002 and 2010; excerpted in Harvey Kubernik, *Hollywood Shack Job: Rock Music in Film and on Your Screen* (Albuquerque: University of New Mexico Press, 2006), and *Treats!*, 2010.

Del Breckenfeld: Interview, 2019.

## 10: '69 Turned Out to Be Fine

Barrie Wentzell: Interview, 2019.

George Varga: Interview, 2019.

Hugh Banton: Interview by Kenneth Kubernik, 2019.

Fred Schuster: Interview, 2019.

Kirk Silsbee: Interview, 2019.

James Williamson: Interview, 2019.

Kim Simmonds: Interview, 2019.

Elizabeth Darrow Jones: Interview, 2019.

Paul Diamond: Interview, 2019.

Gene Aguilera: Interview 2019.

Toulouse Engelhardt: Interview, 2019.

Ken Resser: Interview by Kenneth Kubernik, 2019.

Larry LeBlanc: Interview, 2019.

Gary Pig Gold: Interview, 2019.

Robert Knight: Interview, 2017, for *Record Collector News*, 2017.

Glenn Archambault: Interview, 2019.

Ed Cassidy: Interview, 1975, for *Melody Maker*, 1975.

Glenn Archambault: Interview, 2019.

Mark Roman: Interview, 2019.

Roger (Jim) McGuinn: Interview, 2005; excerpted in *Goldmine*, 2005, *Record Collector News*, 2015, and CaveHollywood.com, 2019.

John York: Interview, 2019.

Jimmy Robinson: Interview, 2006.

## 11: Woodstock and Them Changes

Mel Lawrence: Interview, 2011; excerpted in Kubernik and Kubernik, *Perfect Haze*.

Henry Diltz: Interview, 2011; excerpted in Kubernik and Kubernik, *Perfect Haze*.

Eddie Kramer: Interviews, 2007 and 2019; excerpted in *Goldmine*, 2007, and *Record Collector News,* 2019.

Billy Cox: Interview, 2015, for *Record Collector News,* 2015.

Jerry Wexler: Interview, 2007, for *MOJO*, 2007; excerpted in Kubernik and Kubernik,
   *Perfect Haze*.

Janie Hendrix: Interview, 2011, for *Record Collector News*, 2011.

James Williamson: Interview, 2019.

Allan Arkush: Interview, 2019.

Jimmy Robinson: Interview, 2006.

Billy Cox: Interview, 2015, for *Record Collector News*, 2015; excerpted in Gillian G. Gaar, *Hendrix:
   The Illustrated Story* (Minneapolis, MN: Voyageur Press, 2017).

Prescott Niles: Interview, 2019.

Bill Graham: Interview, 1976. *Melody Maker*, 1976.

Michael Simmons: Interview, 2015, for *Record Collector News,* 2015; excerpted in Gaar, *Hendrix*.

James Cushing: Interview, 2019.

## 12: Walkin' on Gilded Splinters

Ken Resser: Interview by Kenneth Kubernik, 2019.

Pat Baker: Interview, 2019.

Denny Bruce: Interview, 2019.

John Storyk: Interview, 2019.

Elizabeth Darrow Jones: Interview, 2019.

Bruce D. Henderson: Interview, 2019.

Eddie Kramer: Interview, 2007, for *Goldmine*, 2007.

Abe Jacob: Interview, 2013.

Billy Cox: Interview, 2015, for *Record Collector News,* 2015.

Janie Hendrix: Interview, 2011, for *Record Collector News,* 2011.

Nils Lofgren: Interview, 2019.

## 13: The Sky Is Crying

Murray Lerner: Interview, 2010, for *Record Collector News,* 2010.

Bob Johnston: Interviews, 2007 and 2014, for *Record Collector News,* 2007, and
   CaveHollywood.com, 2014.

Carmine Appice: Interview, 2019.

Richard Williams: Interview, 2019.

Justin Hayward: Interview, 2019.

James Cushing: Interview, 2007. *Goldmine*, 2007.

Anya Wilson: Interview, 2019.

Bobby Womack: Interview, 2009, excerpted in CaveHollywood.com, 2019.

Rosemarie Patronette: Interview, 2019.

Nils Lofgren: Interview, 2019.

David N. Pepperell: Interview, 2019.

## 14: See You in the Next Life

Eddie Kramer: Interview, 2019, for *Record Collector News*, 2019.

Bob Say: Interview, 2019.

Johnny Echols: Interview, 2019.

Patti Smith: Interview, 2004, for *HITS*, 2004.

Daniel Weizmann: Interview, 2019.

Celeste Goyer: Interview, 2019.

James Cushing: Interview, 2019.

Michael Des Barres: Interview, 2019.

Del Breckenfeld: Interview, 2019.

Prescott Niles: Interview, 2019.

Billy Cox: Interview, 2015, for *Record Collector News*, 2015.

Janie Hendrix: Interview, 2011, for *Record Collector News*, 2011.

Carlos Santana: Interview 2016, for *Record Collector News*, 2016.

## Appendix I: Jimi and Jazz—A Marriage Never Consummated

Gil Evans: Interview, "Hendrix Lives! Tribute to a Genius," *Guitar World,* March 1988.

James Newton: Interview by Kenneth Kubernik, 2019.

## Appendix II: Room Full of Gear

Del Breckenfeld: Interview, 2019.

Richard Bosworth: Interview, 2019.

Michael Bloomfield: Interview, "Michael Bloomfield Reminisces," *Guitar Player,* September 1975.

Frank Orlando: Interview, 2015.

Glen Laughlin: Interview by Kenneth Kubernik, 2019.

Michel Delville: Interview by Kenneth Kubernik, 2019.

Hugh Banton: Interview by Kenneth Kubernik, 2019.

John Etheridge: Interview by Kenneth Kubernik, 2019.

Nels Cline: Interview by Kenneth Kubernik, 2019.

# Suggested Reading

Jimi Hendrix's life has been exhaustively (exhaustingly?) documented, leading to the inevitable challenge for any new biographer: What on earth could you possibly add to the conversation? We grew up with Jimi, following him from his U.S. debut at Monterey AM station KRLA in Los Angeles, broadcasted live from the festival; every minute of that fabled weekend was spent nestled by a portable radio, listening for reports from the front. When word came that his majesty, Brian Jones, was seen strolling the grounds with England's newest sensation, Jimi Hendrix, a new tab was started in the Kubernik record collection. From that point on Jimi was a central part of our lives.

The voices you hear in this book are from fellow travelers who experienced Jimi in real time. What they have to say, we believe, sheds an invaluable, fresh perspective to the multitude of books that have chronicled his life and times. Below are a snapshot of some of these works that were helpful in providing context, perspective, and a rigorous chronology that keeps the missteps and counterfactuals to a precious few. All these titles are praiseworthy for their contributions to the Hendrix canon, and would reward readers of our book who want to pursue his life down to its studs.

Etchingham, Kathy, with Andrew Crofts *Through Gypsy Eyes: My Life, the Sixties and Jimi Hendrix*, London: Orion, 1998.
(Memoir by Jimi's girlfriend, whom he lived with in London.)

Hendrix, Jimi, and Peter Neal, ed. *Jimi Hendrix Starting at Zero: His Own Story*. New York: Bloomsbury, 2013.
(Only Jimi's words, culled from every interview that could be cited.)

Mitchell, Mitch, with John Platt. *Jimi Hendrix: Inside the Experience.* New York: Harmony, 1990.
(Mitch provides a running commentary that enlightens the corresponding text.)

Roby, Steven, and Brad Schreiber. *Becoming Jimi Hendrix: From Southern Crossroads to Psychedelic London, the Untold Story of a Musical Genius*. Philadelphia: Da Capo, 2010.
(An in-depth, well-researched, and well-reviewed biography.)

Shadwick, Keith. *Jimi Hendrix Musician*. New York: Backbeat, 2003.
(Insightfully focuses on Jimi's music. And don't forget to check out the author's terrific 2002 biography of jazz piano icon, Bill Evans, *Bill Evans: Everything Happens to Me—A Musical Biography*.)

Shapiro, Harry, and Caesar Glebbeek. *Jimi Hendrix: Electric Gypsy.* New York: St. Martin's, 1990.
(A deep, deep dive; a completist's dream.)

Stubbs, David. *Jimi Hendrix: The Stories Behind Every Song*. London: Carlton, 2002.
(Covers his complete body of work.)

# Index

### Pages in *italics* are illustrated

Germany
    1967 performance, *148–49*, 170
    1969 performance, 170–72, *171*
    1970 performance, *232–33*, 233–34
*Get That Feeling—Jimi Hendrix Plays, Curtis Knight Sings*
    (album), 21
*Getting Ready* (King), 33
Gibb, Russ, 114
Gibbons, Billy, 114
Gibson Flying V, 148
Gilroy, Paul, 5, 6, 8
"God Save the Queen," 229, 230–31
Gold, Gary Pig, 188–89
Goldberg, Barry, 28, 71
Golden Gate Park (1967), 79–80, *80*
Gold Star studio, 16, 139
Gomelsky, Giorgio, 52
Gordy, Barry, 58
Goyer, Celeste, 248–49
Graham, Bill, 63, 79, 103–5, 146, 204–5, 207–9, *208*, 224, 256
Grande Ballroom (Detroit; 1966, 1968), 114, 142–43
Greensboro (NC), 96–97
Griffin, Rick, 104
Grimshaw, Gary, 114, *115*
Grin (band), 227
Grossman, Albert, 220
Gruber, Freddie, 135
Gunnell, Johnny and Rik, 36
Guy, Buddy, 43
Gypsy Sun and Rainbows, 197–203

Hacker, Michael, 159
Hadani, Ami, 140
Hagstrom basses, 272
Hall, Ace, *22*
Halliday, Lisa, 255
Halverson, Bill, 137
Hammond, John, Jr., 28, 72, 242
*Handel to Hendrix* (Chanan), 257
Hanley, Bill, 205
*Happening for Lulu* (TV show), 169, *169*
"Happenings," 59–60
Hare, Pat, 51
Harlem Benefit concert (1969), 203
Harper, Colin, 259
Harrison, George, 102, 137
Harrison, Robert Pogue, 124–27, *125*
Harrison, Sandra, 124, *125*, 126, 128
Harrison, Thomas, 124–27, *125*, *129*
Harry, Bill, 43
Harte, Jenni Dean, 60, 61
Hartman, Phil, 180
Hauser, Carl, 23
"(Have You Ever Been to) Electric Ladyland," 261, 262
Hawaii (1969), 189, *236*
Hayward, Justin, 232
"Hear My Train a Comin,'" 224, 248
Heider, Wally, 137, 206
Heller, Jerry, 76
Henderson, Bruce D., 222–24, *223*
Henderson, Jan Alan, 92
Hendrix, Bob, 249–250
Hendrix, James "Al" (father), 7, 11, 34, 241, 245
Hendrix, Janie (sister), 11, 12, 144, 161, 189, 203, 226, 241, 245, 250, 252–53, *252*
Hendrix, Jimi
    about: life trajectory, 1–9

Cherokee heritage of, 7–8, 32
death of, 5, 234–40
Jimi Hendrix Experience formation, 30–31. *See also* Jimi
    Hendrix Experience, the
drug bust in Canada, 177, 186–89, *187*
European tour (1970), 228–34
funeral and memorial for, 238, 241–42, *241–43*
gear preferences, 121–22, 148, 263–69, 272–73
guitar destruction by, *44*, 60, 63, 68–69, 148, *148–49*
Gypsy Sun and Rainbows, 197–203
on his own funeral, 238
jazz and, 211, 256–62
Jimmy James and the Blue Flames, 2–3, 21, 23, 24, 28, 191
as left-handed guitarist, 17, 86–87, *87*, 186, *250*, 265, 266
legacy of, 244–253, 275
Little Richard tour (1965), 2, 14–17, *14*, 18–19, 90
London (1966–67), 3, *4*, 5–6, 8–9, *9*, 29
London (1970), 212, 234–35
military service of, 2, 13, 34, 197
musical influences, 2, 5, 8–9, 11–17, 33, 139, 153–61, 188
New York (1965–66), 2–3, 19–29, *20*, *26–27*, 30–36, 37–47, 48–52
New York (1970), 212, 215–21
record contract settlement, 203–11. *See also Band of Gypsys*
on retiring, 177
science fiction interest of, 7, 32, 116
singing voice of, 35, 52, 110, 159–61, 248
social injustices and, 8, 29, 42, 69–70, 88–90, 150, 157, 177, 197–99, 222, 248
song composition analysis of, 261–62
sonic artistry of, 5, 71–74, 145, 254–55, 269–75
US tour (1970), 212–14, 222–27
Hendrix, June, 241
Hendrix, Leon, 241
Hendrix, Lucille (mother), 7
Herd, *98*
"Hey Joe"
    1966 performances, 28, 40, 248
    1968 performances, 130, 141
    1969 performance, 172
    Chandler on, 29
    guitar sound, 35, 268, 272
    legacy of, 248
    recording of, 29, 48, 49
    on UK charts, 48
    US music industry's interest in, 54
Hidley, Tom, 120, 140
Hillman, Chris, 17, 67, *67*
Holden, Randy, 265–66
Hollywood Bowl (1967), 79, 84, 91–96, *93*, *95–96*
Hollywood Bowl (1968), 133–37, *134*, *136*
Hollywood Palladium (1969), 175–76
Honolulu (1969), 189
Hooker, John Lee, 43
Hopper, Hugh, 145–48, *145*
Hough, Stephen, 255
"Hound Dog" (Presley), 11, 155
"House Burning Down," 153, 261
Howlin' Wolf, 9, 51–52, 234
Hughes, Jimmy, 207
Hulett, Tom, 241
Humperdinck, Engelbert, 52, 77

Ike & Tina Turner Revue, 84, 190
Isle of Fehmarn (Germany; 1970), *232–33*, 233–34
Isle of Wight (England; 1970), 228–33, *231*
Isley, Ernie, 19–20, 90

# Picture Credits

Alamy: AF archive: 169; John Bentley: 40, 41; dpa picture alliance: 171, 233; Eagle Visions/Craig Lovell: 260; Everett Collection: 118, 236, 237; Philippe Gras: 145, 231; Gijsbert Hanekroot: 33, 139; Heritage Image Partnership: 39; MediaPunch Inc.: 198; Moviestore Collection Ltd.: 166, 167; Pictorial Press Ltd: 2,3, 38, 42, 43, 44, 98; Mick Sinclair: 50; Trinity Mirror/ Mirrorpix: 24, 25, 152; United Archives GmbH: 31; ZUMA Press, Inc.: 53

Courtesy of Allan Arkush: 205

Courtesy of Brian Auger: 36

Maryanne Bilham: 253

Peter Blecha/Northwest Music Archives: 13

Ed Caraeff/Iconic Images: 96, 112, 138

Annette Del Zoppo: 132

Courtesy of Michel Delville: 269, 270

Courtesy of Dave Diamond: 54

Jim Dickson, courtesy of the Henry Diltz Archives: 17

Henry Diltz: cover, vi, 12, 14, 32, 46, 47, 55, 59, 61, 63, 64, 66 top, 67, 69, 70 bottom, 71, 72, 73, 74, 75, 77, 82, 83, 85, 86, 88, 93, 94, 95 bottom, 99, 106, 107, 134, 166, 176, 199, 200, 201, 202, 208, 235, 246

Courtesy of Fender: 250, 251, 265

Courtesy of the Gary Grimshaw Legacy Foundation: 115

Courtesy of Gary Pig Gold: 188

Deborah Gee: 268

Courtesy of Jeff Gelb: 116, 117

Getty Images: Apic/Hulton Archive: 7; Atlantic-kid/ iStock Editoriall/Getty Images Plus: 4, 5; Cyrus Andrews/Michael Ochs Archives: x, 1; Donaldson Collection/Michael Ochs Archives: 187; Jack Manning/Archive Photos/New York Times Co.: 26; Frank Mastropolo/Corbis: 122; Fred W. McDarrah: 219; Michael Ochs Archives: 15, 16, 20, 21, 22, 158; Bob Peterson/The LIFE Images Collection: 241; PoPsie Randolph/Michael Ochs: 66 bottom; David Redfern/Redferns: 173; Rolls Press/Popperfoto: 56; Peter Timm/ullstein bild: 149

George Goad: 183

Courtesy of Jeff Gold: 103, 154

Heather Harris: 70 top, 247

Courtesy of Thomas Harrison: 125, 129

Bruce D. Henderson: 223

Robert Knight: 106 top

Robert Landau: 101

Courtesy of Dennis Loren: 80, 104, 142

Mark Roman Archives: 113, 192, 193

Michael Miller Archives: 135, 175

Mickey Dolenz Archive: 87

Courtesy of Marina Muhlfriedel: 110

Zoran Orlic: 273

Rosemarie Patronette: 143 right, 206, 252

Courtesy of Prescott Niles Archives: 143 left, 251

Courtesy of Ray Randolph: 89, 136, 159

Eron Rauch: 262

Courtesy of Kenneth Resser: 133, 184 top, 213, 214

Courtesy of Mark Roman: 190, 194

Courtesy of Jim Salzer: 81, 97

Courtesy of Seattle Municipal Archives: 226, 227

Howard Sherman: 217

Shutterstock.com: Harold Matosian/AP: 184 bottom; Mariusz S. Jurgielewicz: 243; Marc Sharratt: ii; Herb Shmitz: 9

Courtesy of Kim Simmonds/Jim Summaria: 43, 183 bottom

Roger Steffens: 163, 164

Courtesy of Howard Storyk: 216

Richard Upper: 105

John Van Hamersveld: 108, 109

Guy Webster: 68, 95 top

Courtesy of Wikimedia Commons: 157, 221

Nurit Wilde: 62

ZUMA Wire: ©Globe Photos: viii

Textures by Lost and Taken

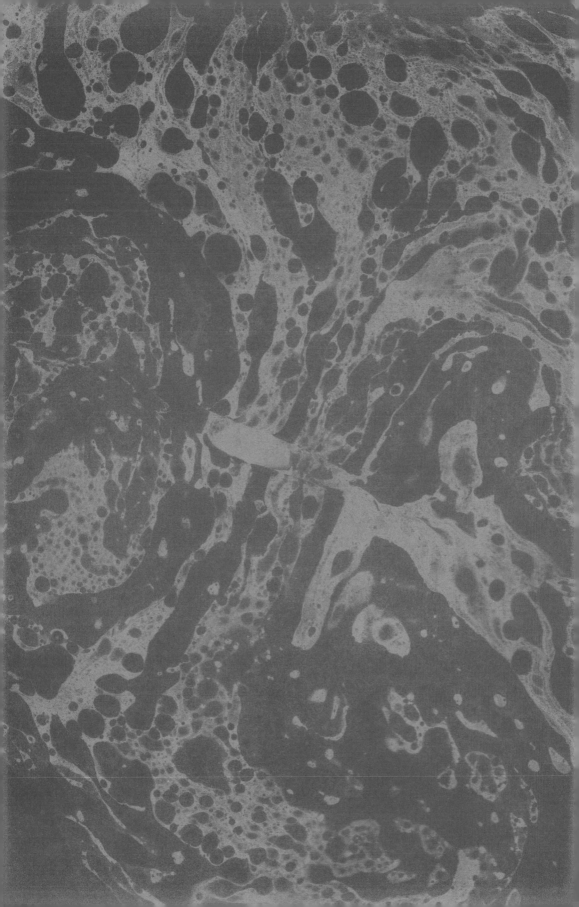

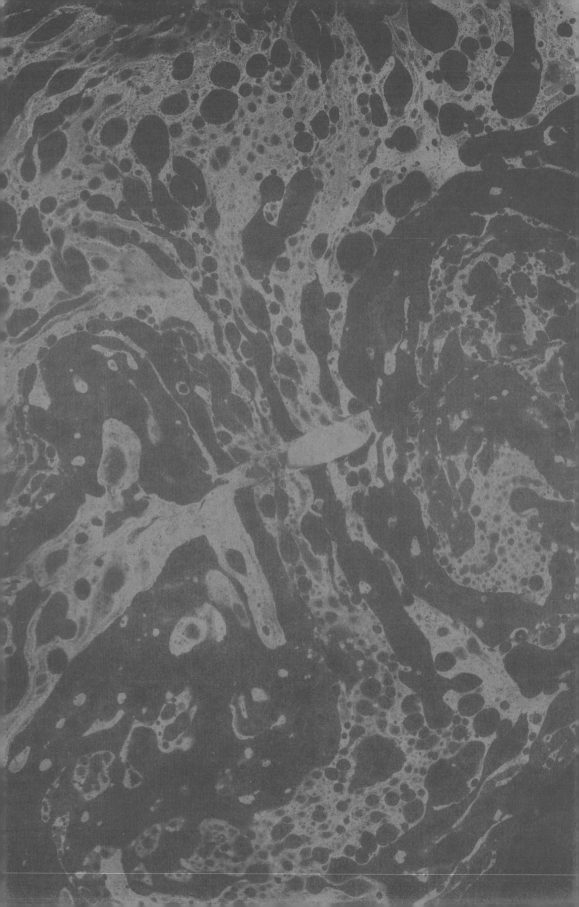